Extraordinary
Art Dealers

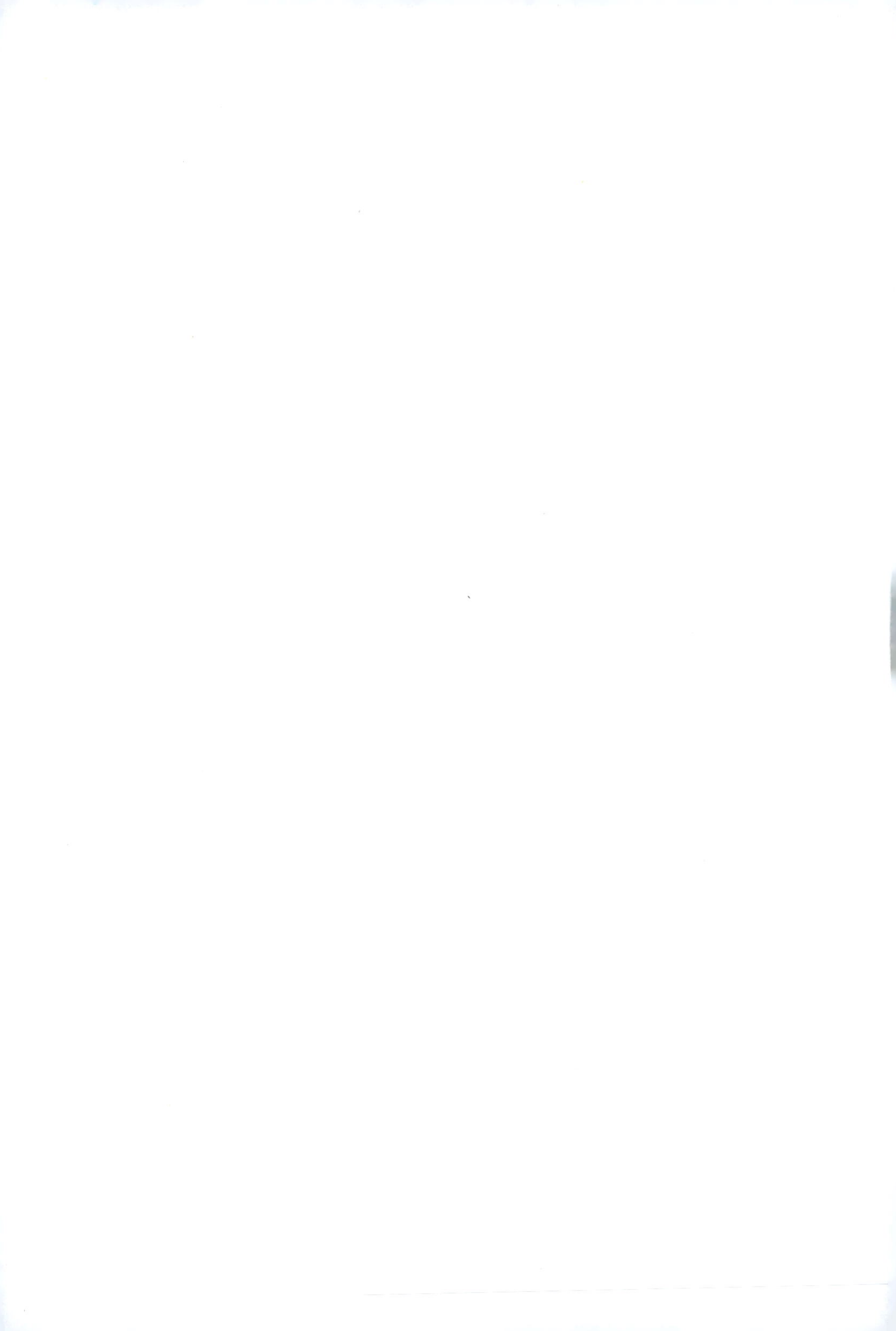

Catherine Ingram

Extraordinary Art Dealers

Stories of Obsession, Innovation and Creativity

HENI Publishing, London

First published in 2024
This edition published in 2026
Text © 2026 HENI

ISBN 978-1-911736-33-2

Edited by Sara Harrison, Rebecca Morrill,
Vincenza Napoli and Kirsty Watling
Preliminary research by Simona Pignataro
Research by Alice Blow, Lois Haines and
Meghan Montgomery
Proofread by Alison Wormleighton
Designed by Sylvia Ugga
Cover illustration by Celyn Brazier
Production by Sarah McLaughlin

Printed in Bosnia & Herzegovina by GPS
Typeface: Söhne, Chronicle

Publisher: HENI Publishing, London, United Kingdom
EU Authorised Representative: Easy Access System
Europe - Mustamäe tee 50, 10621 Tallinn, Estonia,
gpsr.requests@easproject.com

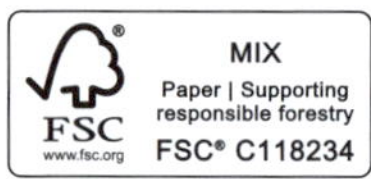

Contents

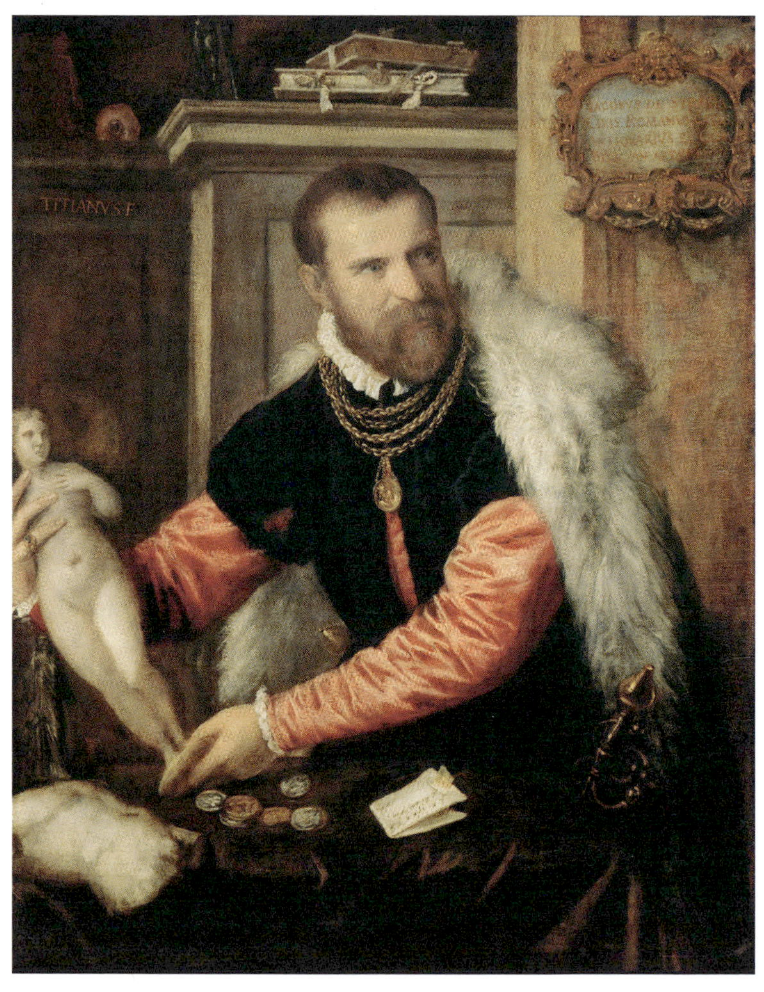

Titian, *Jacopo Strada*, c. 1567/68,
oil on canvas, 126 × 95.5 cm, (49 ⅝ × 37 ⅝ in.),
Kunsthistorisches Museum, Vienna.

Introduction

Titian is known for his tender portraits, but his painting of the art merchant, Jacopo Strada, from 1567/68 has a different psychology. Dressed in silk and fur, and adorned with a sparkling gold chain, the dealer is uneasy. The fur drops off his right shoulder. His eyes have a greedy glint. Holding a statue of Venus, he looks away from the sculpture, oblivious to its beauty, as his attention is caught by something beyond the frame. The diagonal thrust of the composition makes him appear to be moving in the direction of his gaze as if he is about to address a potential buyer out of view. Focussed on a possible transaction, Strada's furtive behaviour reflects the common low regard for art dealers. Marcel Duchamp certainly shared this view, disparagingly referring to them as 'lice on the backs of the artists'.[1]

Selling art is a unique business. Art lacks a practical function and is appreciated for attributes like beauty and originality, which are esoteric and immeasurable. It is the dealer who has the nerve to give these unfathomable ideals a monetary value, but ironically their part in introducing money into the art practice has led them to be vilified. The eighteenth century saw the birth of aesthetics. Immanuel Kant argued art was a profound activity removed from everyday concerns like money.[2] This premise had enormous influence on the art world, and supported the idea that art dealing was a tawdry affair which contaminated the sanctified practice of art.

Dealers are in fact caught in a double bind. While money seems to taint their practice, their success is evaluated on sales. The most written about dealers tend to be the most moneyed, the ones who sell top-dollar artists, operate an international network of galleries and have become so intoxicatingly successful that they themselves have become a brand – their very names securing high prices. This elite group has become known as 'branded dealers', and articles and books have forensically dissected their sales techniques – indeed, Leo Castelli's dealership style has come to be known as the 'Castelli Method'.

The branded dealer plays to their buyers' longing to be part of the enchanting world of the moneyed. This allure is evoked elegantly by the character of Daisy Fay in F. Scott Fitzgerald's *The Great Gatsby* (1925): 'Her voice is full of money... That was it. I'd never understood before. It was full of money – that was the inexhaustible charm that rose and fell in it, the jingle of it, the cymbals' song of it.'[3] And as these buyers hum to the same tune, they expect access to the most valued artists and their best work.

However, evaluating success solely by financial metrics provides a limited perspective on this rich subject. It fails to recognise the dealers' sensitivity, and their interest in the art. Betty Parsons reflected on what led her to support the undiscovered Abstract Expressionists: 'I fell in love with them. They were just marvellous. I just couldn't understand why people didn't understand that.'[4] These dealers were pioneers. Castelli was to sell the *first* Jasper Johns's flag paintings, the *first* comic strip paintings by Roy Lichtenstein and the *first* shaped canvases by Frank Stella. And Kekoo Gandhy spotted an emerging art scene in Mumbai, India, where he played a part in achieving international recognition for Indian modern artists. The question that arises is why these dealers saw talent where others couldn't. To answer this, the conversation around dealership needs to open up.

This book aims to explore the various motivations of art dealers. It is in no way a comprehensive study. The focus is the modern period (1870–1960), with an introductory chapter on early dealerships. There is an attempt to tackle the negativity around the profession by isolating controversial figures whose practice has misrepresented art in some way. Beyond this, it is a celebration of dealerships and their different manifestations. Arranged by theme, the book aims to provoke conversation. For example, one chapter explores the idealists who were on a similar spiritual journey to their artists, while a later chapter on cultural stewardship relates how certain dealers promulgated the values of their immediate milieu. And then there is the personality dealer, whose character shapes their unique approach while simultaneously capturing the public's attention.

The advantage of broadening the conversation is that the originality and creativity of these dealers can be appreciated. André Breton, for instance, has never been considered in the literature on art dealing. His gallery was short-lived and failed to turn a profit, and one might ask why he should be included here. However, his curation was radical – at his gallery, he immersed the visitor in a Surreal fantasy and explored uncharted territory, selling works that bridged the gap between art and design. Meanwhile, the cultural stewards represented artistic production outside the traditionally spotlighted cities of Paris, London and New York, which have monopolised attention for too long.

Another reason for challenging the opinion that dealers are scoundrels is that it misrepresents the typical relationship between dealer and artist. Generally, artists consider their dealers to be their allies, and appreciate the critical role they play in their careers. For Castelli, dealership had a civic purpose: 'Well, the function of... a good art dealer who really cares for art and not about money should be to find new artists and make them known to the public.'[5] Indeed, Titian's presentation might echo the mainstream narrative, but it is not how artists typically represent their dealers. These are usually very positive, and often reverent. Indeed, there is the joyous double portrait by Jean-Michel Basquiat, *Humidity* (1982), which shows Andy Warhol with his Swiss art dealer Bruno Bischofberger. The sun is shining, the artist has his arms in the air, and looks ecstatically happy to be with him.

When Larry Rivers had an exhibition with Virginia Dwan, he visited her, and had the opportunity to enjoy sunny California. His time with her was more than an occasion to sell his art. It was an uplifting, transformative experience. At the end of the trip, he gave Dwan a portrait he'd drawn of her, on which he inscribed the words, 'to my Great Dealer + her sun + surf'.[6] It could be claimed that special relationships of this kind between artist and dealer are the beating heart of art dealerships.

Chapter 1

Early Dealings

Introduction

This story begins in the eighteenth century when the art trade was experiencing unprecedented expansion. From this dynamic environment emerged what we now recognise as the prototype of the modern art dealer. What is interesting is that even in these nascent circumstances, art dealing had a heterogenous identity, and all manner of activity can be related to it. The five art dealers examined in this chapter have been chosen for their distinct visions.

Of course, art dealing originated before the eighteenth century. For a long time in Western Europe, art was centred around the Catholic church, with works commissioned by church authorities and rich donors who wanted to win favour for the afterlife. However, in the early Renaissance, there started to be a small trade in artworks with secular subject matter. This happened via busy stalls which flourished first in Flanders. From 1460, a market ran in the grounds of the Church of Our Lady in Antwerp where artists would sell their own work, with a few of them also trading work by other artists.

The writer Philip Hook reinforces that this early art trade was led by artists, 'carving out for themselves the role of art dealers,'[1] and this continued to be the case for a long time. The two eighteenth-century art dealers examined here were also artists. Significantly, the model of the artist-dealer persists into the modern period, albeit to a lesser degree, and case studies later in this book explore two twentieth-century artist-dealers: the Malian photographer Malick Sidibé, who sold his own work, and the Mexican dealers Lola and Manuel Álvarez Bravo, who ran a gallery from their home.

A secondary market was established via the Antwerp stalls when merchants bought the work and then sold it abroad for inflated prices. Through the seventeenth century, the art market diversified rapidly. As art became a way of asserting one's social status, royal houses and aristocracy looked to agents to source supreme works of art. Before being toppled from the throne and beheaded in 1649, Charles I was one of the largest trophy hunters. Taking a Grand Tour of Italy to study the classical past had become a rite of passage for the wealthy, which generated a demand for art treasure souvenirs – another factor to fuel the international trade. Meanwhile, auction houses were opening and, at the other end of the market, sellers of popular prints were trading cheap copies on the high street.

This chapter opens with the two eighteenth-century dealers Arthur Pond and William Hogarth, who had very different approaches. From a wealthy background, Pond was interested in the connoisseurship tradition. Believing art was an ideal state, he created a rarefied, luxury transaction for his aristocratic buyers. While the connoisseur dealer was the dominant model in this period, there were rebels. Despising the gentlemanly pretensions of connoisseurship, Hogarth brought the brassy energy of the common tradesmen to the art market.

The nineteenth-century dealer Ernest Gambart would take up the baton from Hogarth, operating as a popular dealer focussed on selling affordable prints. This century saw an emerging professionalism that would transform the art trade, with dealers establishing permanent gallery spaces and producing catalogues raisonnés. There was also greater financial expertise. Paul Durand-Ruel was one of the first to offer artists monthly stipends, making the very practice of art financially viable. And William Buchanan became renowned for his astute use of speculative art buying, using his keen eye to foresee trends and acquire pieces poised for significant appreciation.

While all these dealers brought a new level of professionalism, their approaches were nonetheless truly individual.

Arthur Pond

(1701–1758)

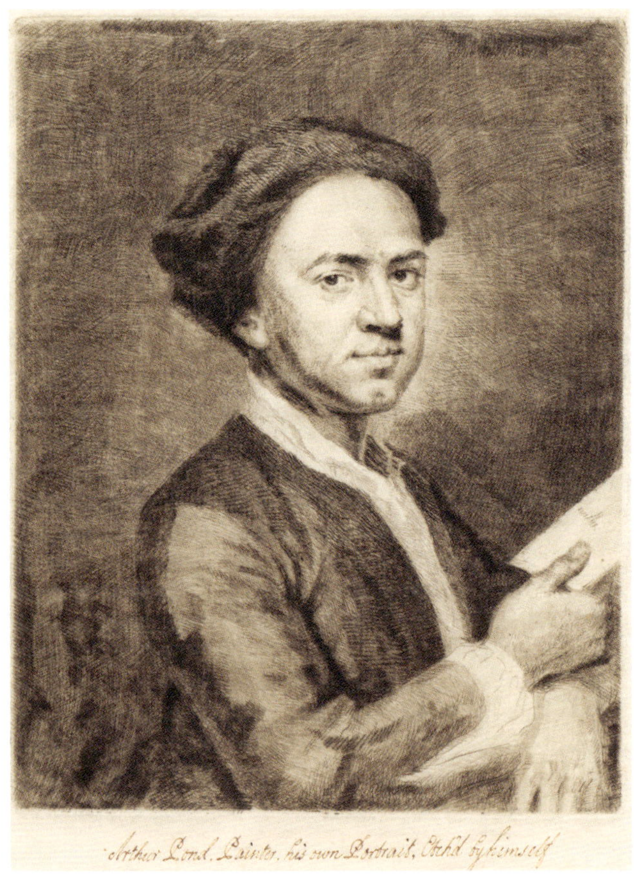

Arthur Pond, *Self-Portrait*, 1751, etching,
22.1 × 16.4 cm, (8 ¾ × 6 ½ in.), Yale Center
for British Art, New Haven, CT, USA.

The career of English art dealer Arthur Pond spanned the early decades of the eighteenth century, a transitional phase in the art market when trade opened up between Britain and Continental Europe, and art was becoming valued very differently than in previous times. While establishing himself within the art world, Pond explored the 'connoisseur' tradition – a concept that would deeply influence his approach to selling art.

The eldest son of a London surgeon, Pond began his career as a painter, studying under the portraitist John Vanderbank (1694–1739). Early on, he befriended fellow painter George Knapton (1698–1778), who was also from a wealthy city family, and together with some other friends they set up the Roman Club in 1723 – a group of young writers and painters who were deeply influenced by discussions around connoisseurship. The concept of connoisseurship had been gaining significance since the beginning of the century with Anthony Ashley Cooper, the 3rd Earl of Shaftesbury (1671–1713), being an authoritative voice on the subject. Cooper emphasised that the appreciation of art had a philosophical purpose, leading one to a deeper understanding of beauty and nature. Significantly for him, beauty was not to be found in the everyday and the incidental, but was an ideal state, concerned with 'the admiration and love of order, harmony and proportion'.[1] He saw these values expounded in classical times and in Renaissance art, and was known to dress in classical garb. The more contentious aspect of his connoisseurship was that it came to be parcelled up as an 'aristocratic attitude'; his advocation of beauty became a pursuit for the leisured class.

The Roman Club was also influenced by the more pragmatic connoisseur Jonathan Richardson (1667–1745), who had constructed a rating system of 0 to 20 to value the relative beauty or sublimity of a work of art. It became a tool for the Club's budding connoisseurs to start a discussion around art. For Pond, connoisseurship offered far more than just a conversation starter. Its principles would influence his dealership, shaping both what he sold and how he presented the works on sale. Central to Richardson's ideology was his recommendation to spend time in Italy, studying the ancient and Renaissance past – advice Pond took seriously. In 1725 Pond started out on a Grand Tour of Italy.

Pond's subsequent career selling European Old Masters benefitted from a coincidence of circumstances. For decades, the English art market had been stultified by a law prohibiting the import of works of art from abroad. A small domestic market was driven by royalty and wealthy aristocrats seeking high value art as trophies or statements of their power. Then in 1695, the law was repealed, opening the way for dealers to trade internationally. Concurrently, the trend for the Grand Tour among the wealthy was fuelling a fashion for the type of Old Master paintings the tourists encountered in Italy. Somewhat fortuitously for Pond, many Italian collectors were struggling financially and were open to selling their Old Master artworks. Essentially, Pond had the perfect market: secure sellers in Italy and interested buyers back home.

In London, Pond had started out acting as an agent for collectors, bidding on their behalf at public auctions to prevent prices being artificially raised on account of the known wealth of a collector. His more lucrative ventures began during his time in Italy between 1725 and 1727, when he worked for collectors back home and handled work by highly-respected artists; his journal mentions works by Italian masters including Giovanni Castiglione (1609–1664) and Giovanni Passeri (*c.* 1610–1679) and prestigious artists from elsewhere in Europe including Rembrandt van Rijn (1606–1669) and Claude Lorrain (1604/5–1682). By the end of his trip, Pond had acquired some original works to sell on and while most were small pieces – mainly prints and drawings – he nevertheless made a healthy 100 to 200 per cent profit on each work.

In 1727, en route back to London, Pond stopped in Paris. There he met the art dealer and connoisseur Pierre-Jean Mariette and witnessed the scope of his trade in Dutch, French and Italian prints and drawings. Mariette's international reach probably inspired Pond to establish a greater number of connections overseas. He later facilitated the alliance formed between the Society of Dilettanti in Rome with the Roman Club in England, which undoubtedly helped his own business affairs in Italy.

From Mariette's connoisseur circle, Pond learnt the process of identifying an artist by his 'hand' and the idiosyncrasies in drawing styles. This method had a commercial advantage, allowing dealers to claim a work of art was by a certain master without a signature or definite provenance. Pond became very skilled at identifying artists' styles, and cleverly created his own provenance mark, writing the word 'true' beside his signature on the back. Using the word 'true' was ingenious for it implied a moral value – truth – thus endorsing the high values of the connoisseur. Amongst his contemporaries, it became the mark of authentication. There are many works in major museums that still bear his imprint.

The connoisseur-dealer is in some ways an oxymoron since the connoisseur believes art should be removed from everyday concerns including the monetary value of a painting. Pond was acutely aware of the conflict this posed as a profiteer from art, yet successfully negotiated his way round it. In the first instance, he presented himself foremost as an artist. In his day, this was a far more respected position than a dealer. He also distanced his own dealership from commercial enterprises, especially the street printseller. Pond never owned a shop; instead, he brought potential buyers to his imposing home in Covent Garden. And unlike William Hogarth, he didn't set up a shop sign outside his home; for a connoisseur it would be considered vulgar to openly display one's trade.

Within his home, Pond orchestrated the buyer's experience as a polite exchange between like-minded thinkers, engaged in 'a quest for beauty', rather than a commercial transaction. He would often speak in Italian to emphasise his knowledge of the classical tradition. Later, when he moved to Lincoln's Inn Fields, he furnished the public rooms with dark mahogany furniture, and had the walls covered in green wool damask, with such luxurious decor adding a further layer of refinement. This superficial divorce from trade ended up being a winning commercial strategy, allowing the buyers to imagine the artwork in their own homes.

Although his trade in original works secured his reputation, Pond also successfully sold painted copies of Old Masters as well as his own art, and he had other strategies to reach buyers in these instances. In 1837, he started touring grand homes, in order to meet wealthy clients to whom he would then offer his services as an artist, making portraits and drawings of their family members. He also gave drawing lessons, mostly to women. This move into education proved to be very successful; several women became advocates for his art, and he secured many commissions through them.

In his dealership of prints, Pond was focussed on another market – one with mass appeal. In many ways, this venture contradicted the rarefied atmosphere he created when selling original art from his home. His largest trade came from selling reproductions of Old Master works and here Pond was prepared to use more overt strategies. He placed adverts for his latest print release in newspapers such as the *Daily Advertiser*. His first publication, *Prints in Imitation of Drawings* (1735), however, was a financial disaster. It was littered with amateurish mistakes – during printing many of the images were erroneously reversed. After this flop, Pond went into partnership with Knapton booksellers who had printing presses. He diversified into more popular subject matter, releasing two series of caricatures. He also ventured into celebrity culture, and made engravings of famous people of the day, such as the actor and theatre producer David Garrick; this type of work was especially successful.

An assessment of Pond's career reveals the fundamental issues that face art dealers. His varied marketing schemes demonstrate the extreme polarities in his dealership, with his rarefied sales of original Old Master art at one end, and his popular reach selling prints at the other. Positioning himself as a 'connoisseur-dealer' opened up an inherent problem: how to talk about money. This perceived conflict between art and money is not exclusive to the connoisseur and is reflected in the emerging tradition of aesthetics. The German philosopher Immanuel Kant (1724–1804) considered the appreciation of beauty to be a disinterested activity, removed from real-world concerns, such as work and money. Kant would have a long-standing influence on the art world. His values reinforce an uncertain status for dealers whose profession could be seen by some to muddy the values of art by introducing pecuniary concerns.

Looking forward to the twentieth century, several dealers would adopt a similar approach to Pond and try to hide the commercial aspect. However, there were also those that rejected this position entirely, and embraced commerce. Indeed, William Hogarth (1697–1764) shaped his dealership in opposition to the high-minded values of his contemporary, Pond, and presented himself instead as a popular art dealer.

William Hogarth

(1697–1764)

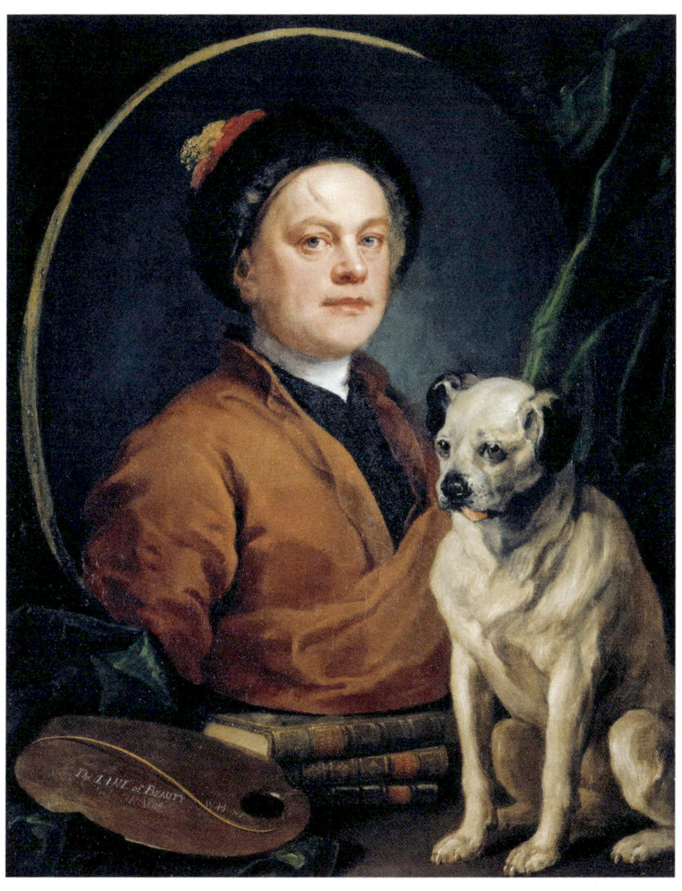

William Hogarth, *The Painter and his Pug (Self Portrait of the Artist and his dog 'Trump')*, 1745, oil on canvas, 90 × 69.9 cm (35 ½ × 27 ½ in.), Tate, UK.

Irrefutably one of the best known English artists of the eighteenth century, William Hogarth also acted as his own dealer: a radical move that has been largely passed over. In 2008, Damien Hirst (b. 1965) shocked the art world when he decided to bypass dealers, avoiding their significant cut, and sell his work at Sotheby's auction house. In his lifetime, Hogarth met the same outrage when he held a private auction of his own artworks. It seems critical to understand why Hogarth chose to circumvent the traditional commercial route, and establish himself as his own dealer.

Hogarth's move into sales was motivated by his frustration with the existing market, and his dislike for the connoisseur-dealer. Hogarth was clear about his feelings: 'the connoisseur and I are at war... I hate them.'[1] The artist disliked everything about the connoisseur, from their fascination with foreign travel to their preference for the Old Masters. In many ways, his position fits the model later used by the twentieth-century French sociologist Pierre Bourdieu, of the disruptive prophet overturning the 'convention of the habitus'[2] – the established order. Hogarth's radical move was to reject the classical tradition and establish himself as a popular art dealer.

Hogarth had a very different background to the rich connoisseur-dealers like Arthur Pond. He was born in Bartholomew Close, near London's Smithfield meat market, and anticipating a career in printmaking, 'next doore to Mr Downinge's printers'.[3] Every Monday, the farmers brought livestock to the market to be slaughtered and sold. The family faced great difficulties when Hogarth's father, a teacher and coffeehouse owner, was convicted of debt and the whole family were interned in Fleet Prison. Years later, Hogarth would show the bleak reality of a debtor's prison in his satirical painting series *A Rake's Progress* (1733–35). Having experienced such terrible poverty and suffering, Hogarth was determined to succeed commercially.

Unlike the connoisseur-dealer who aimed to mask the financial aspect from the sale, Hogarth embraced the commercial side and unashamedly exploited the type of marketing strategies used by street tradespeople. He entered the art world as an engraver, which associated him with the popular print trade, at the time largely controlled by booksellers. From the beginning, he was keen to establish himself as an independent trader. In 1720 he created his own shop card (fig. 1) which elegantly advertised 'W. HOGARTH – Engraver'. His aspiration to be a fine artist is reflected by the Greek muse on the left of the card, who represents Art and holds her hand up to Hogarth's

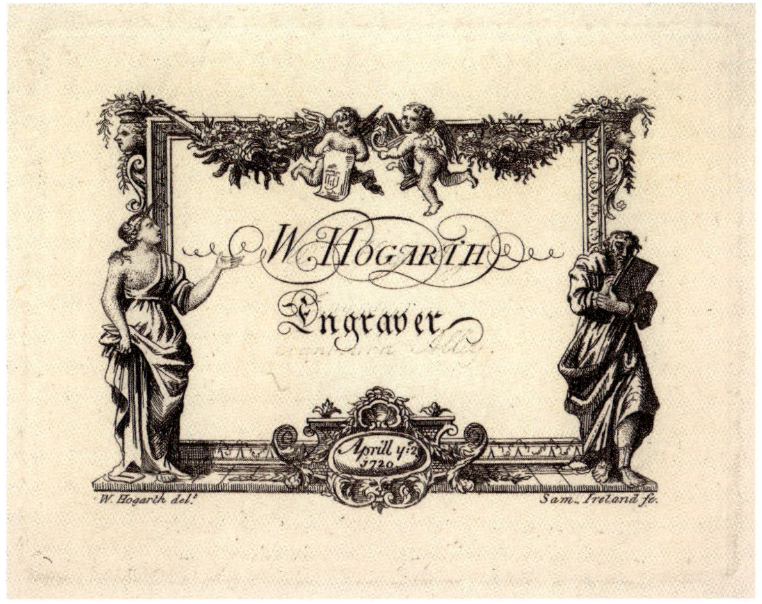

Fig.1 After William Hogarth, engraver Samuel Ireland, Hogarth's
Shop Card, 1790s, etching and engraving, sheet: 13.4 × 16.9 cm
(5 ¼ × 6 ⅝ in.), The Metropolitan Museum of Art, New York.

name. Such pictorial cards were common among shop traders and Hogarth would produce cards for other tradesmen including Ellis Gamble, a silversmith who Hogarth had been apprenticed to for six years from 1714.

While the connoisseur market was focussed on Old Master prints, depicting scenes from the classical past or views of foreign places, Hogarth sold images of contemporary life. He would often represent stories from the press. In 1726, he created a print based on a notorious news story about Mary Tofts who claimed she'd given birth to rabbits. The print has great comedy and combines a graphic birth scene with jumping bunnies. Selling very well, it confirmed to him that following the pulse of contemporary affairs was a winning strategy. In contrast with the idealised images marketed by the connoisseur-dealer, which were intended to put the viewer in a position of awe, Hogarth's audience could identify with the scenes he created and recognise the newsworthy characters. He would often hold back prints temporarily in order to add topical characters as they appeared in the press, and infuse images with the very latest cultural currency.

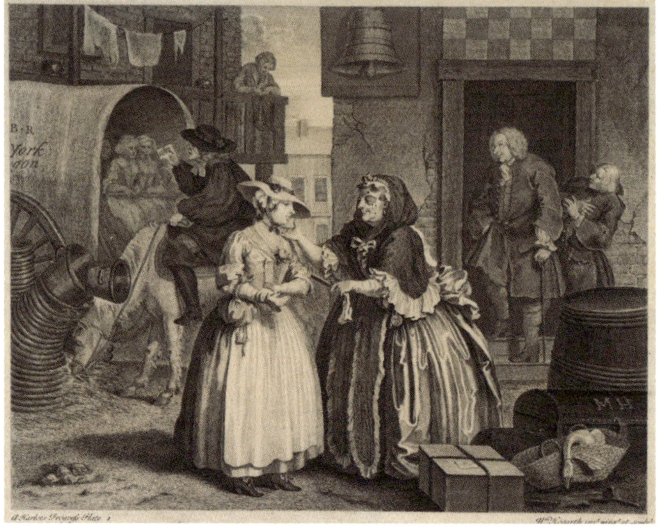

Fig. 2 William Hogarth, *A Harlot's Progress*, Plate 1, before April
1732, etching and engraving, first state of four, 31.3 × 38.4 cm
(12 ⅜ × 15 ⅛ in.), The Metropolitan Museum of Art, New York.

Hogarth continued to use popular subject matter to market his work to
a larger audience. In 1732 he made a print series, *A Harlot's Progress*, drawn
from his suite of six paintings from the previous year (now destroyed), which
told the story of a young woman who arrives in the city, falls into prostitution
and suffers a miserable death. Each print featured public figures for the
contemporary audience to identify and brimmed with anecdotal detail
for them to decipher. From the first print (fig. 2), the viewer can anticipate
the future demise of the young woman from telling signs such as a strangled
goose in a basket and the crumbling state of the buildings. The format of
the series, with its drama unfolding across a sequence of six images, created
value by its sheer volume. In a sense, Hogarth was offering entertainment
rather like cinema would some 200 years later.

Keen to separate his business from the street printseller, Hogarth made
the decision to market *A Harlot's Progress* himself. Eliminating the middle-
men – the print dealers and booksellers – was a bold move. Indeed, it is rare
in the history of dealing to find an artist acting independently like this. The
sales were run through a subscription scheme, with 1,240 subscriptions put
up for purchase; the buyers were asked for a down payment of half a guinea,

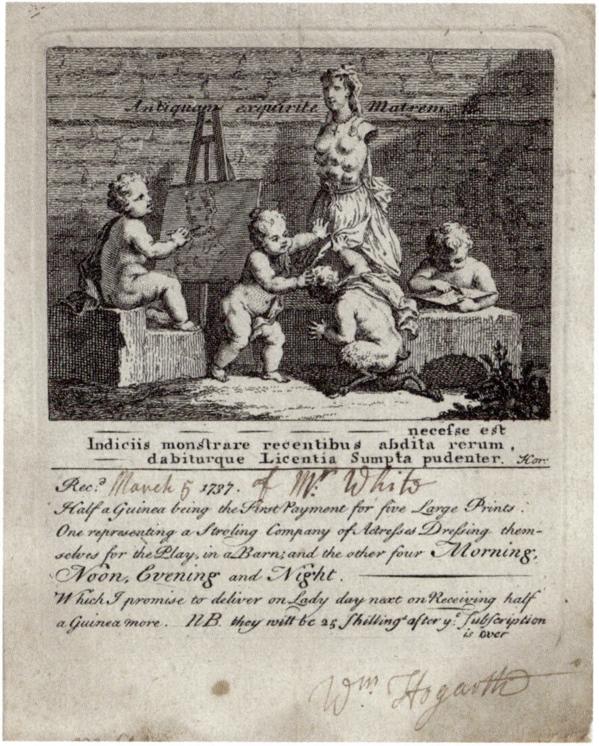

Fig. 3 William Hogarth, *Boys Peeping at Nature*,
subscription ticket dated 1737, etching, 17.6 × 13.8 cm
(7 × 5 ½ in.), The Metropolitan Museum of Art, New York.

with a further half a guinea due on collection. Proving highly popular, all subscriptions were sold. The success was partly down to brilliant marketing, with Hogarth adding on bonus extras. For example, when the buyers made the down payment, they were issued with a subscription ticket that had an engraving by the artist. The ticket for *A Harlot's Progress* (fig. 3) bore the engraving of *Boys Peeping at Nature* (1730), which showed a lecherous satyr peering up the skirt of Diana of Ephesus.

Hogarth also ran an aggressive advertising campaign in the press. In January 1732, a notice in *The Craftsman* announced a two-month delay because, 'being disappointed of the Assistance he approved, he is obliged to engrave them all himself'.[4] The wait built excitement and picked up straggling buyers, and the decision had clear financial benefits for the artist. The advert also emphasised the added value of the works being executed by him, and is an early instance of Hogarth distinguishing himself as an 'artist' printmaker.

In 1735 Hogarth petitioned Parliament to grant the 'artist' printmaker the same copyright protection awarded to authors in 1709. In an angry letter, he singled out printsellers who copied original prints without the permission of the 'Sculpture-Engravers' and robbed them of their due profits. His plea was heard and, in 1735, Parliament passed an act protecting printmakers' rights. It was a momentous event in the history of printmaking, recognising the artistic value of prints, but also providing the potential for artists to secure a secondary source of income from their original artwork. The nineteenth-century dealer Ernest Gambart (1814–1902) would capitalise on this law, and the potential profits from prints, often prioritising the securing of copyright before buying the original painting.

Interestingly, Hogarth gave permission for an authorised copy (for which he received a royalty) of *A Harlot's Progress* to be made by the printmaker Giles King, which sold at the much cheaper price of 4 shillings through booksellers. It was a canny way to make more money from the series, and reach lower-income clients, while not offending his subscribers who owned the high-quality artist edition. Still, Hogarth was frustrated at having to rely on the bookseller to sell these copies. He would solve this problem by opening his own shop.

In 1733, Hogarth and his wife, Jane, moved to a tall townhouse on Leicester Fields (now Leicester Square). He converted the front room into a gallery and, disrupting the neighbourhood's residential air, he boldly erected a shop sign outside. It depicted a lacquered bust of the Flemish artist, Anthony van Dyck (1599–1641), and soon Hogarth's shop became known as the 'Golden Head'. The premises had a large window through which prospective buyers could peer in at Hogarth's work. The spectacle functioned like the crowd-drawing window displays of the popular printsellers, which had the lure of Instagram today, drawing audiences into a visual platform purporting to be on trend. Hogarth's topical characters and newsworthy stories served to reinforce this currency.

Asserting further independence, Hogarth made the provocative decision to sidestep the grand, public auction houses, and hold a private auction at his shop. Hogarth's contemporaries were shocked by this audacious plan. Playing up to the spirit of provocation, Hogarth staged the auction as proof of the supremacy of English art. The invitation was adorned with *The Battle*

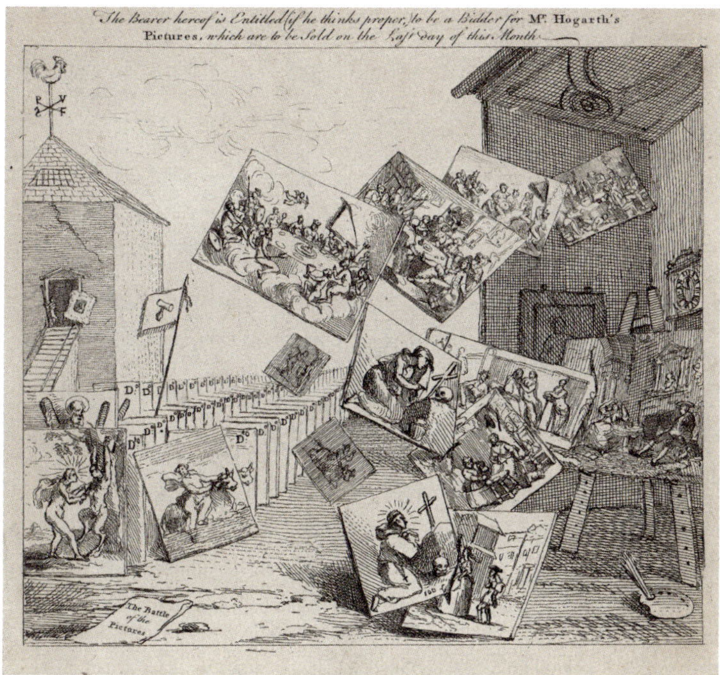

Fig. 4 William Hogarth, *The Battle of the Pictures*, 1745, etching,
19.5 × 21.1 cm (7¾ × 8⅜ in.), The Metropolitan Museum of Art, New York.

of the Pictures (1745, fig. 4) which depicted a windswept scene with Old Master paintings and Hogarth's own artworks caught in the wind stream and battling to bring each other down. The auction was successful: Hogarth's 19 canvases sold for £500 in total, a respectable fee given a modern portrait sold for around £8. However, in reality, the Old Masters still had the edge, with a single such painting selling for the price of Hogarth's entire lot.

A remarkable consistency ran through Hogarth's practice. His art was rooted in contemporary culture just as his dealership was integrated into modern, commercial life. In terms of dealership, Gambart would pick up the baton from Hogarth and market homegrown art on the same popular axis. In 1753, Hogarth made another attempt at securing the position of English art, publishing his treatise *The Analysis of Beauty*, which he sold at his gallery. In it, he attacks the generalised forms of Old Master art and delivers a concept of beauty with qualities of the living world. The theoretical framework added another dimension to Hogarth's independence.

William Buchanan

(1777–1864)

Boastful and canny, the Scottish dealer William Buchanan was his own spin doctor, always presenting his art business in the best light. He was to reap riches from the turmoil of the French Revolution (1789–99) and the Napoleonic Wars (1803–15) when major foreign collectors lost their wealth and were forced to sell their works of art. In his writings, he reframed this as an enterprise of national importance, saving art treasures from war zones. Yet his opportunism was boundless. On hearing Napoleon was purchasing art in Rome, he advised his agent to approach the Emperor and offer him a painting by Nicolas Poussin (1594–1665). Disregarding the fact that Britain was essentially at war with France, he was prepared to sell to the enemy.

Born in Glasgow, Buchanan was a lawyer before he turned to art dealing. From the outset, he was attentive to his public image. Like the eighteenth-century dealer Arthur Pond, he was keen to differentiate his dealership from the street print trader. However, their approaches were very different. While Pond orchestrated his sales as a high art experience distanced from monetary concerns, Buchanan positioned himself as the speculator, the financial maverick able to sense the market and predict the future value of artworks.

Although Buchanan missed being involved in the sale of the Orléans Collection in 1798, the event left a deep impression on him. Originally amassed by the French prince, Philippe II, Duke of Orléans, part of the collection had been bought up by a syndicate of English aristocrats with the aid of the art dealer, Michael Bryan. A huge stimulus to the English art market, Buchanan wrote about the sale in his book *Memoirs of Painting with a Chronological History of the Importation of Pictures by the Grand Masters* (1824). This publication reveals a metanarrative; it emphasises how the selling of the French royal art collection had created a rare opportunity for Britain to build an art collection of national importance. By February 1803, Buchanan had assembled a group of Old Master paintings, which he offered to the government to purchase, with a view to them becoming part of a new national art gallery. By acquiring such art, he felt the government could raise the level of British art, since, he claimed, 'it holds out a bright example for imitation, and rouses and calls into action the native talents of those who feel the sacred flame of emulation.'[1]

The government missed this opportunity. However, Buchanan would continue to use the example of the Orléans sale, and capitalise on the escalating troubles abroad. The French Revolution, and Napoleon's invasion of Italy, had impoverished aristocrats in these countries, and they were looking to sell their art collections. Buchanan had an agent in Italy – a Scottish artist called James Irvine (1757–1831) – who sourced Old Master works to ship to London. And when Napoleon invaded Spain, Buchanan again swiftly moved in and worked with an agent in Madrid. Revered works of art passed through his hands including *Bacchus and Ariadne* (1520–23, fig. 6) by Titian (*c.* 1490–1576) and *The Toilet of Venus ('The Rokeby Venus')* (1647–51, fig. 5) by Diego Velázquez (1599–1660).

Buchanan's early years as a dealer (1802–6) are well covered by his correspondence. Sometimes his inflated pronouncements sound like a brilliant advertising pitch. Certainly in advertising today, the story behind the product is everything. Hugh Brigstocke, who edited a volume of

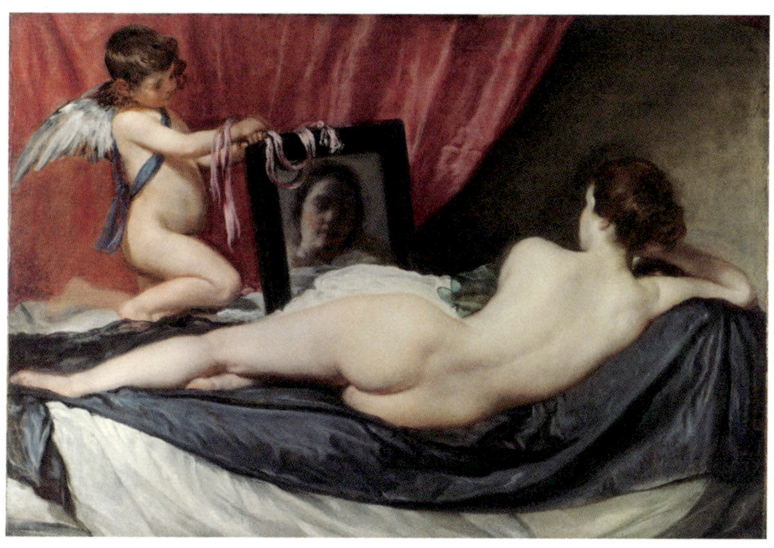

Fig. 5 Diego Velázquez, *The Toilet of Venus*, 1647–51, oil on canvas, 122.5 × 177 cm (48 ⅛ × 69 ⅝ in.), National Gallery, London.

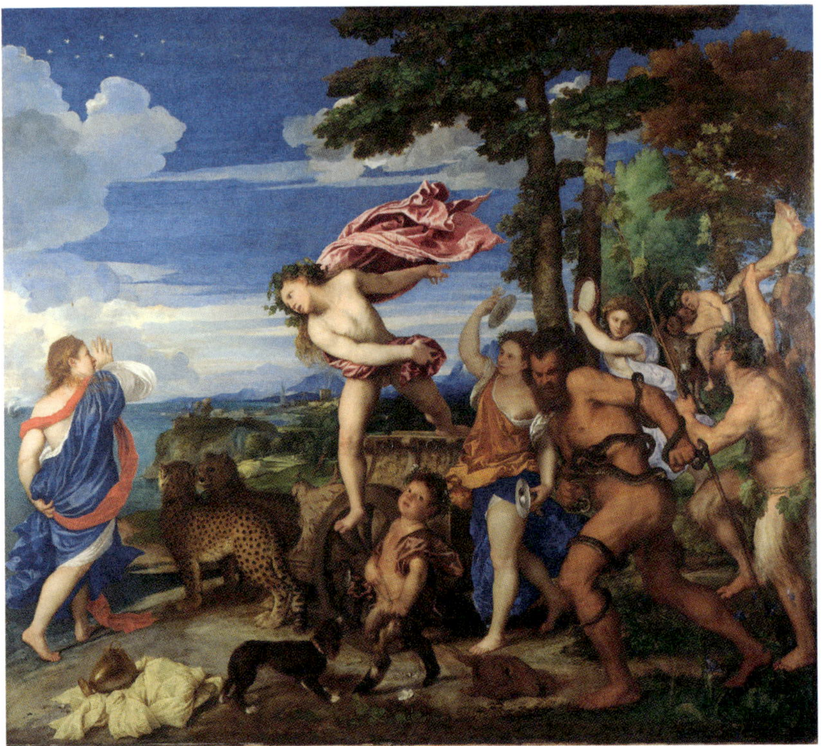

Fig. 6 Titian, *Bacchus and Ariadne*, 1520–23, oil on canvas,
176.5 × 191 cm (69 ½ × 75 ¼ in.) National Gallery, London.

Buchanan's correspondence, describes the dealer as being totally ignorant about art and contemptuous of his buyers. Indeed, it is true that Buchanan had a low opinion of some of his clients; he was especially disdainful of the Earl of Wemyss and his 'rage for naked beauties'.[2] However, Buchanan's humorous evaluation of the 'lecherous Old Dog'[3] is also strangely progressive.

Though Buchanan remained distant with his clients, he was deeply involved with his London agent, David Stewart, who was responsible for sales. He would send Stewart lists of recommendations, and practical advice on how to approach the buyer. In one letter, he advises him:

It is of great consequence to know the taste of the purchasers
for the different Masters, and the individual Master each
Collector is most fond of, for all have a favourite Master. And

it could be a great point gained from their own mouths by asking, 'What master are you looking for at present?' And note down the answer.[4]

Buchanan also cunningly told his agent not to sell too many big pictures that would fill buyers' walls and thereby limit future sales.

Far from being ignorant as Brigstocke suggests, Buchanan's writing on the Orléans Collection sale indicates he had a sound understanding of art history, and was sensitive to the distinctive qualities of the Old Masters. And this knowledge was critical to forming an understanding of the market. Buchanan had an acute sense for the moment and English taste. In these early, well-documented years, he marked out an interest amongst buyers to purchase a few select masterpieces, a practice which anticipates the buying of 'trophy art' today. He was also practical, and unafraid to admit when he'd misjudged the market. He managed to secure two works by Raphael (1483–1520); however, the works were early pieces by the artist and, as Buchanan recognised, too 'hard, brown, early, and Gothick'[5] for English taste. When they failed to sell, Buchanan sent them back to Rome to be sold; years later the art dealer Joseph Duveen (1869–1939) would express his deep regret at these canvases being lost from Britain.

To optimise sales, the Scottish dealer brazenly experimented with different marketing strategies. Realising the lure of a fresh-to-market sale, he encouraged Stewart to tell his buyer they were being shown the work first. Of course, Stewart would be speaking to several buyers at the same time, but he'd conjure the idea with each of them that they were being offered an exclusive look. When Buchanan first hired rooms in 1803, on Oxendon Street, right in the heart of London, he bombarded Stewart with more recommendations, this time on how to showcase the works. He suggested, for example, the most favourable lighting conditions for a particular artist. And cannily, he considered how the space could be used to tailor the sale to each buyer. The dealer writes, 'We must in future keep all our pictures arranged in another room to whom nobody can have access but yourself, and pull them out one by one into the front room, as you find they are likely to suit your callers.'[6]

Buchanan recognised another advantage of focussing on a single work: the picture could be shown to its best advantage, and unfortunate clashes with surrounding pictures could be avoided. Another nineteenth-century dealer,

Ernest Gambart, would exploit the single-picture exhibition to great effect and it is a practice that continues to be used in contemporary galleries today.

In 1804 Buchanan opened his own gallery, close to where he'd hired rooms. This establishment was a far grander affair. Buchanan liked to boast that the principal room of 2.8 square metres (30 square feet) had the exact same proportions as Christie's rooms, only on a smaller scale. Initially, Buchanan struggled to make the gallery work: he had overextended himself financially and the market was suffering a serious downturn. He had always been careful to manage risk. To minimise losses, he'd tried to gauge interest from buyers first, but this was difficult as sales were coming from overseas and communication was poor. He mostly relied on prints of masterpieces, or sometimes he'd have a local artist make a sketch. With the market in free fall, Buchanan reconsidered his career, and started a crash course in dealing jewellery.

Before the market crisis, Buchanan had speculated to his Italian agent about a burgeoning taste for vibrant colour, stating how 'the English are more caught by the fascination for colour than by any other means, provided drawing and composition are in themselves correct, and the subject good. This renders the works of Rubens, Titian, Van Dyck... and the other great colourists so much sought after.'[7] In Buchanan's opinion, it was Titian who 'carried the brilliancy of colouring to its highest perfection.'[8] And he had advised his Italian agent, 'A fine Titian is probably the greatest object at present of any master for people appear Titian mad.'[9]

As the art market recovered, Buchanan's predictions proved correct. The sale of Titian's painting *Bacchus and Ariadne* to a private individual in 1807 could be considered the crowning glory of Buchanan's career as a speculative dealer. The sale corroborated Buchanan's vision; as the writer Philip Hook describes, '[It] simultaneously confirmed all his theories: the taste of English buyers for bright colour, their mania for Titian; their willingness to pay exceptional prices for exceptional quality.'[10] In 1826, the painting would be sold on to the newly established National Gallery, a jewel in the crown for Buchanan, whose ideal was to build a public art collection of national importance.

Ernest Gambart

(1814–1902)

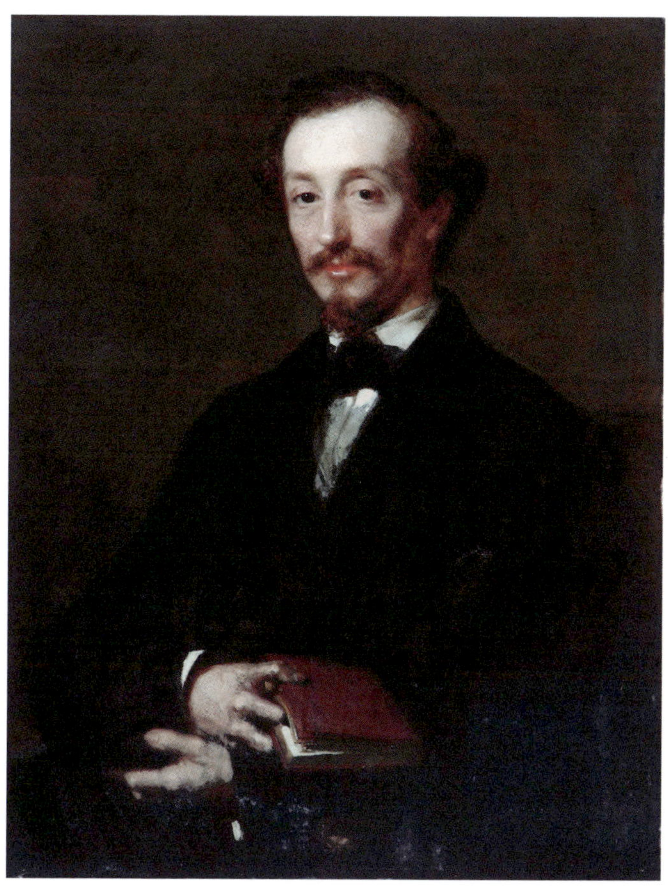

John Prescott Knight, *Mr Ernest Gambart*,
oil on canvas, 90.2 × 71.1 cm (35 ½ × 28 in.),
Atkinson Art Gallery, Southport, UK.

The Pre-Raphaelite painter Dante Gabriel Rossetti (1828–1882) nicknamed the dealer Ernest Gambart 'Gamble Art'. Certainly, Gambart took risks, and reaped great profits from selling art. Meeting the prevailing taste for accessible art, he shrewdly sold works by living artists, and his business flourished during a commercial boom. In fact, contemporary art had never been so valuable, and Gambart played a leading role in this development, demanding ever-increasing prices. Rossetti, and the many other contemporary artists whose work Gambart represented, did very well from the situation.

Born in Belgium in 1814, Gambart moved to London in 1840. At this point, he had been acting as an agent for the French print publisher Goupil & Cie., who'd sent him a portfolio of their Old Master and French School prints to sell. However, he struggled to make sales even though the art market was flourishing in Britain and this made him question trading in the Old Masters. He decided to change tack and specialise in art by living artists. Branching out on his own, in the mid-1850s Gambart opened the French Gallery on 120/121 Pall Mall – one of the first commercial galleries dedicated to selling contemporary art.

In the early part of the nineteenth century, the Royal Academy of Arts was the main route for living artists to find buyers. However, increasingly frustrated by its monopoly, artists had begun to look for alternative venues, running exhibitions on an ad hoc basis in their studios and through print-sellers. Dealers were also organising independent exhibitions. However, their profession was not widely respected at that time because of the significant number of fake Old Master artworks that had been sold through their channels. Gambart was determined to distinguish his practice from this poorly regarded trade.

Art historian Pamela Fletcher has revealed how Gambart infused his sales with the newly emerging language of professionalism.[1] In this respect, he managed to ease the uncomfortable relationship between money and art, for as sociologist Pierre Bourdieu has argued, the art business functions in terms of 'the economic world reversed',[2] where aesthetic value demands a disavowal of economic interest. Professionalism sidestepped the conflict, by bringing values of trustworthiness and expertise.

In terms of Gambart's professionalism, he offered a permanent exhibition space for contemporary artists who had previously had an itinerant existence. The French Gallery was a clever choice of name, distancing his establishment from trade printsellers, who typically marketed their business under their own name. It also added an allure by invoking France's long-respected art tradition.

Projecting a sense of expertise, Gambart positioned himself as a specialist of a single period. He also introduced respected practices from the Royal Academy. For example, he copied their crowd-drawing annual fixtures and held a Winter Exhibition. This was very successful: the 1854–55 Winter Exhibition sold £6,000 worth of works (around £625,000 today). His gallery released catalogues for the exhibitions, which, following the Royal Academy's example, didn't mention prices. This approach encouraged buyers to engage with gallery staff who could then discuss the artwork's significance, and enhance the perceived value of the sale.

The market had transformed in the nineteenth century. While the aristocrat buyer had waned, the Industrial Revolution had created great wealth for the mercantile middle class who were gaining interest in art. Gambart appealed to this new buyer with his unpretentious manner. Chiming with middle class values, he spoke of art in terms of workmanship while also recognising their taste for familiar, everyday scenes, packed with incident and drama.

As well as selling the major Victorian artists including William Powell Frith (1819–1909), Edwin Landseer (1802–1873) and the Pre-Raphaelite group, Gambart would hold regular exhibitions of contemporary artists from abroad, and would tour Europe to source artists. One of his most successful finds was the Dutch artist Lawrence Alma-Tadema (1836–1912), who combined a photographic realism with historical subject matter. The dealer may have subsequently influenced the artist's style, which became lighter and more suited to the taste of his English clients.

Gambart had two standout practices: one was exhibiting a single work of art, and the other was selling prints of the original painting. Both came together when he showed the 2.4 by 5-metre (8 by 17-foot) painting *The Horse Fair* (1852–55, fig. 7) by Rosa Bonheur (1822–1899). The painting had failed to sell at the Paris Salon of 1853, but Gambart sensed its subject matter would be popular with British horse lovers. In the summer of 1855, he built up a sense of excitement, with the artist being treated as a celebrity. On the 16 July there was a grand feast attended by the President of the Royal Academy, Sir Charles Eastlake, and the following day a select group of collectors were shown Bonheur's work. The artist herself received much press attention, which often highlighted her appearance: her short hair, and decision to wear male clothes. This public interest in the artist and

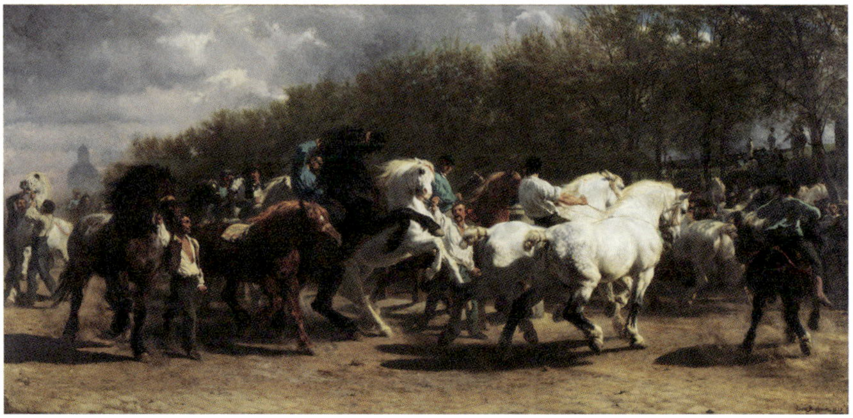

Fig.7 Rosa Bonheur, *The Horse Fair*, 1852–55,
oil on canvas, 244.5 × 506.7 cm (96 ¼ × 199 ½ in.),
The Metropolitan Museum of Art, New York.

the spectacle of the single work brought huge crowds. Adding to the fervour, Queen Victoria expressed an interest in buying the painting and it was sent to Buckingham Palace for one day. While royal approval immediately piqued interest, the empty wall at the gallery created further sensation.

Ultimately, the Queen did not buy the work and after exhibiting it in New York, Gambart sold it in 1857 to New Jersey-based collector William Wright. However, Gambart had already generated an income from the painting. The entrance fee to the London exhibition of 1 shilling added up to around £20 to £30 a day (equivalent to around £2,300 today), and after London, the painting was taken on a triumphal tour around cities in the UK including Liverpool, Manchester and Glasgow, generating further income from entrance fees in every location.

Gambart also owned the copyright for *The Horse Fair*, allowing him to issue prints, and he commissioned artist Thomas Landseer (1795–1880) to create it. The popularity of the exhibitions and press attention helped secure a long list of subscribers. Gambart would later continue to follow this business model and in some cases, after reaping the profits from the subsidiary rights, he would gift the painting to the nation – an ingenious strategy that raised the profile of the artists and, ultimately, the value of their art. It also associated Gambart with philanthropy, building his reputation as a principled, professional dealer.

Early on, Gambart had his eyes set on William Powell Frith who had enormous popular appeal. Brimming with detail, his panoramic canvases had the scope of a cinema screen and, like Hogarth's audience, the viewer played an active role, deciphering the unfolding dramas. Commissioned by the chemist Jacob Bell, Frith's painting *The Derby Day* (1856–58) already had a home, but Gambart snapped up the copyright at £1,500 (the same price as the painting) and the exhibition rights for four and a half years. Much to his irritation, he lost Frith's next blockbuster, *The Railway Station* (1862), to his rival, Louis Victor Flatow, who secured both the painting and its copyright.

Gambart also sensed the potential of the emerging Pre-Raphaelite group, and secured many successful deals for them. John Everett Millais (1829–1896) describes how, '[he] overwhelms me with small commissions which after all pay mightily well.'[3] Gambart's handling of William Holman Hunt's (1827–1910) career is especially interesting. At the beginning, he was reticent about Hunt's religious subject matter and decided against buying his painting *The Light of the World* (1853, fig. 8) – something he likely regretted

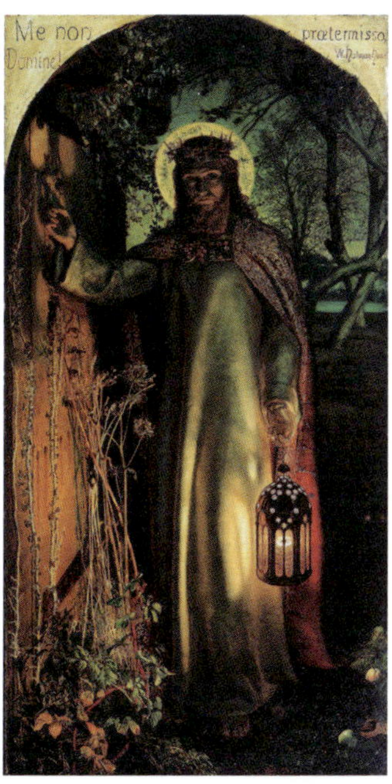

Fig. 8 William Holman Hunt, *The Light of the World*, 1853, oil on canvas, 121.9 × 61 cm (48 × 24 in.), Keble College, Oxford, UK.

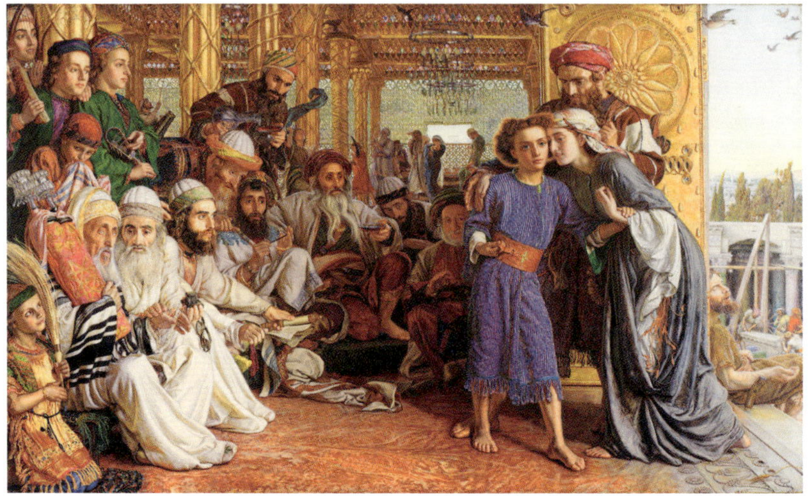

Fig. 9 William Holman Hunt, *The Finding of the Saviour in the Temple*, 1854–60, oil on canvas, 85.7 × 141 cm (33 ¾ × 55 ½ in.), Birmingham Museums and Art Gallery, UK.

since it went on to become an iconic image of the Victorian age. Unusually for him, Gambart had missed a key factor in English taste: an underlying religious piety that came to drive interest in Hunt's paintings. However, he did buy the copyright for the painting, and the engraving by W. H. Simmons (1811–1882) was highly valued; one critic wrote, 'it is one of the most perfect things modern art has produced... a great triumph.'[4] The earnings from this print alone could have kept the dealer comfortable for the rest of his life.

After this success, Gambart bought Hunt's painting *The Finding of the Saviour in the Temple* (1854–60, fig. 9) alongside the copyright and exhibition rights for £5,500. This was the highest sum paid for a painting by a living artist, and Gambart put his full promotional machinery into action. To appeal to a larger market, he released three price points for the prints (£3, £5 and £8), based on size. He also carefully managed the exhibiting of the painting. When Eastlake requested it be shown at the Royal Academy, Gambart refused. His strategy here was to position Hunt as an alternative to the humdrum of the Royal Academy, and something modern, and fresh. Hunt reveals the dealer's determination on this, '[Gambart] says if I will let him have my pictures to exhibit separately from the Royal Academy, he will give me as much again for them: it would be worth his while.'[5]

The situation contrasts with the formation of an avant-garde in France, where artists began to show their work in independent venues after it was refused by the Académie française. Gambart was offering this independence instead as a lucrative option to artists.

It appears that Gambart came to understand the potency of Hunt's religious subject matter; the presentation of *The Finding of the Saviour in the Temple* had the solemnity of a religious encounter. With the room in semi-darkness and the painting behind a thick canopy, a diffuse light illuminated the image of a young Christ. The exhibition was a sensation and drew crowds. Diarist and civil servant Arthur Munby described the impact of the painting: 'I cannot trust myself to speak of it... it is unique and simply wonderful... one should sit before it in quiet for hours.'[6]

Hunt had brought an emerging Realist language to religious subject matter. The dealer put pressure on the artist to write an article and explain his vision. When Hunt refused, Gambart turned to the critic F. G. Stephens (1827–1907) who wrote a piece in the *Athenaeum*. Perhaps directed by Gambart, Stephens's article emphasised the meticulously detailed setting, and Hunt's archaeological research in the Middle East. This sheds light on the delicate relationship between critic and dealer in a period when new art required contextualisation. Gambart continued to appeal to critics, also convincing the writer John Ruskin (1819–1900) to include reviews of his French exhibitions in his *Academy Notes* (1857–59, 1875).

Focussed on the popular art market, Gambart's art business functioned like a well-oiled machine, with his trade in prints and spectacular, crowd-pleasing exhibitions working in symphony, each promoting the other. Indeed, his professionalism had a slickness that anticipated the polished commercialism of the branded dealer.

Paul Durand-Ruel

(1831–1922)

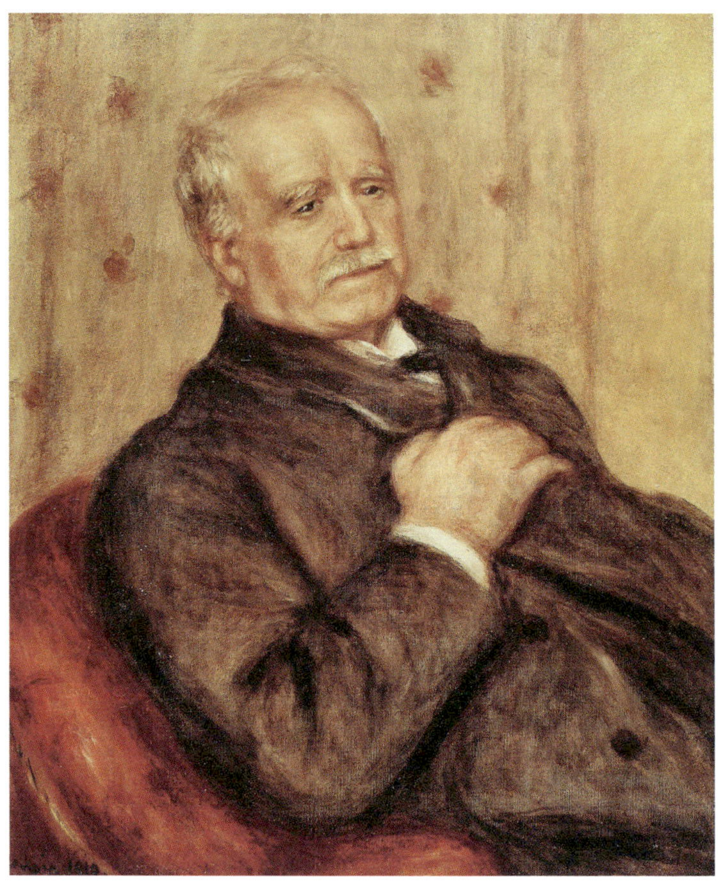

Pierre-Auguste Renoir,
Paul Durand-Ruel, 1910, oil on canvas,
65 × 54 cm (25⅝ × 21¼ in.).

Around 1910, Pierre-Auguste Renoir (1841–1919) painted a portrait of his dealer. Paul Durand-Ruel appears a tender, melancholic figure. Now celebrated for building the careers of the Impressionists, during his lifetime he was mocked for supporting them. In his memoirs, Durand-Ruel relates how people called him 'a madman'.[1] He would consistently play the outsider. A monarchist and a Catholic, he deeply mourned the society before the French Revolution, and the Impressionists stood in opposition to such ideals; most were radical thinkers, and a few even had revolutionary sympathies. Yet somehow, the contradictions worked. To quote Renoir: 'We needed a dyed-in-the-wool reactionary to defend our work, which the Salonards were calling revolutionary. At least Durand-Ruel wasn't someone they'd shoot as a Communard.'[2]

Durand-Ruel had grown up surrounded by art. His parents ran a stationery and art supplies shop in Paris, which they gradually transformed into a gallery, and which Durand-Ruel eventually inherited. Significantly, his parents had run a barter system whereby they supplied artists with materials in exchange for work. For Durand-Ruel, this early contact with living artists, witnessing their struggles to survive, was a crucial experience. As a dealer he would be attentive to his artists' welfare, paying many of them a monthly stipend so they could afford to paint. While wealthy art patrons had long offered this type of financial support, it was exceptional for a dealer, especially at this time.

Durand-Ruel's first career thoughts were to join the military or be a missionary. The common motivation running through these vocations and his dealership is a rescuer mindset. Pierre Assouline, in his biography of Durand-Ruel, notes that he 'was obsessive, even frenetic in his pursuit of a complete oeuvre, even one that he knew would later be completely dispersed at auction'.[3] His compulsive buying likely stemmed in part from the collective trauma of the French Revolution and the continued political instability and violence that permeated society and culture. As the radical poet Arthur Rimbaud willed the Communards to burn the Louvre down, Durand-Ruel was intent on protecting an emerging French art tradition.

Working from his parents' gallery, Durand-Ruel's focus on French art resonated with shifting attitudes in the art world. As Arthur Pond's dealership exemplified, eighteenth-century taste had centred on the classical tradition and Italian Renaissance art. While the Académie française would aggressively perpetuate classicism as the ideal, there were glimmers of a democratisation of taste in the nineteenth century. The newly established national museums were organising their collections according to country of origin and were introducing the public to different art. Durand-Ruel drew on this discourse on nationality, marketing his artists abroad as the French School. He discovered the canvases of Eugène Delacroix (1798–1863) at the Exposition Universelle of 1855, and their 'splendid colour' convinced him of the 'triumph of modern art over academic art'.[4] His focus was to remain on contemporary art.

Durand-Ruel's first dealings were with what he called the 'beautiful School of 1830', which included the Barbizon artists Théodore Rousseau (1812–1867) and Jean-François Millet (1814–1875), as well as Delacroix and Gustave Courbet (1819–1877). Essential to his early business was the securing of a financial backer, Charles Edwards, which allowed him to buy up substantial quantities of artworks and establish exclusivity with some of his artists. Between 1866 and 1872, he purchased 102 works by Delacroix, and was prepared to pay above market prices to secure his monopoly; he spent 96,000 francs for *The Death of Sardanapalus* (1827, fig. 10) in 1873.

In 1881, the artist Eugène Boudin (1824–1898) reported the extent of Durand-Ruel's activity: 'Here I am being completely monopolised by Durand-Ruel. Yes! He has bought up all my pictures scattered among the dealers. He has forbidden me from painting any for the collectors and especially for his colleagues.'[5] The strategy seemed to work, for Boudin adds, 'In spite of myself, I'm becoming very important: they can't get enough of Boudin.'[6] Because those in the 'beautiful School of 1830' were established artists and their prices were high, there wasn't much room to make large profits at this point.

Early on, Durand-Ruel sensed that this new art needed a critical context. He had come to revere individuality, somewhat ironically given the concept was strongly associated with the French Revolution. In 1867, he bought 91 works, mostly *plein-air* sketches by Rousseau – their unfinished state being a mark of the artist's temperament. At the time, drawings were not valued highly: the Académie française considered them mere studies for a final painting. Intent on changing attitudes, in 1869 he published his short-lived *Revue Internationale de l'Art et de la Curiosité*, which was distributed in many European cities. The art critic Alfred Sensier (1815–1877) contributed a series of articles on Rousseau in which he discussed the artist's drawings, and the individuality of his expression. As the dealer sowed

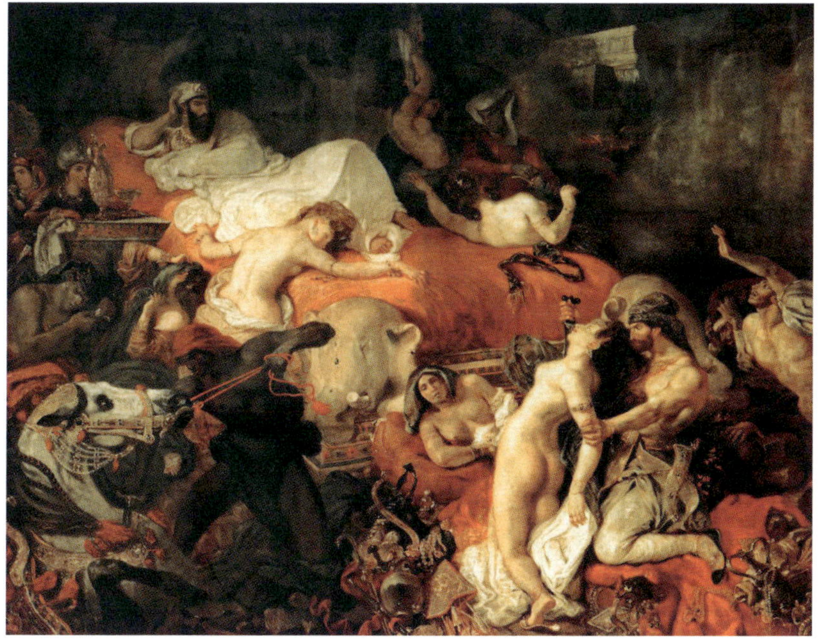

Fig. 10 Eugène Delacroix, *The Death of Sardanapalus*, 1827,
oil on canvas, 392 × 496 cm (154 ⅜ × 195 ¼ in.), Louvre, Paris.

this context for his 'beautiful School of 1830', he prepared the ground for Impressionism, and their raw canvases with their sketch-like execution.

When the Franco–Prussian War broke out in 1870, Durand-Ruel sought safety in London. Shipping his collection over, he established his business at 168 New Bond Street. There, he marketed his narrative of a 'French school' of painting. Naming his business The Society of French Artists, his catalogues boasted an imaginary committee of famous French artists which included Courbet, who had no knowledge of his assigned position.

While living in London, Durand-Ruel met fellow refugees Claude Monet (1840–1926) and Camille Pissarro (1830–1903) and bought his first of their works from them. He returned to Paris after the war in 1871, and was then introduced to Renoir, Alfred Sisley (1839–1899) and Edgar Degas (1834–1917). He also discovered two paintings by Édouard Manet (1832–1883) at the studio of the British sculptor Alfred Stevens (1817–1875) and immediately purchased them. The next day he swept up everything in Manet's studio, buying 23 canvases for 35,000 francs.

What distinguishes this phase in Durand-Ruel's dealings is that he was catching artists early in their careers: a painting by Monet could be bought for as little as 200 francs At the time, the novelist Émile Zola anticipated the potential profit, stating, 'I am so sure that Manet will be one of the masters of tomorrow that I should believe I had made a good bargain, had I the money, in buying all his canvases today. In fifty years, they will sell for fifteen or twenty times more.'[7]

A key reason for securing these monopolies was to drive up the prices. Durand-Ruel would stress the value of this to his artists. When Pissarro wanted to sell his work independently, Durand-Ruel insisted the artist price his works higher. The dealer was prepared to go to extreme lengths and, for example, would send agents to bid up works at auction.

In the early 1870s, Durand-Ruel entered a manic phase of buying, partly prompted by the tragic death of his young wife Eva. He admitted it became a perilous path; in the case of Monet alone, he spent 9,000 francs in 1872; the following year this increased to 19,000F. During this time, he was relentlessly promoting his artists. In 1876, echoing Ernest Gambart's rival exhibitions, he supplanted the established exhibition route of the Salon, and held the Second Impressionist exhibition at his own gallery. He asked the critic Théodore Duret (1838–1927) to write an essay for the catalogue. And chiming with the dealer's marketing, Duret placed Impressionism within a tradition of French landscape art while also emphasising the individual genius of each painter.

Despite these efforts, no paintings were sold, and the critics wrote caustic reviews, describing the art in pathological terms. One newspaper warned people to stay away as it would harm their health. Even literary figures were dismissive; the Symbolist novelist Joris-Karl Huysmans (1848–1907) compared the effect of Impressionist art to a retinal disorder. The lack of sales in combination with the huge outgoings from purchasing Impressionist art in such volume brought the dealer to the brink of financial disaster. Fortuitously, in 1880 he managed to find a new financial backer, Jules Feder, the director of the Union Générale bank. This brought temporary stability, and he was able to resume buying.

Durand-Ruel struck out with another ambitious strategy, rethinking the tradition of the solo retrospective exhibition. Typically held at the end of a prestigious career, Durand-Ruel used it to highlight individual early or mid-career artists. In 1883 he staged a series of one-man shows of Boudin, Monet, Renoir,

Pissarro and Sisley. Though few sales were generated, these monographic exhibitions were an important moment in the history of curation.

By February 1882, the Union Générale bank had collapsed, and Feder needed to recover his loan from Durand-Ruel. Near bankruptcy again, the dealer's situation was to transform when, in 1886, James F. Sutton (1843–1915), founder member of the American Art Association, a New York art gallery and auction house, visited Durand-Ruel's gallery and offered him an exhibition in the United States. Sutton promised to cover everything from insurance to transportation. Even more importantly, he negotiated favourable import duties whereby Durand-Ruel only had to pay 20 per cent tax (typically it was 33 per cent), and moreover this sum was only to be levied on works that sold. The French dealer took 289 paintings and sold his vision of a French naturalist art, exhibiting works from the 'beautiful School of 1830' alongside Impressionist art. Marketing Impressionism in relationship to these older, established artists was a strategy he had used previously in art publications, and it worked well here. Although only 49 works sold (raising around $40,000), for the first time the Impressionists received positive attention. As the dealer recognised:

> Without America, I would have been lost, ruined, after having
> bought so many Monets and Renoirs. The two exhibitions there in
> 1886 saved me. The American public bought moderately it is true,
> but thanks to that public Monet and Renoir were able to live and
> the French public followed suit.[8]

Durand-Ruel claimed the Americans had fewer prejudices than the old-world Europeans. Reaping the benefits of this more receptive audience, in 1888 he opened a gallery in New York where he sold his Impressionist and French art to newly wealthy industrialists – one of his major buyers being the chemist, Alfred Barnes. As prices for Impressionist art rose, Durand-Ruel was ready with his stockpile of work to sell to this new market.

Following his success in America, Durand-Ruel entered into an agreement with the German dealer Paul Cassirer (1871–1926) to exhibit Impressionist works at his Berlin gallery, and through this, many of these works found their way into major museums, further increasing the perception of their value. Durand-Ruel was acutely aware of how advantageous this placement was, telling Cassirer, 'Museums are our best advertisements.'[9]

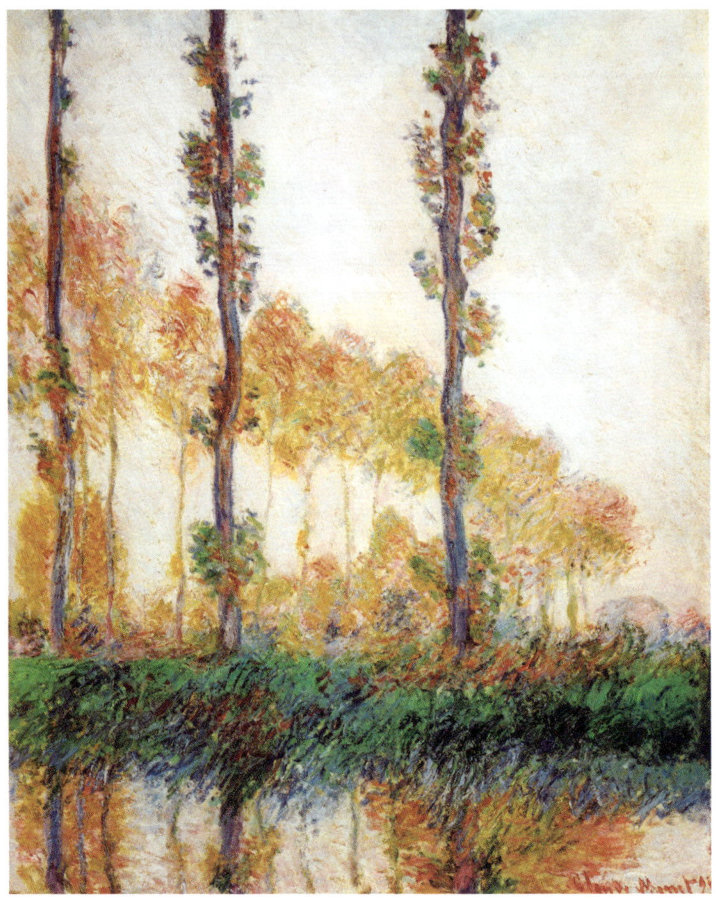

Fig. 11 Claude Monet, *Poplars (Autumn)*, 1891,
oil on canvas, 92 × 73 cm (36⅛ × 28¾ in.).

In Germany, Durand-Ruel also explored an alternative, somewhat eccentric avenue, holding small exhibitions of art in elite hotels. This move into the luxury sector had the polish of the branded gallery.

Ridiculed for investing in the unknown Impressionist artists, by the end of his career Durand-Ruel was able to reflect, 'My madness had been wisdom.'[10] By the 1890s he was achieving high prices for his Impressionist canvases, his biggest seller being Monet, and in 1892, he opened an exhibition of Monet's series *Poplars* (fig. 11). In many ways, it was a refinement of the one-man show, focusing on a single motif in the artist's oeuvre. The exhibition demonstrated a great synergy between dealer and artist. Durand-Ruel had consistently attempted to sell the idea of an artist's temperament, something dealers of modern art would continue to reinforce. And the series form developed this idea, each canvas conveying a different mood and acting as a beat in the artist's unfolding experience. Just as time plays a central role in Monet's series, time was a key element in the dealer's success. He bought undiscovered artists and waited. As Durand-Ruel advised, 'You should never be in a rush to sell.'[11]

Chapter 2

The Branded Dealer

Introduction

The psychology of the brand is highly effective: that Nike swoosh across a trainer sets it apart as a premier product. And the branded dealership holds the same promise of excellence. When buyers are taking a risk, especially on an unknown artist, brands are reassuring. Don Thompson explains the logic, 'Friends might go bug-eyed when you say, "I paid five point six million dollars for that ceramic statue." No one is dismissive when you say, "I bought this at Sotheby's" or "I found this at Gagosian" or "This is my Jeff Koons."'[1] The dealer's role is to make their brand desirable and certainly, with the nineteenth-century dealer Joseph Duveen, buyers were prepared to pay more for a 'Duveen' painting.

The sophisticated selling methods of the branded dealers reflect the ongoing professionalisation of the art market that began in the nineteenth century. They emerged as modern advertising was taking shape, and their businesses were informed by this new discipline. A key principle in advertising is maintaining a consistent brand across all platforms, a standard the early dealers embraced. Duveen had a seamless look, with his salubrious gallery complementing his smart suits, and prestigious sales of Old Master art. Later, dealers brought more elaborate marketing strategies to cultivate their brands, including advertising campaigns and endorsements from celebrities. They would attract buyers with desirable 'extras': the allure of being part of an elite social group, being invited to openings, and having priority for future purchases.

In our capitalist-driven market, the branded dealer has become an exclusive term, applied to the most financially successful. Thompson argues, 'Gagosian and White Cube and maybe twenty others are the branded galleries at the peak of the dealer pyramid. They represent artists who have achieved the greatest success – but these are far less than 1 per cent of all contemporary artists.'[2]

Valued as the gold standard, writers have attempted to define the qualities of the branded dealership, and according to them, it's about securing the top artists, and raising their profiles to secure higher prices. It has also come to be identified with a particular type of gallery space, known as the white cube. Writer Brian O'Doherty describes its austere style of curation:

The outside world must not come in, so windows are usually sealed off. Walls are painted white. The ceiling becomes the source of light. The wooden floor is polished so that you click along clinically, or carpeted so that you pad soundlessly.[3]

Historically, it was a reaction to the cheek-by-jowl display at the Royal Academy in London and the French salons where the walls were covered top to bottom with paintings. Now the standard curation style in commercial galleries has a Kantian premise, positioning art in an autonomous field – in a world apart. In the ethereal, white space, the displayed art is sanctified and endowed with a sense of posterity. Accorded these higher values, it becomes 'priceless' and sells for large amounts.

In his landmark collection of essays, *Inside the White Cube* (1976), O'Doherty criticised the sterility of the white cube space, how everyday life is shut out, and how the visitor becomes an intruder. Later chapters in this book will look at dealerships which challenge this model, and instead actively engage with the world. For example, Virginia Dwan supports art that literally happens outside, in the landscape. Meanwhile, Chapter 4, 'Cultural Stewards', addresses dealers who have an almost anthropological viewpoint, and exhibit artists who are tapping into the vital currents of their local cultures.

The important question here is whether our understanding of the branded dealership even works for its considered followers. Certainly, it is an exciting chase following how these dealers advance their image and create ever more desirable associations for their business. However, 'branded dealership' has been oversimplified, and now primarily signifies exclusivity. Choosing dealers for this section has been about reflecting the different character of the branded dealers. Indeed, if we think of just two of them in terms of vehicle brands, Ambroise Vollard would be the Beatnik VW Kombi whereas Leo Castelli is more the slick Rolls-Royce. To date, the psychological motivations for creating a brand have been sorely overlooked. And the cornerstone of any great brand lies in the story behind it.

Joseph Duveen

(1869–1939)

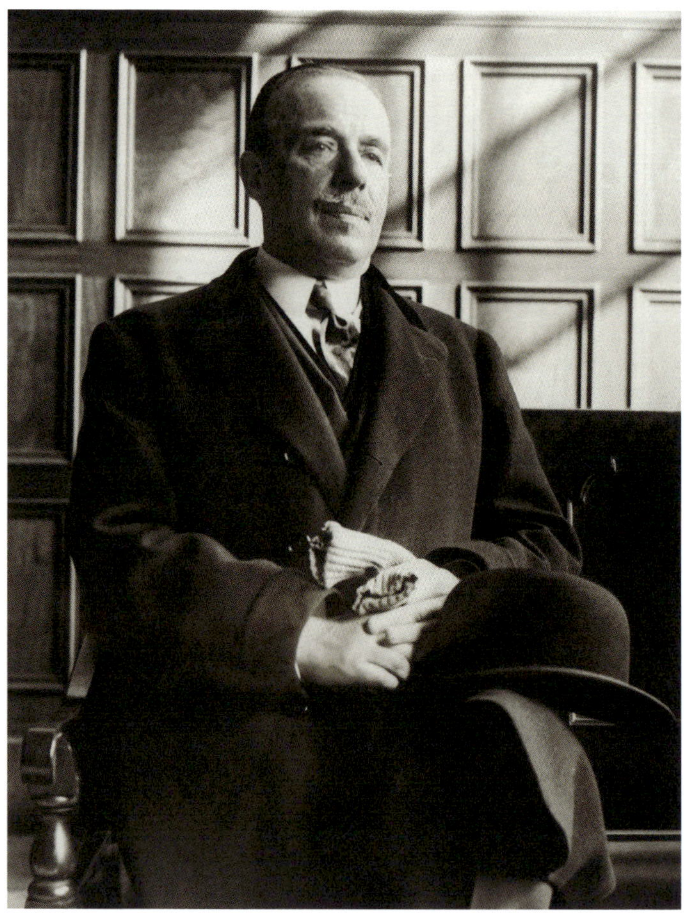

Sir Joseph Duveen, c.1929.
Photographer unknown.

Always impeccably turned out, Joseph Duveen was a potent combination of disarming friendliness, and great theatre. There's a spectacular tale from the time he was first courting J. P. Morgan (1837–1913) as a client and Morgan summoned the dealer to his grand house to test him out. Pointing to five identical vases on the floor, Morgan challenged Duveen to identify the two fakes amongst the precious sixteenth-century Ming vases. Duveen lifted his cane and smashed two of them to bits. Fortunately, he'd made the right choice.

One collector, Andrew Mellon (1855–1937), once forlornly expressed to Duveen, 'Ah yes, the pictures always look better when you are here.'[1] Duveen inspired confidence. From the gallery's ambiance to his debonair dress, every detail of his business exuded sophistication. His clients bought into the mythology of his brand, and were prepared to pay exorbitant prices.

Duveen was the eldest of 12 children; his family was originally from Holland. His father and uncle moved to England and began dealing in Delft pottery in Hull, and over time grew this into a thriving art business specialising in decorative objects, with shops in London and New York. Primed to work in the family business, Duveen became interested in fine art. In 1901 he persuaded his father to spend 14,050 guineas on a portrait by the English artist John Hoppner (1758–1810). An extremely high price for the artist's work, Philip Hook argues, it revealed a core equation in Duveen's thinking: high prices conferred value.[2] In this respect, he was different to Ambroise Vollard (1866–1939) who rooted out bargains, buying up undiscovered modern artists at low prices. Duveen instead bought expensive Old Master art, and then inflated its value.

Duveen's success was partly down to his understanding of the market and his early realisation 'that Europe has a great deal of art, and America a great deal of money'.[3] The transatlantic art trade flourished after 1909 when a law was passed in America which abolished import duty on objects over 100 years old. Rival dealerships, Thomas Agnew & Sons in London, and M. Knoedler & Co. in New York, took advantage of this and were also trading Old Masters in the United States. Duveen established himself as a leading player by securing high-profile European art collections.

Between 1905 and 1908, Duveen purchased the art collections of Rodolphe Kann (1845–1905) and Maurice Kann (1839–1906) in Paris, and the collection of Oscar Hainauer (1840–1894) in Berlin. The immense value of all three collections, and the quality of the works, secured the identity

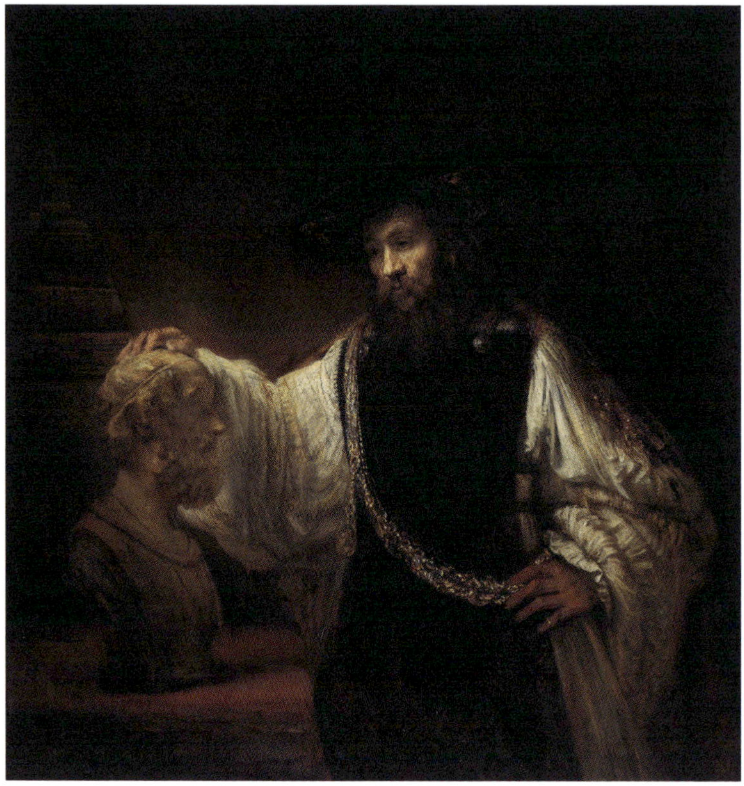

Fig. 12 Rembrandt van Rijn, *Aristotle with a Bust of Homer*, 1653, oil on canvas,
143.5 × 136.5 cm (56 ½ × 53 ¾ in.), The Metropolitan Museum of Art, New York.

of his dealership. Rodolphe Kann's collection, which Duveen bought for around $4 million (about $107 million today), had works by Frans Hals (1582/83–1666) and Johannes Vermeer (1632–1675), and key paintings by Rembrandt including *Aristotle with a Bust of Homer* (1653, fig. 12).

Duveen artfully convinced America's tycoons, 'When you pay high for the priceless, you acquire it cheaply.'[4] His marketing spin tapped into the desires and social aspirations of these new wealthy industrialists. Duveen's biographer S. N. Behrman described the dynamic: 'While the American millionaires of the Duveen Era could not become lords and ladies, they could buy the family portraits and other works of art... [and this] strengthened their feeling of identification and equality with British nobility and with the great rulers and the merchant princes of the Renaissance.'[5]

Amongst his clients, Duveen deliberately fostered a social hierarchy. His elite buyers included Morgan, Mellon, John D. Rockefeller (1839–1937), Henry Clay Frick (1849–1919) and Samuel H. Kress (1863–1955), and these men got the best pickings. Even with this group, Duveen emphasised his unique position, asserting that he alone had access to the best art. At the bottom ranks were the novice buyers who were expected to pay higher prices. Duveen once refused to sell a Rembrandt to a Californian buyer on the basis that, 'I can't possibly sell Rembrandt to a man who owns no other pictures. The Rembrandt would be lonely.'[6]

This frustrating loop for new buyers exists today in blue-chip galleries, which earmark their iconic works for high-profile collectors or their most loyal clients. In the case of early buyers, Duveen advised them to build up a collection of more modest work first before buying a masterpiece. The sense one gets is that the underdogs were delighted just to be in the dealer's orbit. As one novice buyer relates, 'Duveen has the greatest men in the world as his clients. He has Mellon. Why should he give a first-class picture to me when he can sell it to Mellon?'[7]

Duveen had galleries in Paris, London and New York, the considered epicentres of the art world. Up until this point, dealers typically established galleries in old shops and retail premises, but Duveen chose to have purpose-built galleries constructed. Designed from scratch, they were imprinted with the psychology of his brand, and stood as bastions of luxury. In 1911, he erected his New York gallery on Fifth Avenue and 56th Street. The elegant exterior in limestone had a restrained classicism. Inside, skylit galleries bathed the paintings in natural light and offered the best conditions for viewing art, while the sumptuous, soft furnishings and rich wallpapers endowed an element of opulence. Arguably, the most interesting element was the orchestration of the visitor's experience; the galleries, befitting their elevated status, were on the top floor. There were also private rooms to which Duveen could usher his top collectors, and offer a bespoke experience, putting them in front of a select few paintings.

Duveen's elite experience has the qualities of the age-old metaphor of the swan – the bird moving gracefully on a lake, all the while kicking furiously under the water. To maintain the illusion of effortless luxury, Duveen worked extraordinarily hard. He took enormous financial risks, once recounting to a client, 'I get [these masterpieces] because people know I will pay the highest prices in the world.'[8] He deliberately fostered the impression of being extravagant in his offers: on one occasion, a collector asked $18,000 for a portrait, and Duveen responded by complimenting the piece, and offering $25,000. Another winning quality was his patience. Duveen would let his clients live with the art before they purchased it. Rockefeller was once delivered a trio of sculptures by Andrea del Verrocchio (*c.* 1435–1488), Donatello (*c.* 1386–1466) and Desiderio da Settignano (*c.* 1430–1464) and given a whole year to contemplate their beauty. Of course, by the end of the period, he couldn't live without them, and paid the high price of $1.5 million.

Duveen became indispensable to his clients, organising marriages, securing passages on trains and boats, commissioning architects to build luxurious homes for their masterpieces, and even ensuring their favourite cigars got to them. All the time, he furtively kept his buyers on brand and made sure their walls were showing high-profile Old Master art. At a dinner party held by one of his clients, he was in raptures about a Monet painting hanging on the wall, and convinced his client to sell it to him. While flattering his client's taste, he explained his real intentions: 'I didn't want that fellow to get used to buying modern pictures.'[9] Duveen did the same if he spotted poor-quality works on the walls of collectors' homes. Such paintings were treated as business expenses, and stashed away in his cellar.

The dealer projected the idea that he could answer every desire. When Henry and Arabella Huntington told Duveen they wanted to buy *The Blue Boy* (1770, fig. 13) by Thomas Gainsborough (1727–1788) the painting wasn't on the market.[10] But, in 1922, the dealer managed to convince its owner, the Duke of Westminster, to part with the painting for the staggering sum of $728,800. Before it left the United Kingdom, the painting was exhibited for three weeks at the National Gallery in London. *The Times* reported 90,000 people went to see it, and before the painting left, the director of the National Gallery sorrowfully inscribed on the back of the painting 'au revoir', hoping for the return of this national treasure. With this final exhibition gathering such public attention, Duveen stood as the figurehead of this sale of international importance.

There were two key people associated with Duveen, who also worked hard to maintain an illusion. The first was the fabulously named Bertram Boggis (1887–1958), an earthy character who befriended the collectors' households and gathered vital information. For example, Maurice de Rothschild was known to suffer constipation and Boggis would call the butler to check whether Rothschild had been to the toilet before any business was brought to

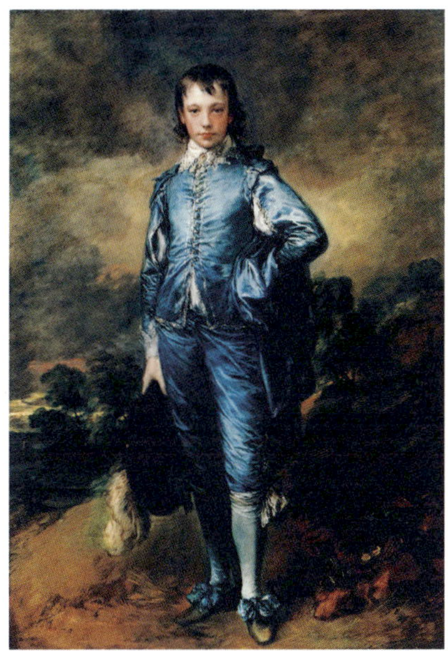

Fig. 13 Thomas Gainsborough, *The Blue Boy*, *c.* 1770, oil on canvas, 177.8 cm × 112.1 cm (70 × 44 ⅛ in.), The Huntington, San Marino, CA, USA.

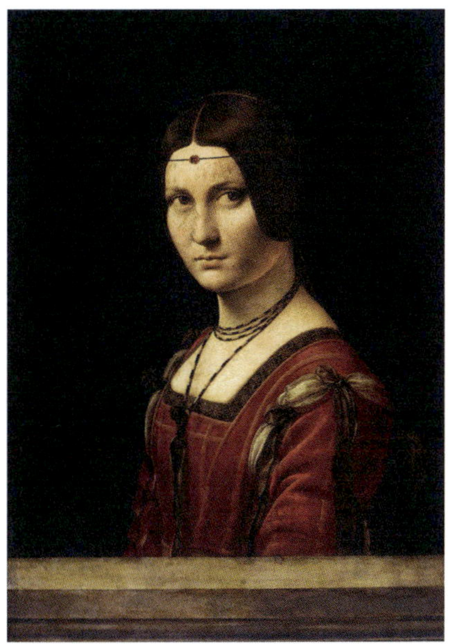

Fig. 14 Leonardo da Vinci, *La Belle Ferronnière*, *c.* 1495, oil on panel, 63 × 45 cm (24 ¾ × 17 ¾ in.), Louvre, Paris.

him. The other important figure was the Renaissance art historian and connoisseur Bernard Berenson (1865–1959) who was responsible for attributing some of the works that were on sale – a crucial task since many of the Italian paintings lacked a clear provenance. However, with a vested interest in making the largest profit, Berenson's attributions were often over-optimistic. In 1913, Berenson vouched that the Renaissance painting being sold to Benjamin Altman was a Giorgione (*c.* 1473–1510), an artist who carried an especially high price tag because of his short career. Rather suspiciously, only a few years earlier, he'd attributed the painting to Titian.

Thriving on risk, Duveen courted controversy throughout his career. There were several lawsuits against him. The 1920s saw the affair of *La Belle Ferronnière* (fig. 14) when Duveen refuted that a painting owned by Andrée Hahn was by Leonardo da Vinci (1452–1519).[11] Hahn sued the dealer for prejudicing the sale of the painting, and Duveen eventually settled out of court. The affair brought a frisson of danger to his enterprise, and according to Philip Hook, 'It was almost as if Duveen orchestrated it as entertainment to brighten his otherwise monotonously successful progress through the decade.'[12]

Duveen's business continued to prosper. Between 1908 and 1917 the heiress Arabella Huntington, one of his many clients, spent $21 million with Duveen. Endlessly resourceful, towards the end of his career he faced the challenge that the walls of his collectors' homes were now filled with art. At this point he pushed them to think beyond their personal collections and immortalise their names by contributing to national museums. Mellon financed the building of the National Gallery in Washington, DC and bequeathed his collection to the museum. Frick, the Huntingtons and Kress all donated works to American public museums.

Knighted and later made a baron, Duveen's career flourished during the decadent 1920s. He offered priceless beauty, and challenged his collectors to step up to the big game: 'You can get all the pictures you want at fifty thousand apiece – that's easy. But to get pictures at a quarter of a million apiece – that wants doing!'[13]

In the last five years of his life he had cancer. When first diagnosed, and told by the doctors to stop smoking, the debonair dealer had an ivory cigarette with a phosphorous red tip made so he could appear to be smoking. His image had to be maintained to the end.

Ambroise Vollard

(1866–1939)

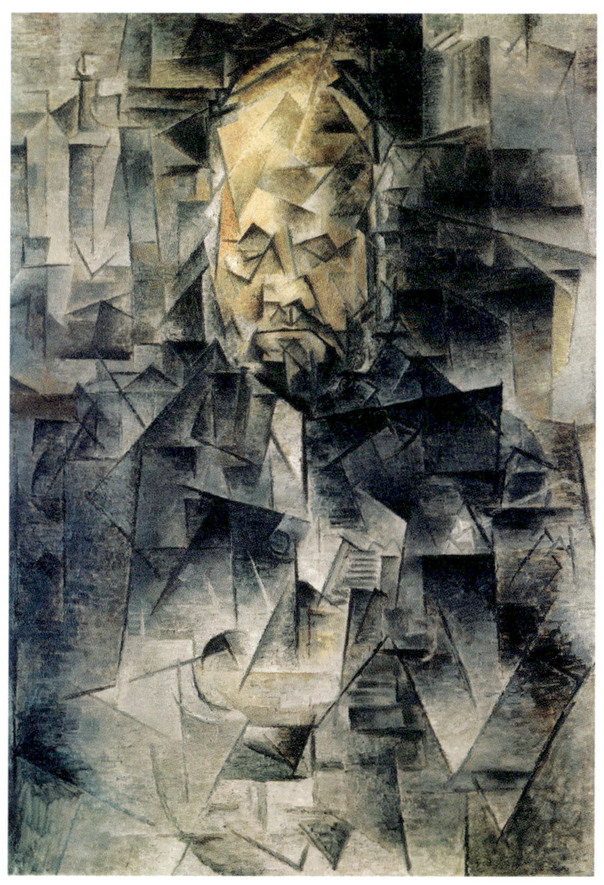

Pablo Picasso, *Portrait of Ambroise Vollard*, 1910,
oil on canvas, 92 × 65 cm (36 ¼ × 25 ⅝ in.),
Pushkin Museum, Moscow.

Ambroise Vollard was painted by a pantheon of celebrated artists. Pablo Picasso (1881–1973) reflected, 'The most beautiful woman who ever lived never had her portrait painted, drawn or engraved any oftener than Vollard – by Cezanne, Renoir, Rouault, Bonnard, Forain, almost everybody, in fact.'[1] He was a tenacious character. A prototype of the branded dealer, he was intent on selling modern art when this market was in its infancy, and the public were hostile to it. Buyers were looking for reassurance, and his endorsement came to signal whether an artist should be taken seriously.

Born in Saint-Denis, the capital of the French overseas department of La Réunion, Vollard exhibited a collector's impulse from a young age, amassing collections of pebbles and bits of broken blue crockery. In 1885, aged 19, he left the island to study law in Montpellier in the South of France. He later moved to Paris and looked for work with an established art dealer. Rejected by Georges Petit because he knew no foreign languages, Vollard started at L'Union Artistique, a gallery which specialised in academic paintings. Around 1900, he struck out on his own, and started dealing out of two small rooms in an apartment in Montmartre.

The alluring aspect of any brand is how it conjures a narrative, and Vollard's dealership was bound up with his character. The writer Gertrude Stein (1874–1946) described this force of nature as 'a huge dark man, glooming',[2] wittily adding, 'This was Vollard cheerful.'[3] His gruff manner suited the ethos of avant-garde artists like Paul Cezanne (1839–1906) and Picasso whose art was premised on authenticity and self-expression. Vollard offered them an unvarnished, grassroots experience. He turned up to Picasso's dilapidated studio in the Bateau-Lavoir with a horse and cart ready outside to load up his purchases. He had an extraordinary confidence when it came to modern art. While Paul Durand-Ruel employed schemes to give context to the new art, such as hiring critics to write articles to explain it to viewers, Vollard was less accommodating. His audience had to catch up.

Vollard was known to be contrary with his customers. If a buyer asked to see a work by Cezanne, they were unlikely to see one; the chances were slightly better if they asked for another artist. Writer Philip Hook laments Vollard's 'no frills' customer service, which he argues goes against 'the very precepts of salesmanship now taught so religiously to operatives in the great auction houses... [which] emphasise the simple central lesson that the client comes first.'[4]

But Vollard was not being naive: by withholding paintings, he made them more desirable to his customers. His haughtiness implied that the art being looked at was of a higher order. Indeed, one has to question whether the customer ever comes first in the branded gallery where it is engineered that the buyer is fortunate to even be allowed to buy the art. These galleries are typically psychologically daunting places. Certainly, Vollard's new gallery had an unnerving atmosphere.

In September 1893, he rented a small shop on Rue Laffitte, known as the 'street of pictures' where Durand-Ruel and Alexandre Bernheim (1839–1915) also had their galleries. In contrast to these luxurious establishments, Vollard's was deliberately underwhelming. The dusty front window obscured views of the modest interior. As Stein described, 'It was an incredible place. It didn't look like a picture gallery. Inside, there were a couple of canvases turned to the wall: in one corner, there was a small pile of big and little canvases thrown pell-mell on top of one another.'[5] In terms of what his customer expected, it was shocking but the austerity focussed attention on the serious matter of art.

One of Vollard's key innovations was to drive sales by marketing 'newness' as a critical selling point. In his memoirs, there are many references to an 'advanced art'. The most significant passage comes towards the end: 'When I opened my shop... the Impressionist movement had won the day, but by then fresh adventurers were exploring fresh paths. For painting is not stationary, it cannot escape the urge to renewal, the incessant evolution that manifests itself in every form of art.'[6] This shows a major shift from Durand-Ruel's marketing of art in terms of nationhood – a value that drove the nineteenth-century art market. Instead, Vollard was focussed on new, emerging art.

Vollard was relentless in his chase for new talent. Durand-Ruel had been the major dealer of Édouard Manet's work, but Vollard caught the scent: there were still rich pickings to be had. He visited Manet's widow and gathered up a collection of drawings, explaining in his memoirs that 'nobody had wanted them because they were merely sketches, and at that time things of that sort were not valued.'[7] It was a shrewd move at a time when drawings were slowly becoming appreciated as an intimate medium. Exhibited in the new gallery in 1894, they received positive critical attention and the show established Vollard's reputation.

Vollard's most epic hunt was for Cezanne. The dealer described his first sighting of one of his paintings as a 'coup à l'estomac' (a blow to the stomach).[8]

He was given a lead that the artist was living in Aix-en-Provence, but when he arrived there he was told that Cezanne had moved back to Paris. Eventually he tracked down his home where he met the artist's son, who became his chief contact in the negotiation of sales. In 1895 Vollard opened his first solo show of Cezanne's work.

During his management of Cezanne's career, Vollard used practices that would become central to the branded dealer. He would invest in undiscovered artists, and would wait until they became established figures, and the prices of their artworks had soared before he sold them. In 1899, the dealer emptied Cezanne's entire studio, and for ten years, up until the artist's death, he had a near monopoly on his work. A total of 678 documented works by Cezanne passed through Vollard's hands. He snapped up Picasso in his early years and was his principal dealer between 1906 and 1910. Vollard also went on to build a large stock of works by other artists, which he typically purchased directly from them.

Unlike the connoisseur-dealer, Vollard had no embarrassment around discussing money: he didn't employ agents, preferring to negotiate himself. He had strategies to dissuade keen buyers and ensure prices had the chance to peak. One of his methods was to ask for a higher sum if a buyer wanted to make multiple purchases. The dealer explained his thinking to a collector looking to acquire three paintings by Cezanne: 'It's perfectly simple. If I sell you one of my Cezanne's, I have two left. If I sell you two, I have only one left. If I sell you all three, I have none left.'[9]

By withholding works, he spiked interest in artists. But the downside of this waiting game was that it stopped them from making profits in the short term. While Vollard paid some a monthly stipend, many artists were impoverished for years. Paul Gauguin (1848–1903), who suffered from this, raged at how 'Vollard... hides the painting, no doubt with an eye to speculation.'[10]

Vollard didn't always make the right call. He was confounded by Cubism, which is likely why Picasso later turned to the German dealer Daniel-Henry Kahnweiler. He also misjudged Vincent van Gogh (1853–1890). He held a solo show of the Dutch artist's work but when nothing sold, he didn't seek out further opportunities, later also admitting, 'I thought he had no future at all, and I let his paintings go for practically nothing.'[11]

In 1901 Vollard held Picasso's first solo show, and he continued to buy his paintings. In December 1910, the dealer held another exhibition of Picasso's work, which shocked people, but not because of the art. Picasso's friend, the poet Guillaume Apollinaire (1880–1918) complained about the lack of staging.[12] Indeed, no invitations were sent; no catalogue accompanied the show; the paintings didn't even have frames! It raises the question of how avant-garde art is best shown. Vollard's pared-back presentation here was consistent with his practice and reflects a desire to be rid of pretensions and market the authenticity of the art. For Apollinaire, however, it was only Picasso's brilliance that ensured the show was a success.

Vollard's monopolies on artists' careers, and indeed his staging of solo exhibitions were not original strategies in themselves – both were shaped by Durand-Ruel's practice. There were, however, unique circumstances which contributed to the success of Vollard's business. In the first place, he faced little competition, especially after Père Tanguy and several other small-time contemporary art dealers died. In addition, Vollard was a bachelor and without family responsibilities, and so he could afford to wait until prices peaked.

Throughout his career, Vollard fostered an avant-garde scene. An author himself, he wrote a series of absurdist essays around the satirical character Ubu Roi, created by Alfred Jarry (1873–1907). The basement of his gallery became known as The Cave. Here, Vollard entertained artists and poets, serving them up his famous chicken curry. Cezanne, Edgar Degas, Henri Matisse (1869–1954), Pierre-Auguste Renoir and Auguste Rodin (1840–1917) all dined there. The Hungarian photographer Brassaï (1899–1984) relates the excitement of these evenings:

> For thirty years, his famous cellar – a white vaulted room
> without a single picture on the walls had been the center
> of Parisian artistic life. What joyful feasts, what parties
> and conferences, what planning sessions had been held
> there with all those artists, writers, critics and collectors
> who are now famous.[13]

With so few modern artworks in the national museums, and art schools still focussed on a classical past, his gallery became a vital resource where artists could see the latest trends. Artists often bartered with Vollard, exchanging their own works for a painting by another artist. Matisse sold his wife's precious emerald ring to secure Cezanne's *Three Bathers* (1879–82, fig. 15), later acknowledging, 'In the 37 years I have owned this painting...

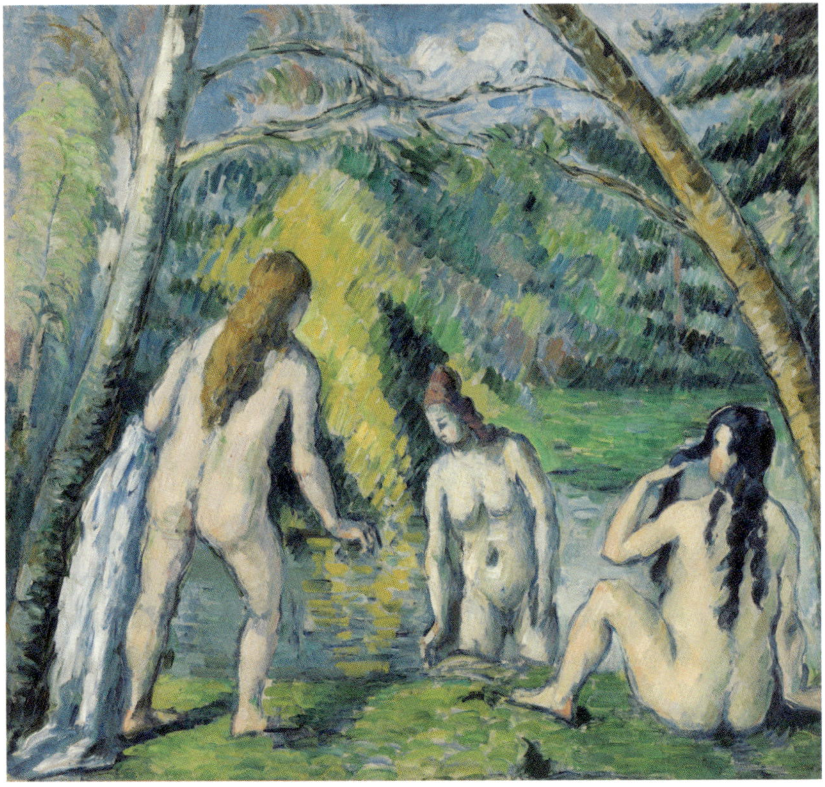

Fig. 15 Paul Cezanne, *Three Bathers*, 1879–82, oil on
canvas, 52 × 55 cm (20 ½ × 21 ⅝ in.), Petit Palais, Paris.

It has supported me morally at critical moments in my venture as an artist;
I have drawn from it my faith and perseverance.'[14]

Vollard's dealership in prints is often overlooked, and yet it is here that
he was perhaps at his most experimental. Dispensing with professional
etchers, he commissioned painters to create prints, and was responsible
for raising the profile of colour lithography, a dormant medium at the time.
Significantly, he marketed a collection of lithographs by Picasso as the
Vollard Suite (1930–37), essentially marking the project with his brand.

He was also the producer of limited-edition *livres d'artistes*. These artists'
books brought together avant-garde artists with poets and writers. It was a
transgressive move to employ painters rather than book illustrators. Usually
unbound, with no text on some pages, they challenged the traditional format

for book illustration. Bonnard illustrated *Parallèlement* (1900), the collected poems of Paul Verlaine (1844–1896). A total work of art, the book is a harmonious marriage of graphics, image and text. Bonnard's rose-coloured drawings sprawl, unconfined, across the gutter of the page, expressing the sensuality and freedom of Verlaine's poems. Vollard's *livres d'artistes* offered a template for the next generation; Kahnweiler and the publisher Tériade would follow his lead and produce their own artists' books.

When Vollard died, his estate was worth $15 million. Somehow his contrary brand, which involved selling difficult art and being difficult himself, had worked. There's a folktale-like charm to his success. Supposedly, he slept a great deal and sometimes customers had to wake him, but his torpor turned out to be a winning strategy. As the French writer André Billy (1882–1971) observed: 'Dreaming and sleeping like this, alone in his shop, Vollard was wasting no time. Month by month, in solitude, the price of his pictures rose.'[15]

Samuel M. Kootz

(1898–1982)

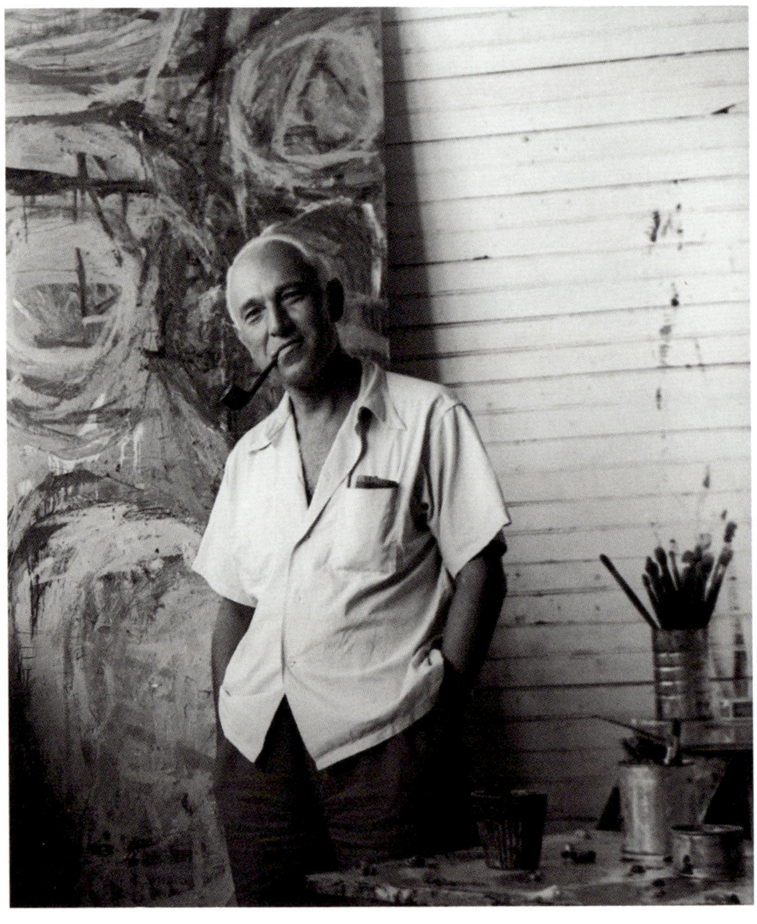

Maurice Berezov, *Samuel Kootz in his studio*, 1950s.

Before Samuel Kootz opened his gallery, he'd already written two books on American art: his second book, *New Frontiers in American Painting* (1943) rallied painters to respond to their time and pioneer a new American art. Prophetically, he observed two emerging trends: abstraction and expressionism – impulses which in time came together in the movement he would be most associated with: Abstract Expressionism. He shared this territory with Betty Parsons (1900–1982), who was also interested in this emerging group, but their two styles of dealership were very different. There was a slickness to Kootz – the cigar-smoking dealer who'd worked in advertising and knew how to sell product.

In the early 1920s, Kootz was a law student in Virginia and it was on weekend trips to New York that he first started to explore commercial galleries. While he was most impressed by the art on show at Alfred Stieglitz's (1864–1946) 291 gallery, he hated Stieglitz's snobbishness and the way he evaluated whether his customers were worthy of the artworks on sale. After practising law for one year, he became an advertising executive for 11 years, and was involved in promoting films for major movie companies. Revealingly, the promotional material for an early exhibition at his gallery has the catchiness of an ad tagline:

> Paintings American, paintings from France;
> Paintings dynamic by Hofmann, Hans...
> a Gottlieb with symbols mysterious;
> It surely will get a reception delirious.[1]

Of more fundamental importance, his work in advertising taught him the potency of a brand, and how to mythologise a product and engineer desirable associations. This prepared him to mastermind his own gallery brand, and present a cohesive narrative through his dealership. However, in retrospect, his first exhibition at Macy's department store created a confusing narrative.

The Macy's art show opened in January 1942; an advertisement appeared in *The New York Times* boasting 179 canvases by 72 American artists.[2] It is questionable whether the ad's promise of bargain prices (from $24.97 to $249 for framed works) was the best pitch for a rarefied item like art, and furthermore, whether a busy shop was the right context for the seriousness of Abstract Expressionism. Mark Rothko (1903–1970) showed several mythical paintings including *Antigone* (1938), which was priced at $200.

Moving forward Kootz would tweak his sales pitch, and associate Abstract Expressionism with more aspirational values.

In April 1945, he opened the Kootz Gallery on 15 East 57th Street in New York. The year before, he'd secured two Abstract Expressionists, William Baziotes (1912–1963) and Robert Motherwell (1915–1991), and put both on a monthly stipend. His inaugural exhibition showcased the French modernist painter, Fernand Léger (1881–1955). The dealer explained: 'The reason we opened with a Léger show was because I wanted to tell people immediately that we were an international gallery interested in quality.'[3] It was a shrewd move, and Kootz would continue to use the prestige of European modernism to add value to his gallery brand, and legitimise the emerging Abstract Expressionist art. His major coup was staging Pablo Picasso's first post-war exhibition.

Picasso was the ultimate brand endorsement for Kootz. In advertising, timing is key, and Picasso was in the spotlight. Having stayed in Paris through the Nazi occupation and endured bullets being fired into his studio,[4] the artist was being heralded as a symbol of the Resistance at the end of the war: intellectuals, creatives and allied soldiers had streamed into his studio on Liberation Day. Sensing the poignancy of the moment, Kootz flew to Paris to meet the artist and convince him to release some of his wartime works. Photos from this period show Kootz with Picasso in the artist's spartan studio. After a couple of visits, Picasso agreed to give him nine paintings, and in 1947 Kootz staged the first one-man show of Picasso's art in America since the war.

In the United States, the story caught the attention of the press, with one paper reporting, 'Mr Kootz made newspaper headlines by flying these canvases out of Paris several weeks ago. The world's most talked-of artist stayed and worked in Paris during the German occupation and most of his canvases in the current show were done at the time.'[5] The exhibition was a sensation: queues gathered before the gallery opened at 9 a.m., and every week over 2,000 catalogues were sold. All the works, priced between $3,500 and $20,000, were snapped up in the first week. In terms of Kootz's brand, the provocative artworks, with their distorted forms and looming colours, served to reinforce the gallery as a site of cutting-edge art. As the newspaper quote above indicates, the American audience were looking for evidence of Picasso's wartime experience, and they found it. One work, *Plant de tomates* (1944) captured the oppressiveness of the occupation. In this piece, nature is reduced to a tomato plant on a windowsill, which, thwarted by the window's prison-like bars, struggles to find light.

While one newspaper heralded Picasso as 'the supreme hero of the hour',[6] the success for Kootz was to be associated with this world-famous artist. Kootz recognised this, and over the next few years, a courtship ensued between the dealer and artist. Enticing Picasso with the riches of the New World, Kootz shipped Picasso a latest-model Cadillac in Nantucket Cream and in return, he received a painting.

More was to come: in an unprecedented move, Picasso suggested to Kootz that he close his New York gallery and exclusively represent him. He offered Kootz a flat in Paris and one in New York from which to run his business. Kootz agreed, and archival photos show his salubrious apartment on Park Avenue, fitted out with elegant furniture, and Picasso's paintings hanging through the space. Selling Picasso from his personal abode, the dealer's identity became synonymous with the Picasso brand – at least for a while. Kootz soon got tired of collectors turning up at his door, despairing when one particularly keen individual disturbed his Saturday morning coffee. This event prompted Kootz to reopen a public gallery at 600 Madison Avenue. Unquestionably, being Picasso's international dealer had raised his profile, and he continued to show his work, but he was now looking to reconnect with what had excited him first: Abstract Expressionism.

Reopening his gallery in 1949, the hiatus provided a pause, which let him refine his identity. Kootz now decided to exclusively represent the 'subjective artist' who, as he explains, 'invents from personal experience, creates from an internal world rather than an external one. He makes no attempt to chronicle the American scene, exploit momentary political struggles or stimulate nostalgia through familiar objects; he deals instead with inward emotions and experiences.'[7] Of course, the leading figures exploring this type of art were his favoured Abstract Expressionists. In 1947, Kootz managed to secure another central figure, Hans Hofmann (1880–1966). Insistent on the consistency of his brand, Kootz didn't resume relationships with several artists from his first gallery.

Kootz would go on to organise two landmark group exhibitions for the Abstract Expressionists: *The Intrasubjectives* (1949) and *New Talent* (1950).[8] Prior to the first one, the Abstract Expressionists didn't have a name, or a group ethos, and Kootz's exhibition pushed for this by showing the artists together, and giving them a collective title, although his name

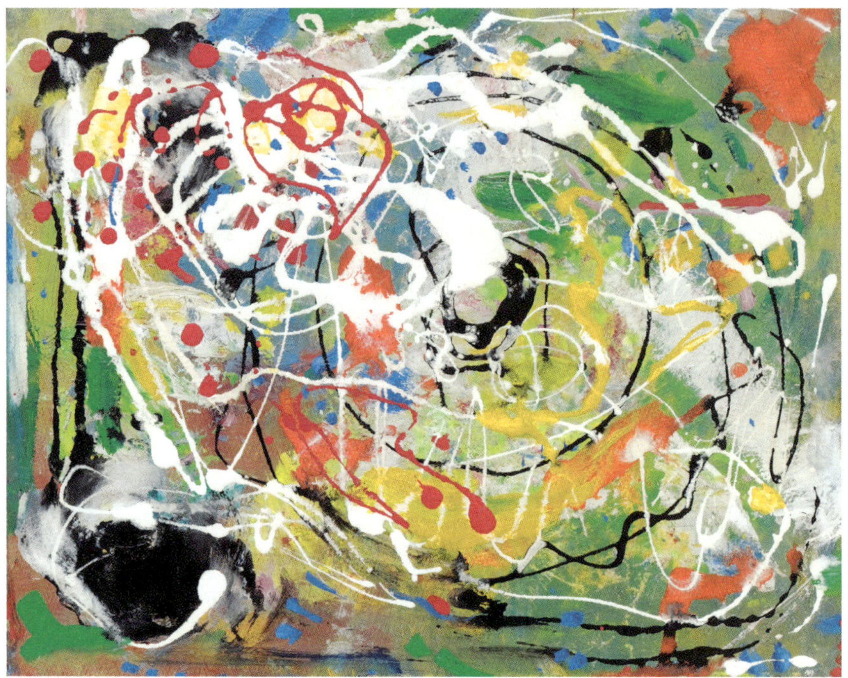

Fig.16 Hans Hofmann, *Spring*, 1944–45 (dated 1940), oil on wood panel,
28.5 × 35.7 cm (11¼ × 14⅛ in.), The Museum of Modern Art, New York.

didn't stick. In *New Talent,* Kootz played his old trick of legitimising new art by bringing in established art world figures. This time, he asked the influential critics Clement Greenberg (1909–1994) and Meyer Schapiro (1904–1996) to curate the show. Greenberg's positioning of Abstract Expressionism was different to that of Kootz, and emphasised the abstract nature of the art, and its attention to form and colour.

In 1955 Greenberg organised a retrospective of Hofmann for Kootz. There was one standout success – a painting from 1940 priced at $150 (fig.16). The director of the Museum of Modern Art in New York, Alfred H. Barr Jr (1902–1981), was drawn to its all-over drip effect, which he recognised as an antecedent of Pollock's iconic drip technique and so he expressed an interest. With Barr firmly on the hook, Kootz suggested to Hofmann that they raise the price to $5,000. An astounded Barr managed to secure a donor to buy the work for MoMA. This moment anticipated the rocketing value of Abstract Expressionism.

Interest from a major museum like MoMA undoubtedly helped draw attention to Abstract Expressionism, and yet, in interview, Kootz couldn't explain why the art market suddenly became so interested.[9] It might be that the available tax breaks on art played a role. These were particularly advantageous when buying new art with a low price tag as the tax deduction was based on artwork's value rather than the purchase price. This loophole enabled canny dealers like Kootz to inflate the value after the sale, and let their collectors reap massive tax rebates.

Kootz constantly thought up new ways of advancing Abstract Expressionism. One early move was to forge a connection with architecture. In 1950, he staged the exhibition *The Muralists and the Modern Architect*. This played a part in depoliticising the mural, which had become a popular medium during the Mexican revolution when it was deployed as a public art of dissension. The exhibition instead foregrounded how the mural could create life-enhancing interiors. Each artist showed a range of items – in Hofmann's case, photos, a ribbon frieze and a large painting – presenting mural art as a flexible commodity that could work in everyone's home.

Kootz would profit from the escalating interest in Abstract Expressionism, and in 1963, he secured over $200,000 in sales of Hofmann's art alone. However, on 9 April 1966, he abruptly shut his gallery, saying he no longer felt culturally relevant. In an interview in 1964, he talked disparagingly of the art world's preoccupation with the new: 'Matisse once said that an artist is born with one idea, and he develops that idea during his entire lifetime. Today if an idea isn't changed every two years, the artist is condemned for being old hat.'[10] Perhaps, his branding was too good, in that he became indelibly connected with the Abstract Expressionists.

In the early 1960s Kootz did look further afield to the European art scene, but his interest was shaped by Abstract Expressionist ideals: he talked of his new protégé, Pierre Soulages (1919–2022), as the French version of Hofmann. It was inevitable that Abstract Expressionism would be superseded by a new art movement, and while Kootz had become old hat, his competitors, Parsons and Leo Castelli (1907–1999), would avoid the same fate by their brand being broader and concerned with the new.

Betty Parsons

(1900–1982)

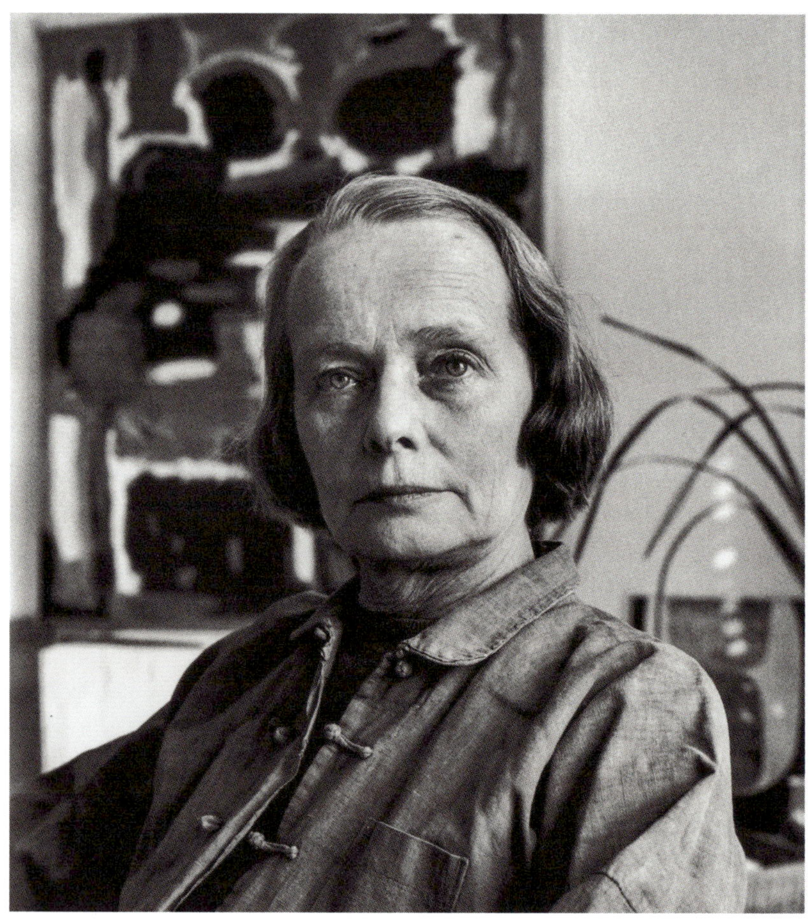

Alexander Liberman,
Betty Parsons, 1963.

Saul Steinberg (1914–1999) once drew Betty Parsons as a majestic-looking dog. Explaining why he imagined her like this, the New York illustrator and artist said, 'Like all the best dealers, Betty has a fictitious quality.'[1] There were many parts to Parsons's story: as well as dealing, she was an artist, a poet and an art collector. She was a conflicted character – a rebel who had social aspirations and an aristocratic manner. Her success as a dealer partly came down to how she expressed these qualities; her non-conformist side led her to seek out the most independent and original artists, while her gallery had an intimidating nobility.

The duality in Parsons's character could have originated in her privileged childhood. The family had homes in New York, Newport and Palm Beach, and a team of servants waiting on them. But as Parsons tells, this all came with expectations, 'Eat this, Wear this. Say this. Think that. Don't do that. Rules, rules, rules.'[2] Her parents liked their children to be dressed in white – indeed there's a photo of the young Parsons which shows a very beautiful child in a white lace dress. However, Parsons chose to revolt. Her writing has a poetic aspect, and often when she is describing her battles, she chimes a word three times. This is evident in the quote above where she repeats the word 'rules' and again when she describes her authoritarian grandfather, 'I was a rebel in my bones – in my family. He was conservative, conservative, conservative.'[3] The repetition of the word 'conservative' gives momentum, underscoring how these negative experiences vivified her, and were something to react against. As her family struggled to accept her bisexuality, and her desire to be an artist, Parsons became insistent. At 15 years old, when attending a finishing school was mentioned, she isolated herself in her room before emerging with her hair slicked to the side, wearing trousers and smoking a cigarette. She entered her father's study and agreed to comply with his wish on one condition: she would attend art classes. Her terms were met.

Irritated by her apathetic parents, Parsons at the age of 13 had discovered a vitality in art at the landmark Armory Show of 1913 where *Nude Descending a Staircase (No. 2)* (1912) by Marcel Duchamp (1887–1968) was on display. She connected to the show's promotional tagline, 'New Spirit', and for weeks after chanted, 'I am the New Spirit.'[4] This mantra reflected the essence of her future dealership and its embrace of the new.

Although Parsons is now best known for picking up unknown Abstract Expressionists, she started out as a practicing artist, training in Paris before working as a portrait painter in California. Supported by her rich friends, she continued with her privileged lifestyle which involved playing tennis with the Hollywood movie star Greta Garbo. In terms of building a luxury brand, while Joseph Duveen worked extraordinarily hard to gather an elite clientele, Parsons's friendship group already had glamour and wealth, and this helped secure Parsons's first job as a dealer.

In 1936 Alan Gruskin offered Parsons a show of her own art at his gallery in New York. The exhibition was successful and 14 paintings were sold, but Gruskin also noticed Parsons's people skills and the set of famous and semi-famous people who surrounded her. Seeing potential there, he offered her a position at the gallery as a dealer. Within a year of working there, Mary Sullivan (1877–1939), a founding trustee of the Museum of Modern Art recruited Parsons to work at her salubrious gallery on Park Avenue. However, Sullivan's clockwatching irritated Parsons, and in 1940 she left to manage the gallery at Wakefield Bookshop on 64 East 55th Street. With more independence, her personal vision emerged, and she started representing a roster of contemporary artists including Joseph Cornell (1903–1972), Hedda Sterne (1910–2011) and Steinberg. At the same time, she started to think about how the space might work.

In a conversation with her friend Annie Laurie Witzel, she described her fantasy for the gallery itself;[5] she imagined the space as having two floors with a spiral staircase between them, and she would operate from the second floor where she would meet only the richest clients like the Rockefellers or royalty. Her elevated position and her desire for rich clients both have the aspirational nature of the branded gallery. Embellishing on her ideal, she added fairy-tale attendants – a joker, a fool and some chivalrous knights – to look after her needs, all of which resonated with her privileged aristocratic background, with its staff of servants. What is fascinating is how this elitist fantasy manifested in her austere modernist gallery.

In 1946 Parsons was invited by the Old Master dealer, Mortimer Brandt, to join his gallery. However, within a year, he had decided to move back to England. Securing loans from friends, Parsons took over the space and opened the Betty Parsons Gallery. There was a professionalism to her enterprise: she held 12 shows a year, including a Christmas show. But it was her orchestration of the gallery itself that was to be instrumental in establishing her brand. When Brandt left, Parsons stripped the space, removing the carpet and every architectural feature. The stark room had nowhere to sit; the dealer's feeling was, 'A gallery isn't a place to rest. It's a place to look at art. You don't come to the gallery to be comfortable.'[6] Writer Don Thompson later pinpoints the psychology of such an unforgiving space: 'The featureless environment is meant to reinforce the idea that what is being viewed is "art" and that galleries are elitist.'[7]

Radically, Parsons decided to paint the walls bone-white and install strong overhead lighting, essentially creating the 'white cube'. Nowadays, this is the standard setting for contemporary art, but it was uncommon in Parsons's day. One is reminded of her childhood dress, and the white clothes that projected class and dignity. Parsons's ethereal interior had the same aspiration. Removing associations with the external world, a monochrome setting also quietens the senses and suggests an ideal realm. The American art critic and poet, Thomas McEvilley (1939–2013), explains the ideology of the white gallery:

> The purpose of such a setting is not unlike the purpose of religious buildings – the artworks, like religious verities, are to appear 'untouched by time and vicissitudes'. The condition of appearing out of time, or beyond time implies a claim that the work already belongs to posterity – that is, it is the assurance of good investment.[8]

With her gallery signalling a timeless worth, Parsons focussed on representing new art, and Indigenous American art. Her first exhibition, *Northwest Coast Indian Art*, opened on the 30 September 1946. Parsons asked the artist Barnett Newman (1905–1970) to write the text for the catalogue. Together, they challenged the problematic categorisation of this art as primitive, with Newman writing to Parsons, 'We have no cause to identify work as primitive and look condescendingly upon it.'[9] Chiming with Parsons's position, in his text Newman pushed the spiritual aspect of the work, and identified a similar impulse in contemporary art.

Parsons soon turned to Abstract Expressionism, holding solo exhibitions for its four giants (as she named them):[10] Jackson Pollock (1912–1956), Newman, Rothko and Clyfford Still (1904–1980). Her attention to this group was provocative, for the art world was focussed on European modernism, and there was a dearth of dealers interested in American art. Suddenly, as her successor Leo Castelli says, 'There was considerable activity at Betty Parsons. Those Rothko, Pollock shows at Betty's were very, very important events.'[11]

Writers often miss Parsons's keen understanding of this movement. From her early visit to the Armory Show, what Parsons looked for was vitality in art, and she found this in Abstract Expressionism. In 1949 she exalted Pollock's work: 'It was a sensation. A total sensation. So full of energy and expansion.'[12] Critically, Parsons was ahead of her time. In the next few years Pollock's art would be central to Clement Greenberg's formalist arguments and discussed purely in terms of abstraction. This drains it of its phenomenological significance, and how his paintings involve the viewer who follows the unfolding labyrinth of improvised lines. Their vibrancy evokes natural forces. And Pollock emphasised this connection with nature, naming two of his paintings after the seasons, *Summertime: Number 9A* (1948) and *Autumn Rhythm (Number 30)* (1950). Parsons allowed her artists to lead the hangs, and for Pollock's show in 1950 his monumental canvases were presented unframed and ran from floor to ceiling, immersing the spectator in their 'energy and expansion'.[13]

Through her career, Parsons faced fierce resistance from art critics and the public, explaining, 'You see they hate you if you are different; everyone hates you and they will destroy you.'[14] There were reports of works being sabotaged and critics poured out scornful reviews. But what really stung was the desertion of the four giants. Early in 1951, Rothko, Pollock, Newman and Still called a meeting with Parsons to propose that she dropped all her other artists to focus exclusively on them, with Newman offering in return, 'We will make you the most important dealer in the world.'[15] Of course, Parsons was never going to march to the beat of someone else's drum, and one by one, her giants defected to the art dealer Sidney Janis, who'd been subletting half her floorspace. With her signature triple emphasis, Parsons raged at how, 'He took, took, took',[16] and indeed Janis continued to take, later secretly approaching her landlord to secure the lease on Parsons's rented space, effectively evicting her from her gallery.

In 1963, Parsons moved to 24 West 57th Street where she continued to represent new art, giving Robert Rauschenberg (1925–2008) his first solo exhibition, and embracing American Minimalists Agnes Martin (1912–2004) and Ellsworth Kelly (1923–2015). There is a prevailing view that Parsons's mission was diluted after she lost the Abstract Expressionists, but it is interesting to consider what happened to these artists post-Parsons. For some, the pattern resembled the recording careers of musicians who are often discovered by a small, independent label, and at the apex of their most critically celebrated work are then lured away to a major label, only to produce less interesting, formulaic work. Pollock's career certainly spiralled into decline. Parsons herself recounts: 'He put himself on the edge. He might be half crazy or even drunk. But he painted like an angel,' significantly adding, 'In my gallery he was never drunk. We were great friends.'[17] Tellingly, Castelli would decide against representing Abstract Expressionism: his feeling was that the best works had been picked up, and the moment had passed.

In 1958, Parsons opened the exhibition *Paintings for Unlimited Space*, which showed art that had the scale and energy she'd first identified in Abstract Expressionism. Her success in bringing attention to this new aesthetic is attributable to the strength of her brand. Her friends added glamour while her austere white gallery evoked a timeless posterity for this new work.

Leo Castelli

(1907–1999)

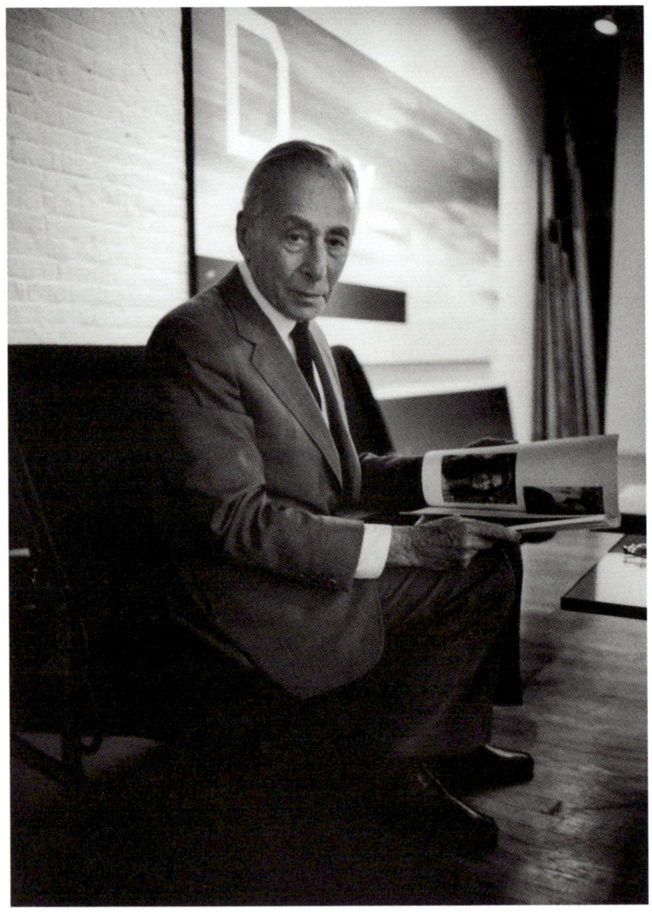

Chris Felver, *Leo Castelli*,
New York City, 1996.

Leo Castelli had the allure of a well-conceived brand. He started selling art when he was 50 years old, projecting a reassuring maturity to a society traumatised by World War II and the horrors of the Holocaust and Hiroshima. Affable and fluent in Italian, French, German and English, he had a European elegance, sealed by his signature look of tailored Milanese suits and Hermès ties. His old-world image was the perfect counterfoil to the new American art he would sell first in New York, and later globally. To the then budding American art theorist Rosalind Krauss, 'Leo was a legend, and I was in awe of him.'[1]

The Castelli mythology stretches back to his childhood. Talking to art historian Paul Cummings in 1969, the dealer describes an enchanted childhood of privilege and globetrotting from his early childhood in Trieste to Vienna where his family lived during World War I. His account never touches on the family tensions, his distant mother and workaholic father, nor does it deal with the terrible discrimination his Jewish family experienced after the rise of fascism and the onset of the war. In 1939 Castelli and his new wife Ileana (née Schapira, later Sonnabend) managed to escape and find safety in New York. However, Castelli's own parents and sister were less fortunate. Living in Budapest, they hid away from the Hungarian Nazis who were deporting Jews to Auschwitz. When a ceasefire was called, his mother and father were hiding in a china cupboard, surviving on two spoonfuls of tomato sauce every day. They tried to cross the Danube, but his mother drowned, and his father died in an infirmary a few weeks later. Castelli buried this appalling history. His own son said he struggled with anything personal: in this sense, the shielding façade of the brand worked for him.

Before the war broke out, Castelli was living with Sonnabend in Paris where they became involved in the art scene. An important experience was seeing the Gravida gallery which André Breton (1896–1966) opened in May 1937 to showcase Surrealist art. The irreverence of this work, and its intersection with everyday life were to shape Castelli's taste. While still in Paris, Castelli opened his first gallery, with the architect René Drouin. They named it Galerie René Drouin, and following the example of Gravida, their first show brought together art, fashion and furniture. Méret Oppenheim (1913–1985) designed a table with bird-like claws for the table legs specifically for the show. This single exhibition would play a key role in securing Castelli's entrance into the New York art scene.

On arriving in New York, Castelli relates, 'When I got there in 1941, everybody knew me from that very brief experience I'd had in Paris. Julien Levy knew me. Dalí knew me. Max Ernst knew me.'[2]

The artists hoped he would open a gallery, but for ten years, Castelli worked at his father-in-law's tie factory. However, he was constantly playing hooky at the Museum of Modern Art, and soon met the director, Alfred H. Barr Jr. Somewhat star struck, the dealer later admitted, 'I've always had a certain involvement in hero worship.'[3] His other idol during this period was Clement Greenberg, who introduced Castelli to what was happening in the American art scene. However, Castelli wasn't entirely in agreement with the primacy Greenberg gave to abstract art. Moreover, from studying MoMA's collection, he'd realised art was an evolutionary process, and he was interested in what was to come next.

Castelli also charmed his way into The Club, a community of American artists that included many of the Abstract Expressionists. Interestingly, in an interview some years later, Castelli emphasised the spiritual dimension of the group and how they were a 'mystical fraternity'.[4] Buddhism was a central interest, and the Japanese Zen monk D. T. Suzuki lectured there. The spiritual aspect of Castelli is rarely noted, and yet it could be said to be latent in his brand, which seeks to endow the ordinary with a higher value.

Through The Club, Castelli became involved in the landmark *Ninth Street Show* (1951). Held in a building soon to be demolished, artists were restricted to entering only one painting. Left alone in the gallery, Castelli picked out the most promising amongst the pile: works by Franz Kline (1910–1962), Pollock and Willem de Kooning (1904–1997). Castelli's action reflects his pattern of identifying 'stars'. After the opening of the *Ninth Street Show*, Castelli met Barr in the Cedar Tavern. He turned up with photographs of all the artworks, and Barr pencilled the artists' names on the back of the photos. In his future galleries, Castelli would keep meticulous archives, which were open to academics and curators, and were a very successful way of extending his influence and promoting his artists. What is significant is that the once star-struck Castelli was now introducing the director of MoMA to new art.

In February 1957, Castelli finally opened the Castelli Gallery in his fourth-floor apartment on 77th Street, converting his L-shaped living room and daughter's bedroom into the gallery space. His first exhibition paired European modernist with Abstract Expressionist works, and the resulting comparisons weren't wholly successful. Nevertheless, people were captivated by the unfathomable Castelli magic. Within the context of the disenchanted post-war society, his gallery exuded an escapism reminiscent of *The Great Gatsby* (1925). Castelli was never didactic. Ivan Karp (1926–2012), who worked for Castelli for many years, described 'a romantic atmosphere, a kind of permanent flirtation around the gallery'.[5]

The Castelli brand soon became associated with the latest art. A few months after opening his gallery, he visited Jasper Johns (b. 1930) at his studio and encountered his encaustic paintings, his flags and targets. Asked later in an interview if it was love at first sight, the dealer responded, 'Total and absolute.'[6] Castelli immediately offered the 27-year-old artist representation. Around the same time, he picked up Robert Rauschenberg. He gave them both a monthly stipend, and in return secured a monopoly on their work. His approach has become known as the 'Castelli method', which fails to recognise that Paul Durand-Ruel used similar tactics many years before. The slick term also misses the connection the dealer felt with these artists.

Johns himself recognised the depth behind Castelli's façade: 'He likes people and he feels very emotionally about them.'[7] In the wake of the Holocaust and Hiroshima, Johns and Rauschenberg were grappling to find a way to connect with the world through their art – Johns reproducing recognisable forms like letters of the alphabet and flags, and Rauschenberg including gritty elements of real life, from broken light bulbs to stained bedcovers. Years earlier, in Paris, Castelli had been drawn to the Surrealists and had appreciated how they connected their art with the living world.

Talking about his two protégés, the dealer admitted, 'I had practically a religious faith in them and that's probably why I succeeded without high pressuring anybody in communicating to the outside world.'[8] His deep sympathy equipped him to promote their work. His early exhibition *New Work* (1957) included works by Rauschenberg and Johns, and the promotional material and the title of the show had the austerity of these artists' works. Castelli also offered them solo shows. Johns's exhibition in 1958 sold well, with Barr buying three paintings for MoMA. And there was a second coup: before the opening, the editor of *Artnews*, Thomas Hess, dropped into the gallery and asked to borrow *Target with Four Faces* (1955); Castelli obliged and several days later, the image made the front page of the January 1958 issue.

Rauschenberg's solo exhibition a couple of months later didn't have the same success as that of Johns. Only one work sold, which was *Bed* (1955), and it was purchased by Castelli. Determined to place Rauschenberg in a museum, he regularly wrote to Dorothy Miller, MoMA's first female curator, proposing different works to buy, and when they were turned down, inventing donors who could purchase work on their behalf. Although he was unsuccessful, it was an innovation in terms of dealership, connecting the museum with the primary market and sales of contemporary art. Castelli would continue to seek external accolades to raise the profile of his artists, campaigning ruthlessly for Rauschenberg to win the Grand Prize at the Venice Biennale in 1964.

The tides, however, changed quickly. When Count Giuseppe Panza di Biumo enquired about purchasing a Rauschenberg in 1959, Castelli somewhat pompously replied, 'It is currently impossible for me to sell you a work of Rauschenberg's – I don't have any.'[9] Like Duveen earlier, Castelli now had a hierarchy, and newcomers were told they were on a waiting list even if they offered a higher price. By refusing to sell sometimes to the highest bidder, Castelli conferred a symbolic value on the art and emphasised its uniqueness and rarity. His top clients, Robert and Ethel Scull, and Emily Hall Tremaine and Burton Tremaine, often found themselves at loggerheads; their most famous battle was over Johns's painting *Map* (1961). In the end, according to Castelli, 'Jasper said nobody could have it. It has to go to a museum, and whoever offers better conditions will get [to live with] it during their lifetime.'[10]

Castelli often projected a naivety with regard to finance, which was somewhat disingenuous, since he'd studied economics as a post-graduate, and worked in finance before becoming a dealer. Like Kootz before him, he exploited the tax benefits on art to motivate sales. Throughout his career, he also expanded his art empire by setting up satellite galleries, supplying dealers around the United States and across Europe with his high-profile artists. It was a winning situation for both parties: the Castelli name and the prestige of his artists immediately raised the profile of his colleagues while Castelli reaped half the commission without much work. It supported the careers of many significant dealers including Robert Fraser (1937–1986).

Castelli's success with Johns and Rauschenberg was blamed for killing off Abstract Expressionism. He was never concerned about the possibility of his own artists being surpassed; instead, he dedicated himself to finding the next wave of talent. In the 1960s he transitioned to Pop art, and represented Roy Lichtenstein (1923–1997). And the chameleon dealer would continue to evolve, later embracing Minimalism and Conceptual art.

In 1971 he formed a cooperative with a group of dealers, including his now ex-wife Sonnabend; they bought a former paper mill on 420 West Broadway. Raw and ungentrified, SoHo's abandoned warehouses had a natural synergy with the new industrial art, and Castelli's 743 square metre (8,000 square foot) space could accommodate the scale of some of this art. Sensitive to the atmosphere, Castelli abandoned the tradition of Tuesday evening viewings, which, in his opinion, had become frivolous events, and opted for open days on Saturdays. Castelli's son remembers the excitement: 'there were Richard Serra's constructions, Dan Flavin's environment pieces, Bruce Nauman's corridors... Phil[ip] Glass and John Cage's concert with twelves radios, Jon[as] Mekas's videos... it was totally unforeseen and certainly, as a child, I picked up the playfulness of those rough experiments at once.'[11]

The Castelli brand stayed on point and had the frisson of being current. Indeed, Castelli believed the dealer had a crucial role to play: 'We are the real vanguard, we are really the lead. We – the good dealers – can make things happen so much more rapidly than if we rely on museums.'[12] In 1989, he made the momentous gesture of gifting Rauschenberg's *Bed* to MoMA in honour of Barr. Despite his repeated efforts, as Calvin Tomkins reflects, 'MoMA and Rauschenberg [had] never quite hit it off.'[13] Castelli had always understood the work's profundity: '*Bed* is one of the important things in a man's life. I mean, he's conceived, he dies [there]... [it is the] symbol of human life.'[14] Indeed, the potency of the Castelli brand rested in this hidden sensitivity, which led him to identify with his artists, and be involved in the sales of some of the most poignant artworks of the twentieth century.

Chapter 3

The Idealists

Introduction

Dealers are risk takers. What motivates them to take a leap of faith and invest in art is complicated and, perhaps surprisingly, often not financially driven. What is rarely acknowledged is the soulfulness of the dealer. It takes great sensitivity to spot new talent, to connect emotionally with the art, and understand the cultural moment the artist is responding to. This section is about idealist dealers who were attuned to their artists and who made a commitment, spurred by their convictions, and vision for art.

Their artist-centred approach manifested in different ways. Above all, these idealist dealers were champions of their artists, holding exhibitions and making sure they received the right sort of critical attention, sometimes playing theorist themselves, publishing articles and books. Many of them took a pastoral role, helping their artists with everyday practicalities, whether that was providing a studio or a meal. In interview, Virginia Dwan emphasised, 'What a great artist does is very significant, and I want to see them have a place on earth, and recognition, and being cared for and supported. That really is meaningful to me.'[1]

Asserting higher values, these idealist dealers typically shunned the commercial side of the industry, and refused to aggressively market their own public images. Indeed, visitors were lucky if they even found Alfred Stieglitz's gallery, for the sign on the door was so small and unremarkable. Sometimes it was not a conscious rejection of monetary affairs: they might have been terrible business people, or their ideologies got in the way of turning a profit. For example, Stieglitz showcased photography at a time when it wasn't valued as an art form, making it a very difficult sale. For whatever reason, most of the galleries discussed here ran at a loss, and this is why for a long time they were not explored in the literature on dealership.

This chapter could have had many entries. One immediately thinks of Erica Brausen, Francis Bacon's first dealer. Bacon was an undiscovered talent when Brausen visited his studio and saw his recently finished *Painting, 1946* (1946). She bought the piece straight away. It has Bacon's raw, agonised emotion and shows a figure isolated in a cage screaming from a fleshy, toothy mouth. The grotesque treatment of the body resonates with the post-Holocaust era, expressing a profound disenchantment with humankind. When Brausen exhibited it, *The Times* described it as 'most alarming',[2] their shock reinforcing the extent of the dealer's leap of faith. Then, there is Berthe Weill who caused a scandal in 1917 when she displayed a painting of an erotic nude by Amedeo Modigliani in her gallery window. Complaints were made, but she refused to take the work down until the police became involved and insisted.

The five dealers chosen here were all on a spiritual quest, and each had a remarkable vision. For example, Topazia Alliata, once a prisoner of war, placed hope in art that had an ethereal lightness. At the other extreme, André Breton valued the macabre and surreal. Their ideals challenged fundamental structures of art dealerships. Indeed, many rejected the rarefied atmosphere of the white cube space, and introduced new ways of viewing art that involved the visitor more.

Spiritually attuned to the artist's vision, the boundaries between dealer and artist were less clear-cut. Dwan describes it as a journey together where, 'They were, every one of them... significant artists and people that made me feel at one in the world. [...] They were on a similar search.'[3]

Daniel-Henry Kahnweiler

(1884–1979)

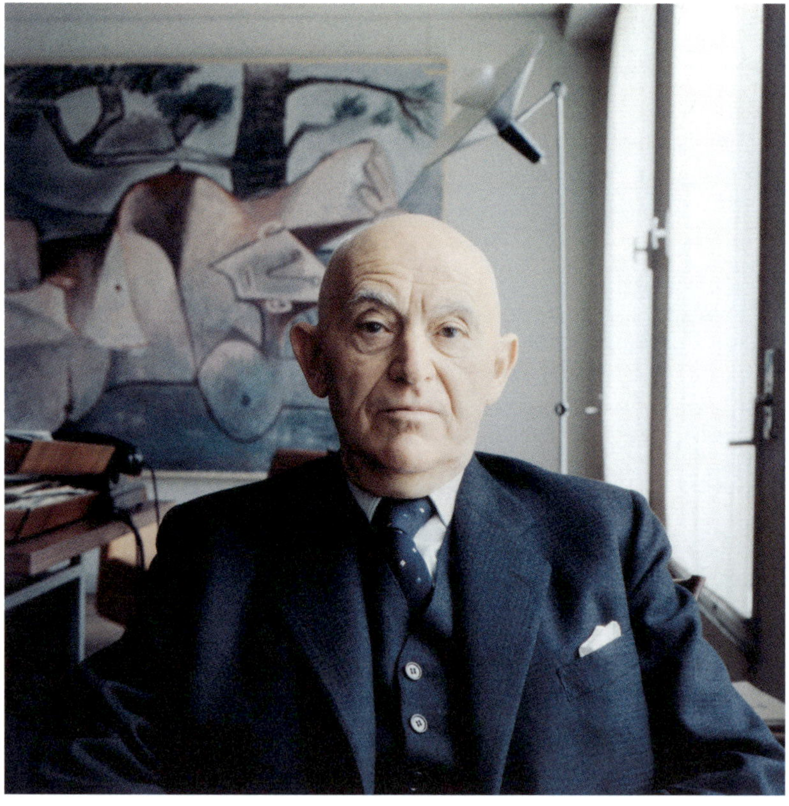

Wolfgang Kühn, *Daniel-Henry Kahnweiler at his gallery in Paris*, c. 1961.

When Daniel-Henry Kahnweiler attended the 1904 exhibition of Claude Monet's London views at Paul Durand-Ruel's gallery in Paris, he was struck by the sight of two cab drivers at the gallery window, apoplectic with rage. With their fists clenched, they yelled, 'Any place that shows such rubbish should have its window bashed in.'[1] The idea that art could produce such strong feelings impressed Kahnweiler. He would later consider outrage as a marker of art's worth, and a signal that it was disrupting convention, and presenting a new way of experiencing the world. On a mission, the dealer related, 'I adore defending what I love.'[2]

Born 1884 in Mannheim, Germany, Kahnweiler was the first son of Betty Neumann and Julius Kahnweiler. The union of his parents' families brought friction; Julius went to work for his brothers-in-law who had amassed great wealth from selling gold. However, he found the situation demoralising and became embittered, and a tyrannical figure at home. According to the biographer Pierre Assouline, Kahnweiler regarded his father as 'thick-headed, violent, incapable of analysing anything.'[3] He came to despise his father's lack of interest in culture, and when the family moved to Stuttgart, he started visiting museums and acquiring art books. Reading *Thus Spoke Zarathustra* (1883–85) by Friedrich Nietzsche (1844–1900) was an epiphany. Kahnweiler identified with the character Zarathustra, who personifies rebellion and decries convention. Perhaps the disruptive prophet inspired him to challenge his family, and their expectations of him.

The parents' plan was that Kahnweiler would be a businessman, and after finishing school, he worked in a bank and trained with a stockbroker in Paris. But it all bored him. He convinced his uncles to loan him £1,000 to open a gallery in Paris, which came with the stipulation that if the gallery didn't succeed within a year, he'd have to work for them. In 1907 he opened Galerie Kahnweiler on Rue Vignon in the 9th arrondissement. The location set it apart from the luxurious galleries on Rue Laffitte, and the shop was extremely modest. Previously occupied by a Polish tailor, it had a tiny storefront. After stripping the 4 by 4 metre (13 by 13 foot) cell, Kahnweiler fitted a carpet, and lined the walls with burlap – the monastic space was a stark contrast to the sumptuous luxury of most commercial galleries.

Kahnweiler's first purchases for the gallery reinforce how little he knew about the business side of the art world. Attending the Salon des Indépendants in 1907, he selected some modern works, paying the full asking price of 100 francs, unaware that dealers were offered substantial reductions. He would never have the ruthless strategy of Durand-Ruel and Ambroise Vollard who waited until their artists' reputations grew and their prices soared before they sold anything.

Whenever possible, Kahnweiler turned works around quickly, selling to faithful clients. The dealer reflected, 'As Picasso later told me, very correctly, "In order for paintings to be sold at high prices, they must first have been sold very cheaply."'[4] These early sales meant artists received an income when their finances were precarious. Paul Gauguin bitterly resented Vollard for making him wait years before he made a profit. Kahnweiler also offered monthly stipends in return for exclusive access to the work and, crucially, he never put pressure on his artists to produce a large volume of work.

In the first two years of opening his gallery, Kahnweiler discovered André Derain (1880–1954), Maurice de Vlaminck (1876–1958), Georges Braque (1882–1963) and Pablo Picasso, and offered them all representation. In many ways these artists embodied the raw energy of Zarathustra, who he so admired. They were physical men – Vlaminck was a champion cyclist and Braque was a boxer. A few of them were explosive characters. Though the dealer, by his own admission, was anti-social, he became part of their lives, visiting their dilapidated studios daily, drinking with them at the famous Au Lapin Agile, and venturing out with Picasso to watch the Cirque Medrano. He was embedded in his artists' lives – their art answered his philosophical quest, and offered new ways to understand the world.

The most controversial painting Kahnweiler defended was Picasso's *Les Demoiselles d'Avignon* (1907). Even the artist's friends were shocked by its brutality, and rumours were circulating that Picasso was insane: Braque said the work looked as if someone was drinking gasoline and spitting fire.[5] For Kahnweiler, this extreme reaction signalled that it was ground-breaking. He was especially interested in the right-hand side of the painting where the geometrical lozenge shapes showed different perspectives of the female figures. The work was the seed of Cubism, and Picasso's *Cubist Portrait of Daniel-Henry Kahnweiler* three years later bears witness to the central role the dealer played in the movement.

There was a strong communal element within Cubism; Braque said of this intense period of experimentation with Picasso that they were 'like mountain climbers roped together'.[6] One could argue that Kahnweiler was the steadying rope. When the two artists left Paris to advance their Cubist landscapes in the countryside, he wrote to them, giving feedback on any new works they sent. Braque's reply from Sourges in southeastern France reflects how much he valued this support: 'Your opinion of my paintings gave me great pleasure, all the more so since it's the only reaction that I have had here, where my isolation has made me lose all critical sense.'[7]

Kahnweiler was one of the first dealers to photograph artists' works. He used a professional photographer to document the artworks, while he also had his own portable camera to capture more informal moments. The archive was a valuable resource, allowing potential buyers to be shown an entire artist's career, and the artists themselves would ask to see images of their earlier sold works to chart their progress. Some of his own photos reveal the artists' studios and the landscapes which inspired their works, and now provide crucial background to their creative process.

At times, Kahnweiler could be over-protective, cocooning his artists from the critics and the public alike. He point-blank refused to engage with any form of advertisement or promotion. After presenting four exhibitions in 1908, he stopped holding shows altogether, giving the explanation, 'we had no desire to expose ourselves either to their rage or laughter.'[8] Instead, he had a group of dedicated, international collectors including the French industrialist Roger Dutilleul, the Russian textile magnate Sergei Shchukin, and the Swiss collectors, Hermann and Margrit Rupf. He also fostered relationships with the Moderne Galerie Thannhauser in Munich, and with the dealer Alfred Flechtheim who had galleries in Berlin, Cologne and Vienna.

Kahnweiler was aware his discerning take limited his commercial opportunities. He was critical of most modern art, dismissing Expressionism and Futurism outright. And while he became the figurehead of Cubism, he only ever rated Picasso, Braque and Juan Gris (1887–1927). He decried the second generation Cubists including Jean Metzinger (1883–1956) and Albert Gleizes (1881–1953) for arranging the geometrical facets in a decorative manner. For him, the true Cubist language had philosophical intentions, and sought to give a fuller understanding of an object, showing various viewpoints, and referencing its texture and colour.

When World War I broke out, as a German citizen Kahnweiler faced the difficult situation that he was now an enemy of the state. He spent the war years in Bern, keeping in contact with his artists from the Swiss capital. He was offered the chance to export the artworks from his Parisian gallery to the USA, but he decided against this – something he later bitterly regretted when they were seized by the French government as war reparations.

For Yve-Alain Bois and Katharine Streip, 'Kahnweiler's exile, for him a tragedy, gave him the opportunity to develop as a critic, aesthetician, and art historian.'[9] He read a great deal, and became interested in Neo-Kantian thinking. He found a natural affinity between Immanuel Kant's ideas on art and his dealership practice. Indeed, his monastic gallery space, and his refusal to hold commercial exhibitions already ratified Kant's position that art is a disinterested activity, removed from life. During his exile, he wrote *The Rise of Cubism* (1920). He interpreted Cubism – and the way the cube-like facets present different aspects of an object (texture, dimension, colour) in terms of the German philosopher's articulation of perception in which our various impressions assemble into a coherent whole.

In the case of Picasso, Kahnweiler also insisted, 'I know no art that is autobiographical to such a degree.'[10] Picasso's experiment in Cubism was driven by his compulsive character, and desire to possess and understand things in their entirety. Unusually, Kahnweiler understood this emotional aspect to the seemingly abstract Cubist work. He highlighted Picasso's hidden inscriptions, and the titles which declare his love for his girlfriend Eva. This depth of interpretation would be later lost in the modernist accounts by Alfred Barr and Clement Greenberg which considered Cubism in terms of abstraction.

In 1920 Kahnweiler returned to Paris where, because of his German citizenship, his entire gallery stock was sequestered as part of the war-time reparation payments. Acting for the government, art dealer Léonce Rosenberg (1879–1947) sold off the works in a series of auctions at Hôtel Drouot which flooded the market with Cubist paintings and devalued their worth for a long time to come. For Kahnweiler, the process of being publicly stripped of his precious art collection was soul-destroying. At the first auction, his artists gathered in support, incensed by Rosenberg's betrayal. Assouline tells how the situation escalated: 'They were shouting and screaming when Braque started kicking [Rosenberg] on the backside as he ran.'[11]

Kahnweiler opened Galerie Simon in 1920, only months after he returned to Paris. To his great disappointment, most of the artists from his first gallery abandoned him, seeking out more lucrative options with other dealers. However, he maintained a good relationship with Picasso, and later became his principal dealer once again. But he would face further trials when France was occupied by the Nazis during the World War II, and Jewish people were prevented from owning businesses. This time, he was more strategic. He retreated to the countryside, turning his business over to his stepdaughter, Louise Leiris, and renaming it Galerie Louise Leiris. On his return, they ran the business together.

An overlooked area of Kahnweiler's career is his venture into publishing. Following Vollard's lead, he produced a series of artist books, bringing together avant-garde artists with contemporary writers and poets. For example, he paired Apollinaire with Derain for *L'Enchanteur Pourrissant* (1909). The poet's fantastical text pushed Derain into new territory; his lurid black and white graphics capture a magical realm.

Kahnweiler defended the artists he represented voraciously. However, his career also demonstrates a dilemma faced by many idealistic dealers, and how their conviction can sometimes affect them commercially. He essentially supported Cubism: very little else satisfied his exacting criteria. He searched for art that had shock value, and while 'the shock of the new' was to become a central strategy to the avant-garde, one wonders if the discerning Kahnweiler would have found the same emotion and philosophical substance in this art.

Alfred Stieglitz

(1864–1946)

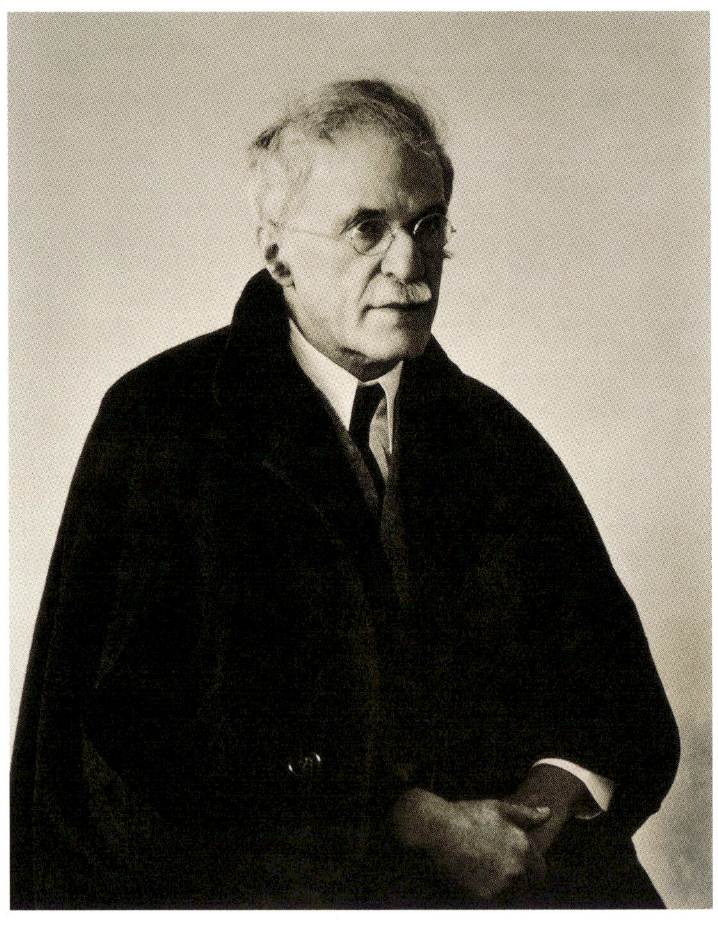

Alfred Stieglitz, c. 1930.
Unknown photographer.

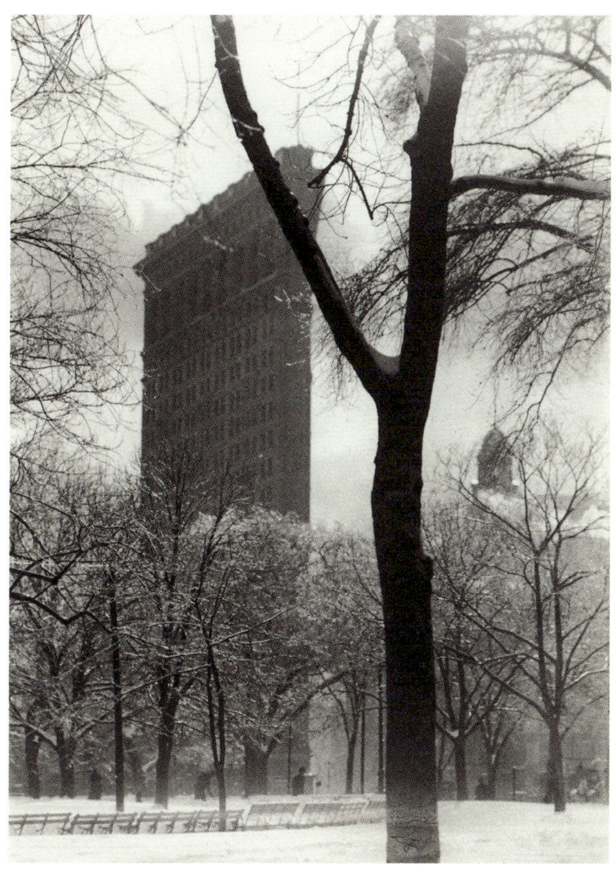

Fig. 17 Alfred Stieglitz, *The Flatiron*, 1903, gelatin silver print,
12 × 8.4 cm (4¾ × 3⁵⁄₁₆ in.), The Art Institute of Chicago.

Alfred Stieglitz considered himself a rebel. He was against artistic convention, and belligerently anti-commercial; if a gallery visitor was overly interested in the price of an artwork, he was likely, as his secretary said, '[to] double the price of the painting'.[1] A renowned photographer himself, there was a symbiotic relationship between his art and his dealership. His priorities are reflected in his iconic photograph, *The Flatiron* (1903, fig. 17). In it, the vertical lines of the tree and the famous New York building give the work a compositional rigour and geometry, while the misty winter scene infuses a sense of otherworldliness. In his dealership, Stieglitz would seek out artists whose work had the same purity of form and sense of the spiritual.

Born in Hoboken, New Jersey, in 1864, Stieglitz was the eldest of six children. His father was a wealthy wool merchant who painted in his spare time, and the family were liberal-thinking, and interested in culture. As a child Stieglitz was jealous of the bond between his twin siblings, and hankered for this spiritual connection for himself. In 1881, the family emigrated to Germany where Stieglitz studied engineering before he became interested in photography. He returned to America in 1890, and settled in New York. Despite despairing at how filthy the city was, the streets also inspired his early photography which captures the energy of modern life.

Stieglitz's first mission was to establish photography as an art form. The contemporary art critic Charles Caffin recognised his efforts, observing, 'Both in his pictures and in his writings, as well as by his personal influence, he has little by little, and in the face of the dead inertia of indifference and of more active opposition... upheld the hands of artistic photographs.'[2] In 1902, Stieglitz joined with a group of pictorial photographers and formed the movement Photo-Secession, although he soon rejected pictorialism on the basis that it manipulated effects in production and betrayed the immediacy of photography. A year later, he released the quarterly magazine *Camera Work*, which brought together texts and high-quality images. Beautifully designed, the cover was an olive green embossed with silver Art Deco lettering. His curation of the content anticipated his approach to his gallery: indeed, the walls of his first space were painted an olive colour.

During his career, Stieglitz ran a succession of galleries including 291 Gallery (1905–17), the Intimate Gallery (1921–29) and the American Gallery (1929–46). They were all small spaces: 291 Gallery measured only 4.6 metres (15 feet) square. The intimate scale suited the close examination of photographs. A year after opening 291, Stieglitz moved a couple of buildings down, but kept the same name. He asked the photographer Edward Steichen (1879–1973) to decorate the new space, painting the walls olive-green and adding burlap curtains around the room. Both played into the intimacy and were cocooning.

Liberated by his father's financial support, Stieglitz was free to follow his ideals. The commercial side of the business was obscured: price tags were abandoned, and the sign on the door was small and unnoticeable. Stieglitz's opinion was 'those who love and understand and have an art-nose will find their way.'[3] Very quickly, a creative and intellectual crowd gathered at the gallery; Georgia O'Keeffe (1887–1986) recounts how tutors at The

Art Students League would send their pupils to see the latest shows. The exhibitions were didactic, but also investigative, as the photographer and writer Paul Haviland (1880–1950) explained, '[The gallery] represents nothing definite; it is ever growing, constantly changing and developing.'[4] The gallery had their own magazine, *291* (1915–16), and in the first issue Haviland presented the gallery as a laboratory, with Stieglitz as the commanding professor.

In the first year of the 291 Gallery, Stieglitz launched a series of photographic exhibitions including one of French artists, and a group exhibition that showcased works by the American photographer Gertrude Käsebier (1852–1934) who was known for her strong compositions, and images of mothers. The shows were well attended, and played a key role in photography being accepted as an art form.

Soon Stieglitz decided to shake things up by introducing his American audience to European modernism. His idea was for it to be a teaching tool, 'We all have to learn how to see. We all have to learn to use our eyes, and 291 [is] here for no other purpose than to give everybody a chance to see.'[5] He held the first exhibitions in America for Auguste Rodin, Constantin Brâncuși (1876–1957), Henri Matisse and Pablo Picasso. In terms of sourcing the art, Stieglitz relied on the help of Steichen, and the Mexican caricaturist George de Zayas (1898–1967) who were both very involved in the Parisian art scene. Because of the small scale of the gallery, he was unable to accommodate large paintings, and exhibited mostly lithographs and drawings. In the early twentieth-century art world, this attention on drawings was somewhat provocative: the Académie française still considered them to be mere studies for the final work. However, the intimate gallery space complemented the more personal medium of drawing.

This emphasis on the personal reflected Stieglitz's interest in the thinking of Sigmund Freud (1856–1939) and Henri Bergson (1859–1941). Both thinkers prioritised unconscious worlds, with Freud emphasising sexual desire. Freud's ideas were circulating in New York at the time, and this may have played a part in the positive reception to Stieglitz's exhibitions of Rodin's intimate drawings in 1908 and 1910.

In his day, Rodin was a radical figure. For the 1908 exhibition, Steichen chose 58 drawings from the artist's studio. While the candid sexuality of these images had disturbed some French critics, Stieglitz and Steichen were impressed by their naturalness, and emphasised this aspect. The curation was minimal: no attempt was made to refine the work. They were exhibited unframed – as it were in their naked state. Stieglitz reported back to Rodin that American women were deeply impressed by 'the elemental beauty you feel to express in things'.[6] Certainly, women were the major purchasers.

Another revolutionary aspect of Rodin's drawings was their vitality. In contrast to the frozen quality of academic nudes, the artist depicted women moving naturally. Using pencil and colour washes of bright red, blue and gold, the forms flowed, their animation evident in his line. Stieglitz reflected the deep impression they made, 'I can only say to have been given the opportunity to live with them constantly for four weeks is the greatest spiritual treat I have ever had.'[7]

Stieglitz himself was learning from these exhibitions. When he first saw an exhibition of Paul Cezanne's watercolours at the Galerie Bernheim-Jeune in Paris in 1907, he sneered, 'There's nothing there, but empty paper with a few splashes of colour,'[8] but later he celebrated the empty white space, and how it flooded Cezanne's scenes with light. Increasingly, Stieglitz played theoretician. He became interested in the fundamental differences between fine art and photography, and started to promote the latter in terms of its objectivity, and ability to directly record nature. This is not to say he disregarded the role of beauty in photography, but this had to be inherent to the scene. Simultaneously, he argued painting should no longer be concerned with representation since photography was better equipped to do this.

Stieglitz became a mentor to younger artists. Paul Strand (1890–1976) showed him his early lyrical photos, and recounted Stieglitz's advice: '[with] the lens wide open… you had a kind of unity because of the softness of the image, but you lost the individual character of all the materials in the things that you photographed. Water looked like grass and grass looked like the bark on the tree.'[9] Strand mentions being convinced by what Stieglitz said. While the dealer would eventually move away from photography exhibitions, he made an exception for Strand, and held a solo show for him in 1916, which included Strand's iconic photo *Blind Woman, New York* (1916). The close-up of the street peddler very much conveys the 'individual character of all the materials'.[10] There's the sharp detailing of the peddler's badge with its licence number, and the placard that reads 'BLIND' – both add to the emotional power of this image.

In 1913, the landmark Armory Show in New York presented the history of European modernism, in a sense justifying what Stieglitz had been doing at his gallery between 1908 and 1912. Publicly, Stieglitz supported and lent works to the exhibition, but he also used his gallery to present an alternate narrative. Running concurrently, he staged a solo show of his own photographs which depicted views of New York, and projected an idea of a national American art. In his later ventures at his Intimate Gallery and An American Place, Stieglitz would abandon European modernism, looking instead to American artists. Perhaps his change of direction was symptomatic of the post-war situation. Art historian Sarah Greenough notes, 'Stieglitz's model was more communal, even familial and intimate, with growing spiritual overtones, he endeavoured to nurture, protect, and promote a community of American artists, writers, poets and critics whose collective voice, he believed, would enrich a spiritually deprived nation.'[11]

In the period 1921 to 1943, his gallery was focussed on seven American artists: Charles Demuth (1883–1935), Arthur Dove (1880–1946), Marsden Hartley (1877–1943), John Marin (1870–1953), O'Keeffe, Strand and Stieglitz himself. In 1925, he presented them together in the group show *Seven Americans* at the Anderson Galleries in New York.[12] With little public interest in American modern art at this point, many of these artists were struggling financially, and Stieglitz often provided them with practical solutions, sometimes offering them financial support.

In O'Keeffe, he found a kindred spirit and the artists became romantically involved. They inspired each other creatively. Between 1918 and 1919, Stieglitz obsessively photographed O'Keeffe, and he exhibited some of these photographs in a solo exhibition at his gallery in 1921. The curation of the show had a proto-Surrealist flavour with works grouped around body parts, in sections titled, 'Hands', 'Hands and Breasts' and 'Feet'. The hang complemented Stieglitz's use of fragmentation in his photographs, with a single detail evoking O'Keeffe's character, and the heady intimacy between the sitter and photographer. Significantly, O'Keeffe eventually withdrew from being his model, and most of the 331 portraits Stieglitz made of her date from these early years between 1917 and 1922. Perhaps she felt that being his muse devalued her own artistic endeavours.

Stieglitz was a great supporter of O'Keeffe's work, but there are similar tensions in how he promoted her. While he was progressive in his assertion that women artists were of equal merit, he positioned her as a 'Great Child'.[13] Rooted in Romantic philosophy, the adulation of the inner child when mapped onto her gender was problematic. He also insistently read her botanical work in terms of female sexuality, and her paintings were appreciated in these terms for a long time, despite the artist herself questioning this narrative.

Stieglitz was always pushing an agenda. In his later career, he started to formulate an identity for American art. Soon, the American Regionalists and Precisionists would be chasing his tail, and advancing alternative ideas for a national art. In the end, the movement that came to encapsulate the American spirit globally would be the Abstract Expressionists. The ideals of this group of artists resonated with Stieglitz's agenda and his fascination for a subjective, vital art. Indeed, the tiny 291 Gallery, and the intimately-scaled works shown there, had expansive horizons.

André Breton

(1896–1966)

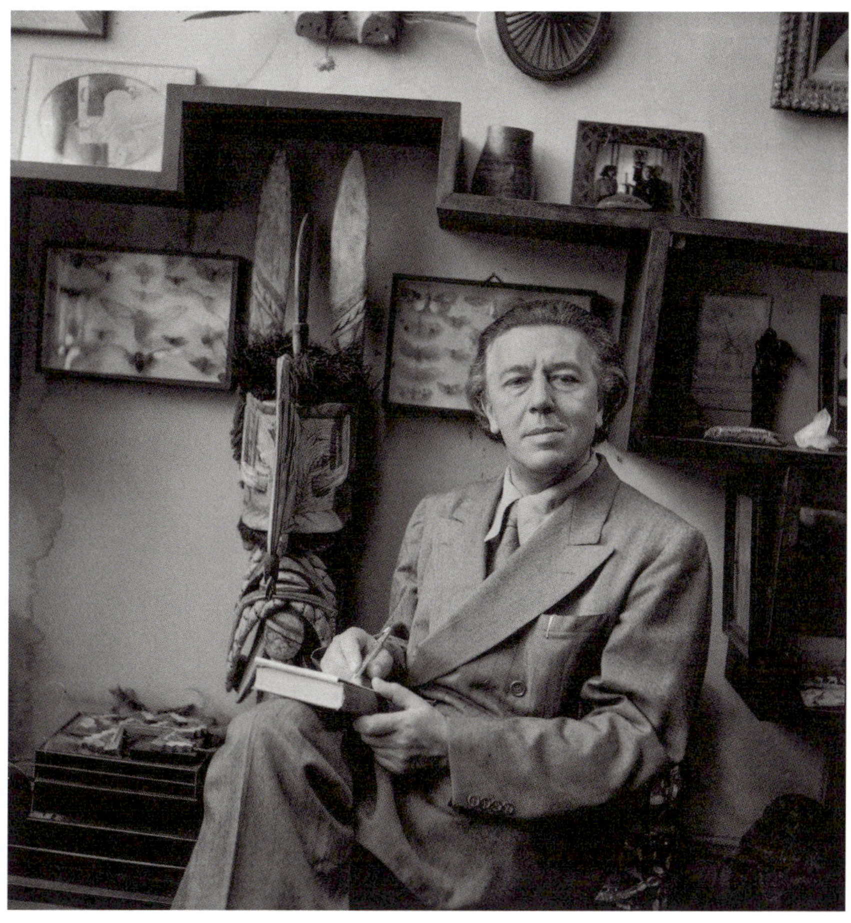

André Breton, 1950.
Unknown photographer.

In 1937, the poet, novelist and leader of the Surrealists, André Breton, opened Galerie Gradiva on the Rue de Seine, Paris. It was an unusual move on his part: he'd always been suspicious of the commercial side of art, once commenting, 'Art is, I repeat, under the sway of dealers and this to the great shame of artists.'[1] His change of heart was likely prompted by his critical financial situation: his obsessive art collecting had drained his family's resources. His wife, Jacqueline Lamba, bitterly remembered the 'Penniless years, surrounded by a priceless collection', adding, 'Collecting to this extent is, as we know, a pathological phenomenon.'[2] But Breton's family obligations were soon forgotten. Instead of looking at ways to make money, he became absorbed in using the gallery space as an extension of Surrealist practices and immersing the visitor in marvellous fantasies.

An only child, Breton had been brought up in a small village in Normandy before his family moved to Paris. As a teenager he became interested in modern writers like Joris-Karl Huysmans whose novels created rich, interior worlds. Although fascinated by literature, Breton chose to study medicine. However, his training was interrupted by the onset of World War I. During the war, he worked for a military hospital in Nantes where he met the poets Guillaume Apollinaire and Alfred Jarry, both of whom were receiving treatment for injuries. Breton had come to despise the violence of war and was exploring Sigmund Freud's ideas on the subconscious. When he returned to Paris, he began collecting, eventually cramming his flat with over 5,000 objects, books and artworks. And in the meantime, he had connected with the artist Tristan Tzara (1896–1963), who would become known for his involvement with the anarchic Dadaists.

The first International Dada Fair (fig. 18), held at Otto Burchard's gallery in Berlin in 1920, was a precursor to Breton's radical curation. The exhibition was a deliberate assault on the Kantian premise that art was a rarefied activity, unconnected to everyday life. The curation embraced the chaos of life. Miscellaneous items, including posters advertising the Dada ethos, paintings and random objects, were scattered across the walls. And adding to the already frantic energy, a mannequin with a pig's head, and dressed as a German officer, dangled ominously over the proceedings.

There would be a discordant curation style at Galerie Gradiva, where fine art, design and furniture were mixed together. Like Dada, Breton was protesting against 'the reign of logic',[3] but he had a different perspective. He had grown to dislike the nihilism of Dada, and was now the figurehead of the

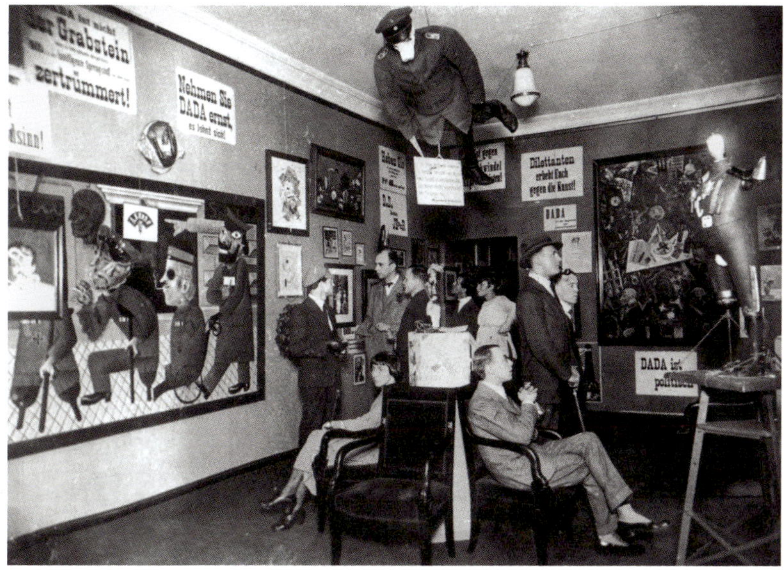

Fig.18 *Opening of the First International Dada fair in the bookshop of Dr. Burchard in Berlin. Standing from left to right: Raoul Hausmann, Otto Burchard, Johannes Baader, Wieland and Margarete Herzfelde, George Grosz, John Heartfield. Sitting: Hannah Hoch and Otto Schmalhausen, 5 June 1920.*

Surrealist movement. In his writings, he connected Surrealism with the unconscious, offering his famous definition, 'SURREALISM. n. Psychic automatism in its pure state, by which one proposes to express – verbally, by means of the written word, or in any other manner – the actual functioning of thought.'[4]

Breton was especially interested in Freud's understanding of our unconscious as a site of repressed desire and this manifested in his gallery's identity. It was named after the novella *Gradiva: A Pompeiian Fantasy* (1903) by Wilhelm Jensen (1837–1911), which Freud had famously analysed from a psychoanalytic perspective. In Jensen's novella, the central character sublimates his desire for his childhood friend, and becomes obsessed with an image of a female figure depicted on an antique Roman relief. Breton wrote to Pablo Picasso, asking, 'My dream would be for you to make a very small drawing of this Gradiva that can be reproduced at will on all the labels and letterhead of the gallery.'[5] It is not known if Picasso even responded, but in the end, Breton had an iron stamp made.

Jensen's exploration of male desire and obsession chimed with the themes Breton was exploring in his own novels. In Breton's second novel, *Nadja*

(1928), the narrator becomes obsessed with a woman he meets by chance in the street. Their writings indicate the troubled role of the female muse within Surrealism where the male is considered a passive innocent, caught up in the alluring sexuality of the female muse. This male fantasy was evoked in the gallery's name and signage. Spelled out over the door, the 'D' of *Gradiva* was enlarged to isolate the word 'DIVA'. Then underneath each letter, was a sequence of women's names – for example, 'COMME Gisele' appeared below the letter 'G'. Reading across, the line of women's names was like a hypnotic mantra to the female muse.

Breton approached Duchamp to design the door to the gallery, and Duchamp came up with the idea of a glass door incised with the silhouette of a man and woman huddled together. The door evolved from Duchamp's *The Bride Stripped Bare by Her Bachelors, Even (The Large Glass)* (1915–23), in which a lower chamber of nine machine-like bachelors compete for the attention of the bride in the upper section. In a sense, in the glass door the now entwined couple represent fulfilled desire.

In terms of curatorship, it marked an important moment when the boundaries between an artwork and the historically 'neutral' gallery space were challenged. The gallery became part of the art experience, setting up a new relationship with the visitor, who was no longer simply a viewer, but an active participant. After passing through the door, they were led into a short, dark passageway created from rubber bellows that connect railway carriages. The interactive nature of this was picked up on in the contemporary press. On 8 November 1937, the French writer Raymond Queneau asked his readers in his popular column, 'In what shop does one enter through a railway bellows?'[6] The extended threshold functioned as a portal into the metaphysical realm that was represented inside by the artworks.

In terms of the display, Breton deliberately juxtaposed different artworks. He mixed books, paintings, furniture and Oceanic and African sculpture together. Works were geographically distant, and genres (fashion, fine art and design) were exhibited together. His thinking echoed the Surrealists' adaptation of a popular Victorian parlour game, the 'Cadavre exquis' (Exquisite Corpse). These were collaborative drawings in which the first person drew a body part on a piece of paper, folded it over to conceal their contribution, before passing it on. When the paper finally was unfolded, a fantastical creature was unveiled.

For Breton, the incongruous display revealed a marvellous, fantastical order. To explain this, he quoted the poet Pierre Reverdy: 'The more the relationship between the two juxtaposed realities is distant and true, the stronger the image will be – the greater its emotional power and poetic reality.'[7] Breton looked for the same qualities in the individual works. Emerging from Duchamp's portal, the first piece one encountered was a sculpture of a human head, by Marcel Jean, featuring zips for eyes, and a collar made from photographic film. The provocative object resonated with the Marquis de Sade's writings, and his fascination with sadomasochism. Breton had heralded this writer in his 1924 manifesto where he posited, 'Sade is Surrealist in sadism.'[8]

With regard to the non-European art exhibited in the gallery, there is little information regarding precisely what was shown. Breton had become increasingly interested in Oceanic art. Less known than African art, it therefore met his criteria of being distant and unfamiliar. Louise Tythacott suggests another possible interest in this work: 'The incorporation of multiple materials on Oceanic masks too may have triggered a visual accord with the surrealists' own processes of assemblage and collage. Just as surrealist collages include a diverse assortment of objects, so shells, human and animal bones, hair, teeth, feathers, fur and debris of all kinds are traditionally used to embellish Pacific artefacts.'[9]

Some of the most challenging works on show were those that blurred the boundary between fine art and design. In a letter to the Surrealist art collector Edward James, René Magritte (1898–1967) mentions visiting the gallery and singles out a 'chair covered in ivy'[10] by Wolfgang Paalen (1905–1959) and a 'cushioned wheelbarrow in which one [can] sit very comfortably'[11] by Óscar Domínguez (1906–1957). Regarding the ivy chair, the artist had employed clever visual metaphors. Specifically, the ladder back of the chair resembles a wooden garden trellis, making it a fitting support for ivy. Yet the object simultaneously appears strange: the twisted branches render the chair uncomfortable, robbing it of its functionality while also imparting a sinister, visceral quality. The piece exemplifies Freud's concept of the uncanny where the familiar is made unfamiliar.

Breton valued the surreal order arising from these juxtapositions. In the case of Domínguez's wheelbarrow (c. 1937), the sumptuous satin fabric played against the rustic wood, giving the visitor a tactile experience while suggesting fairy-tale archetypes like *Beauty and the Beast*. One newspaper critic wrote, 'In fact, we find... images that we can touch, grasp, that we even have the pressing need to grasp in order to be certain not to awaken too quickly with a bitter taste in our mouth and empty hands.'[12]

While Breton was focussed on Surreal possibilities, these works linked fine art with other disciplines, and opened up the idea of collaborations with design and indeed fashion. Man Ray (1890–1976) famously photographed a model dressed in a Vionnet evening gown reclining in Domínguez's wheelbarrow. Breton realised that these surreal objects needed to be marketed differently to paintings, which were unique items bearing the imprint of an artist's hand. He made the pragmatic decision to make two copies of both the wheelbarrow and the ivy chair. In so doing he anticipated the production line for designed objects, and indeed, a year after the opening of Galerie Gradiva, James would commission five versions of Salvador Dalí's iconic Mae West Lips sofa (1938–39).

Galerie Gradiva closed after only a year. It never attracted huge crowds, and it certainly wasn't a roaring commercial success. So why highlight it? The gallery had an extraordinary influence – especially amongst dealers. Peggy Guggenheim (1898–1979) discovered the work of Yves Tanguy (1900–1955) there, and Leo Castelli and Ileana Sonnabend were deeply impressed by the way Breton brought together disciplines and put fine art in dialogue with everyday culture. Beyond this, Galerie Gradiva opened up the idea that the gallery itself could be part of the art experience, in which the visitor played an active role.

Topazia Alliata

(1913–2015)

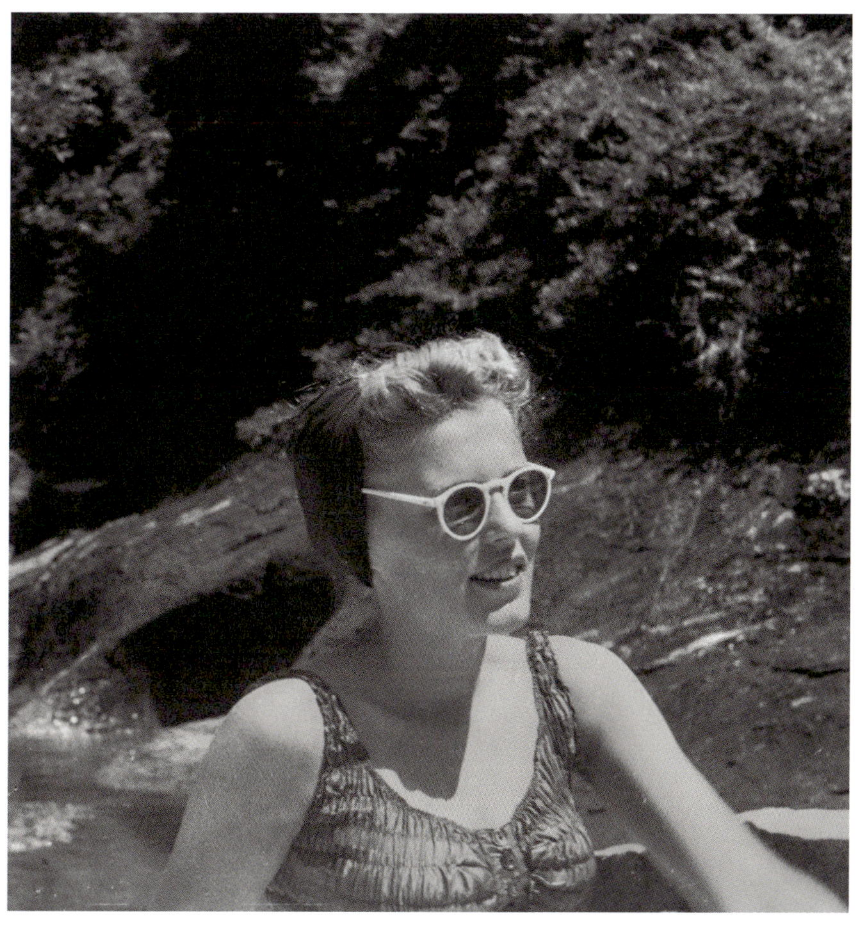

Fosco Maraini, *Topazia Alliata*,
Japan, 1941–43.

In 1955, four years before opening Galleria Trastevere in Rome, Topazia Alliata collaborated with her friend, the poet Emilio Villa (1914–2003), and launched her first exhibition on a barge on the River Tiber. This was a strikingly different context to the commercial galleries in the city centre, and marked her alternative stance. At the launch, Villa positioned a sign outside that read, 'Dogs allowed; bicycles, merchants and critics prohibited.'[1] By humorously ejecting the dealer and critic, they challenged the commercial gallery system. Alliata had a strong sense of freedom, evident in her international vision for art, and her taste for work that had a light-spiritedness. In the case of the latter, she reflected the philosophy of the Italian writer, Italo Calvino (1923–1985), who posed the question, 'Were I to choose an auspicious image for the new millennium, I would choose... the secret of lightness.'[2] Her floating exhibition bobbing on the river embodied this quality.

Born in Palermo on 5 November 1913, Alliata was a painter, diarist, gallery owner and also a princess. Her royal status came from her father, Prince Enrico Alliata di Villafranca, while her mother, Amelia, was a former opera singer. She grew up in Sicily during the oppressive years of Benito Mussolini's fascist reign, but her father stood as a powerful counterforce to this. A liberal thinker, well before alternative lifestyles became popular, he chose to be vegetarian and wrote one of the first Italian vegetarian cookbooks. He also wrote about the Indian spiritual thinker, Jiddu Krishnamurti (1895–1986), whom Alliata met in Naples in 1932. According to Alliata's daughter, Toni Maraini, her mother absorbed Krishnamurti's 'secular, pragmatic... spiritual thinking'.[3] Significantly, Krishnamurti denied guru figures or gods, and argued for personal freedom: 'To be free of all authority, of your own and that of another, is to die to everything of yesterday, so that your mind is always fresh, always young, innocent, full of vigour and passion.'[4]

Alliata first trained to be an artist at Accademia di Belle Arti di Palermo. In 1935 she married the renowned anthropologist Fosco Maraini (1912–2004). Six years later, Maraini was offered a bursary by what was then the Hokkaido Imperial University in Sapporo, Japan, and the couple moved there with their first daughter, and had two more daughters while living there. In 1943, after refusing to declare their allegiance to the fascist state, the entire family was interned in a prison camp. As the only woman and the only children in the camp, they faced daily humiliations, and starving rations, until their release in 1945. Alliata said of this time, 'I have never seen so much hatred and stupidity.'[5] The experience galvanised her pursuit of creative and spiritual freedom.

Alliata's aunt describes the family's return to Sicily: 'they arrived very tested by the period of war and imprisonment, but alive!'[6] Back home, Alliata helped run her family's wine business, but was always frustrated by the mafia involvement. She became involved in activist groups, and was drawn to the cultural scene of Rome where many of her Sicilian artist friends had also become involved. In 1955, after her relationship with her husband broke down, she moved permanently to Rome.

Four years later, in 1959, Alliata opened Galleria Trastevere where she exhibited Italian and international avant-garde art. Liberated from fascism, Rome had been experiencing a cultural renaissance. Her gallery was named after the neighbourhood in which it was situated – a centre of cultural activity, near the Accademia di Belle Arti di Roma, and the vibrant scene around the bookshop, Il Ferro di Cavallo. Art historian and writer Fabrizio D'Amico explains how 'painting in Rome in the 1950s was a civilization at its peak. It blossomed on fertile ground... and mysteriously reached fullness.'[7] Painters from abroad were attracted to this burgeoning scene. In an interview in 2019, the Moroccan artist Mohamed Melehi (1936–2020), who

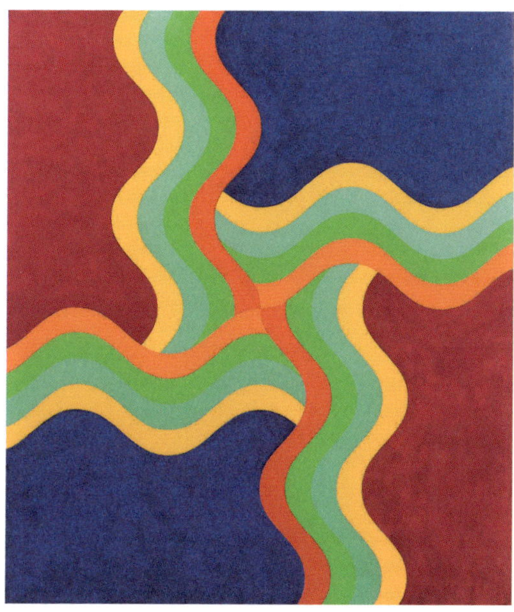

Fig. 19 Mohamed Melehi, *Composition*, 1970, acrylic on panel, 120 × 100 cm (47 ⅛ × 39 ⅜ in.), Collection of Barjeel Art Foundation, Sharjah, UAE.

showed with Alliata, tells how 'Italy was the place to go' since the language of abstract art was 'more open, more advanced in new forms of art'[8] than in Paris where Surrealism still had a dominant hold.

There was a sense of a collective moment at the gallery, that everyone had suffered in some way through the war years, and through the fascist years. A journalist from the Sicilian newspaper *L'Ora* described Galleria Trastevere as an 'an instrument... at the service of freedom for artists'[9] and gave the example of the inaugural exhibition which featured the sculptor Andrea Cascella (1920–1990) who was collaborating with his brother on the *International Monument to the Victims of Fascism* (1958–67). During the first year, Alliata held an exhibition for the Italian artist Alberto Burri (1915–1995) who had been a prisoner of war in a camp in Texas where he made his early canvases on raw burlap sacking. Reminiscent of the privations of wartime experience, the humble sacking would have carried basic food items like rice, and the way they are stitched together suggests worn, patched clothing.

From the beginning, her gallery received international attention. Peggy Guggenheim, Herbert Read and Alberto Moravia all attended the inaugural show. Throughout her career, Alliata forged relationships with many gallerists and critics, including Lawrence Alloway in London, and the German art historian Udo Kultermann, who became interested in the North African artists orbiting the gallery, especially Melehi. During the Vietnam War, many disenchanted American artists found their way to Rome, and sought refuge at her gallery.

For these displaced artists, and many of her other artists, Alliata played a pastoral role. Her house keys were left under her doormat for them to let themselves into her apartment, and her daughter tells how artists were guaranteed a bed to sleep, and there was always a pot of pasta and beans on the stove for them to help themselves. There was also a restaurant in her building where Alliata met her artists, and perhaps, most significantly, she provided a studio for those who couldn't afford to rent one themselves.[10]

The press picked up on Alliata's focus on abstract art.[11] As a mode of expression, abstraction has an intrinsic liberty, unconcerned with faithfully representing the world, and free from systems like illusionistic perspective. She became involved with a new generation of abstract artists who were turning away, as one contemporary critic described it, 'from the deluge of subjectivity',[12] epitomised by the highly expressive mark-making of

Jackson Pollock. Instead, her artists were pioneering a hard-edged abstraction, characterised by razor-sharp edges and flat, bright colour. As Alliata's daughter emphasises, 'Her interest looked to young artists from distant lands and outside of the usual circles, such as the Maghreb and more generally the Mediterranean basin.'[13]

Melehi had a solo show at Galleria Trastevere in 1959 and he was one of the first African artists to have an exhibition in a commercial gallery. Through Alliata, Melehi met key artists including Jannis Kounellis (1936–2017), whose incorporation of everyday materials within his work inspired Melehi to look at his own country's Amazigh heritage. Melehi later reflected that he found his local identity in Rome. In 1962, Alliata supported his application for a Rockefeller fellowship at Columbia University and this exposed him to the hard-edged minimalism of Jim Dine (b. 1935) and Frank Stella (1936–2024). Melehi would go on to develop his own signature take on abstraction, which brought together geometric styles, inspired by Arab rugs, and patterned decoration schemes from mosques, with a sharp minimalism (fig. 19).

Alliata also represented sculptors, and in 1962 held a solo show with Carlo Lorenzetti (b. 1934). His structures, made from thin sheets of metal, had a feather-light quality that consistently attracted the Italian dealer. Lorenzetti refused the weight and materiality of traditional stone and bronze sculpture and by supporting such work, Alliata was playing a part in rethinking the medium. In this respect, the historian Carlotta Sylos Calò has uncovered a significant group show held at Galleria Travestere in 1960, which Alliata invited the Conceptual artist Piero Manzoni (1933–1963) to curate.

The exhibition *Riducibili. Sculture da viaggio ('Reducible. Travel Sculptures')* opened on 8 October 1960. The following year, Manzoni would famously sell cans of his own shit, but he was already breaking new ground for art and questioning the status of the art object. According to Sylos Calò, 'The experimental program of the exhibition, and form of its catalog, are ascribable to Alliata',[14] who had requested something 'sensational'. In a radical rethink of sculpture, works were not shown on pedestals or plinths. More crucially, they were foldable or collapsible, allowing visitors to easily transport them home. Most of them could be popped in a pocket.

Some of the artists ventured into performance. Agostino Bonalumi (1935–2013) made his paper sculptures at the gallery. This focus on his creative act challenged the notion of sculpture as a material object and instead placed value on an ephemeral happening. A sense of impermanence was also latent in the fragile paper structures. Meanwhile, Manzoni contributed balloons, listed for the exhibition as 'Bodies of air in extendable rubber casings up to 80cm in diameter, on a folding base'. Filled with the artist's breath, each one faced the pathetic fate of deflating, and becoming a wrinkled vestige. While this process was marked with a Dadaesque irreverence, it also had poignancy. The ephemeral beauty of balloons conveyed the poetic lightness that had long fascinated Alliata. It encapsulated the fragility of humankind in the era following the Holocaust and the bombing of Hiroshima.

The 'exhibition catalogue' was equally innovative. It bore little relationship to a traditional catalogue, with no illustrations or explanatory essays. In fact, it wasn't even a book: it was a transparent box of thick cards. Beautifully conceived, each one detailed the artwork and artist. Manzoni worked with the typographer Antonio Maschera, and they set a red font on thick, grey card. Extending the premise of the exhibition – of challenging the idea of art being a physical object – they were conceptual pieces that used language to evoke an idea in the visitor's mind, and the text acted as a memory prompt for the performances or temporary artworks they had witnessed.

Alliata said of her time as a prisoner of war that she never knew whether she would see the next dawn rise. When she closed the gallery in 1964, she'd held over 60 shows and supported a galaxy of avant-garde artists, many from outside the European canon. Perhaps more fundamentally, she challenged the role of the commercial gallery – typically a venue for buying rarefied art objects – and posited it as a site of performance and ephemeral experiences.

Virginia Dwan

(1931–2022)

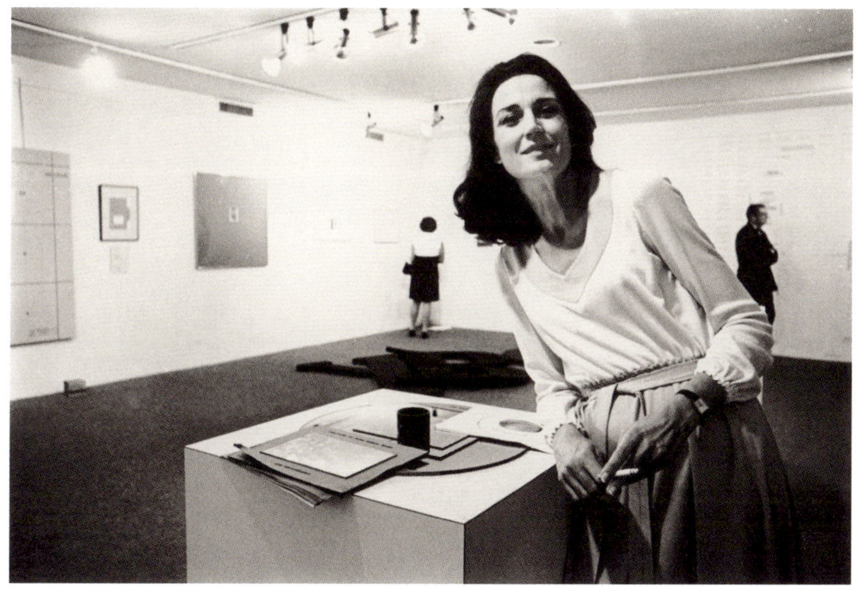

*Virginia Dwan at the exhibition
Language III, Dwan Gallery, New York,
1969. Photographer unknown.*

If there is a situation which perfectly illustrates the intrepid ambition of the idealist dealer, it would be Virginia Dwan sinking into quicksand while the Land artist Robert Smithson (1938–1973) searched for a place to make art on the sun-scorched pit of Usumacinta River, Mexico, in 1969. As a panicked Dwan called out, she was ignored by Smithson who continued his quest. She later reflected that it showed the depth of the artist's commitment. It also revealed hers. On the face of the sandpit, Smithson arranged his *Eighth Mirror Displacement* (1969), with 30-centimetre (12-inch) square mirrors reflecting the surrounding natural world. The artistic statement was lost if the mirrors were moved from the site, and this rendered the piece unsellable. For Dwan, a major challenge would be how to market this unsellable art. But this single trip proved the lengths she would go to for, as well as the quicksand, she had endured a long boat trip in the scalding heat and was bitten raw by mites.

Dwan was born in Minneapolis, Minnesota. Her mother had a daughter from a previous marriage, but with a 13-year age gap between the half-sisters, Dwan was more like an only child. By all accounts, she was very dreamy. When she was ten years old, her family moved to San Fernando in Southern California, and she describes blissful times outdoors, playing on an old oak tree, and taking herself on field trips:

> Our house was near a quarry... and I would find fossil rocks
> up there in the hills, which was an enigma right away, to find
> sea fossil shells up at high elevation. That sort of thing used to
> fascinate me. It wasn't something I thought about in words; it
> was something I like[d] to do.'[1]

These childhood explorations anticipate the wild journeys she would eventually take with her land artists.

Initially, Dwan aspired to be an artist herself and in 1949 she enrolled at the University of California, Los Angeles, to study fine art but, two years later, she transferred to the University of Southern California to study philosophy and psychology. When she turned 21, she acquired a considerable inheritance ($3 million, which today would be worth around $35 million) from her father's estate.[2] This allowed her to open the Dwan Gallery in Westwood, Los Angeles in 1959.

Early on, she was intent on introducing Los Angeles to New York's thriving art scene, especially Abstract Expressionism. It would prove to be a difficult task as Los Angeles lacked a vital art community in the 1950s – one gallery owner went as far as to describe the city as 'Omaha with a beach'.[3] However, the opening of her gallery coincided with a revolution in transport: the new propeller planes halved the flight time between New York and Los Angeles, and President Dwight D. Eisenhower opened his new interstate highways. This all made it much easier to transport art and make studio visits to New York. For the exhibition *15 of New York* in the autumn of 1960, Dwan convinced major artists including Philip Guston (1913–1980), Franz Kline (1910–1962) and Jackson Pollock to contribute works. This exhibition played a pivotal role in establishing Dwan's reputation. And her choice of artworks is telling because they demonstrate her preference for a pared-back aesthetic, with reduced colour and simple forms.

In 1960, she discovered a resonant blue canvas by Yves Klein (1928–1962) in a gallery window in Paris. Leo Castelli had seen the same exhibit and was excited by Klein too, and the two dealers agreed to run consecutive exhibitions in the spring of 1961. Their shows highlight the differences between the branded dealer and the idealist. Castelli pushed Klein as a brand, showing a number of identically sized (apart from one) monochromes in the artist's trademark International Klein Blue (IKB). Meanwhile, Dwan was struck by the spiritual resonance of Klein's art, and how his signature blue suggested an infinite realm. Focussed on the artist, she let Klein lead the vision of the show, and he opted for a broad sweep of his career, which included 'Anthropometry' paintings (created by naked women covered in IKB paint leaving their impressions on canvases), coloured sponges and fire paintings.

Significantly, Dwan hosted Klein in California before the exhibition, and he made works while he was there. This of course had financial benefits, avoiding shipping costs and import duties. And Klein was thrilled by California, the ocean and the immense skies. There's a photo of him making one of his sponges on the beach. It anticipates the next generation of artists who forsake the confines of the studio to create art in outdoor settings.

The romance of Dwan's Californian experience was undeniably a pull for artists living outside Los Angeles. The Pop artist Claes Oldenburg (1929–2022), for instance, describes feeling disenchanted by his urban life in New York, and the adventure of flying over the mountain ridges.[4] The artists' journeys to Los Angeles resonated with the restless road trips of the Beat generation, famously depicted in *On the Road* (1957) by Jack Kerouac (1922–1969). Only Dwan provided a destination. She was very welcoming: artists enjoyed her Californian home, hung out at her pool, and became part of her vibrant social circle. She tells a fabulous story of Robert Rauschenberg turning up in a VW minibus, sliding open the door, and John Cage (1912–1992), Merce Cunningham (1919–2009) and eight of Cunningham's dancers popping out.[5]

Neither Castelli nor Dwan sold anything from their Klein shows. According to Dwan, it was a constant struggle: 'In Los Angeles, I felt I had to defend just about everything I showed.'[6] She had become interested in Ad Reinhardt (1913–1967), a contemporary of the Abstract Expressionists who had rejected their emotional mark-making, and reduced painting to its essentials, foregrounding pure colour and geometric form. Reinhardt was undervalued at the time and at his solo show in 1962, Dwan made a bold curatorial decision to hang one of his vertical paintings above the arch that divided the gallery from the office. The placement mimicked the elevated position of stained glass in a Gothic cathedral, and suggested higher spiritual forces at play. While the gesture aimed to serve the art, it also laid bare Dwan's own priorities, in particular her search for a spirituality in art.

The scale of Reinhardt's paintings reinforced to Dwan that she needed a larger space. She later found a site in Westwood and employed the architect, Morris Verger, to design the new gallery, giving considerable input to the plans herself. Reinhardt's 2.7-metre (9-foot) black canvases helped determine the scale of the building. An important feature was the tunnel-like entrance which marked the transition into the consecrated space of the gallery; the dealer explained: '[it] is the most effective way to wash the eyes and mind of the jumble of daily stimuli and slow the pace to a receptive condition.'[7]

Dwan had solo shows for the Nouveau Réaliste artists Jean Tinguely (1925–1991) and Niki de Saint Phalle (1930–2002), who arrived in advance and created massive works in her studio. Dwan supported their desire to extend their work beyond the gallery. On the hilltops of Malibu, de Saint Phalle invited people to witness the creation of one of her *Tir* pieces. This involved her shooting at sealed pockets of paint on a white canvas which exploded violently, ejecting paint that ran like blood down the canvas.

Dwan also helped Tinguely create a performance element around his motorised water sculptures. The gallerist describes their innovative scheme:

We arranged for a 'progressive' dinner for the fountains that Jean created out of garden hoses and sprinkling devices. Four collectors opened their gardens and their homes to exhibit these works. At each home, one was given an ideal presentation of the fountains in operation as well as a single course of dinner, which was then followed by the next course at the next home. In between, the guests were transported in special buses and served champagne.[8]

For her, this move out of the gallery was momentous, and anticipated her later involvement with Land Art.

Dwan held one of the first Pop art shows and followed it with a solo show for Oldenburg which showcased his oversized foods including *Floor Cone* (1962) and *Giant Wedge of Pecan Pie* (1963). But Pop art was to be more of a flirtation than a deep commitment for her.

In 1965, she opened a New York gallery, establishing the first bicoastal art business. Around this time, she discovered Sol LeWitt (1928–2007) and his skeletal structures, which unfold through space. Through him, she met other Minimalists and in October 1966 she opened her landmark exhibition *10* – a group show of ten Minimalist artists which included works by Agnes Martin and Robert Morris (1931–2018). For Dwan, it was one of her most satisfying experiences. She talked about how their stark works provided a poignant moment of silence amid the social chaos: the Vietnam War, and the continual riots and student shootings.[9]

Through LeWitt, Dwan also met Smithson and became involved with Land Art. In 1968, she opened *Earth Works* at her New York gallery. The first-ever exhibition of Land Art, it tackled the problem of how to bring these site-specific works to a gallery context. On show were maps, photographs and films of the land works. These exhibits had a dual role, functioning both as documentation of the land works and as standalone artworks. Smithson contributed *A Nonsite (Franklin, New Jersey)* (1968), consisting of five trapezoid bins filled with rocks from an industrial site. Meanwhile, Morris produced *Untitled (Dirt)* (1968), which involved him dumping a heap of dirt from a local construction site on the gallery floor. Strewn with peat, bits of rock and metal scraps, the formless trash challenged the preciousness around art. The artist wittily offered the option of buying the work by weight, at $3 per pound; the collector simply had to shovel a portion into a trash bag, and lug it home.

Earth Works opened up new ways for Land Art to work as part of a gallery experience. However, never focussed on the money, Dwan slightly unpicked

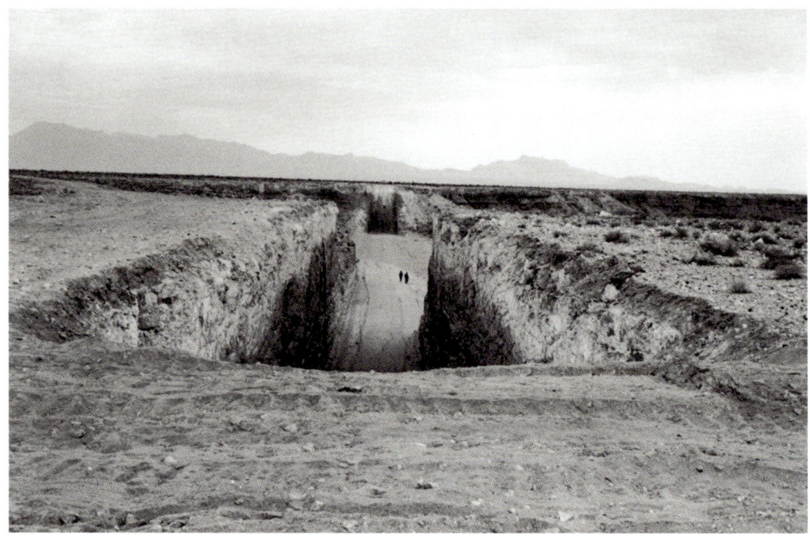

Fig. 20 Michael Heizer, *Double Negative*, 1969, two removals
of 240,000 total tons of earth, rhyolite and sandstone, each:
450 × 9 × 15 m (1,476 × 30 × 49 ft), Museum of Contemporary
Art, Los Angeles, installed at Mormon Mesa, Overton, Nevada.

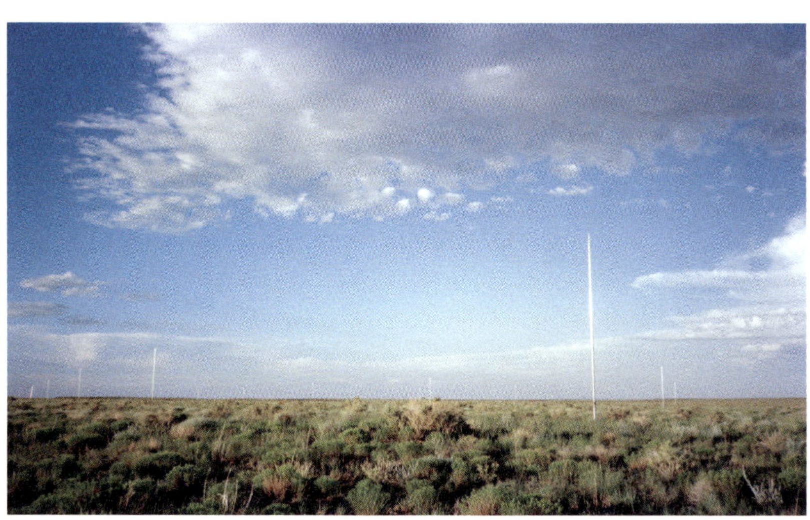

Fig. 21 Walter De Maria, *35-Pole Lightning Field,
Arizona*, 1974, installed near Flagstaff, Arizona.
Collection Dia Art Foundation, New York.

the success of the show by subsequently valuing the site-specific works more. She would go on to support the creation of three of the most iconic pieces of site-specific Land Art: *Double Negative* (1969, fig. 20) by Michael Heizer (b. 1944), *35-Pole Lightning Field* (1974, fig. 21) by Walter De Maria (1935–2013) and Smithson's *Spiral Jetty* (1970). To reach *Spiral Jetty* is a tedious 12-hour car journey from Los Angeles, but the sight of the 450-metre (1,500-foot) curl of black basalt rock against the red hue of the salt lake is quite extraordinary. It has an infernal quality that speaks to the present day and the critical state of our environment.

The endless cycle of debt caught up with Dwan. She closed her gallery in the late sixties, and her New York gallery in 1971. By her own admission, she was hopeless financially, and rarely turned a profit from an exhibition. Perhaps this explains why she's not been included in most publications about art dealers. But this leads one to question what constitutes a successful dealer. Dwan held show after show of ground-breaking art, and she went to extreme lengths to support her artists, venturing out to predator-infested lands for the sake of their work. Moreover, she was instrumental in the production of these artists' work, which addressed her own spiritual longings. She recounts her experience of walking in the trench of Heizer's *Double Negative* in Nevada desert: 'Michael had let me experience it alone. I had sat at the base of the ramp alone, walked alone, and just stood and wondered at it and myself – alone.'[10]

Chapter 4

Cultural Stewards

Introduction

In the modern period, Paris and New York have been considered epicentres of the art world. In the nineteenth century, Paris had the lead, and was associated with iconic art movements like Impressionism, Expressionism and Surrealism. Then, in the 1950s, the focus shifted to New York when monumental canvases by the Abstract Expressionists stole the attention. Clearly, there are inherent problems with this centralised art market – above all its focus on the West. Prioritising these cities also carries the risk of artistic production becoming homogenised as the art produced there comes to signify the progressive current of the time. This happened when New York took up its central role, and modernist theorists such as Clement Greenberg heralded abstract art above all else. In this sense, our cultural stewards could be seen as the rebels who resisted this dominant narrative.

Art historians and museums have striven to offer more inclusive narratives. Anne Helmreich has argued that the commercial gallery, 'can be a valuable and innovative lens through which to examine the global.'[1] In her case study of London-based dealer Kichibei Yamanaka, she argues that, by showcasing Japanese and Chinese art at his gallery, he created valuable global encounters. While she unveils a nuanced understanding of the market, the Japanese tradition is still tautly held within a Western paradigm and observed through the lens of the London art scene. Our cultural stewards instead were trading in the countries where the art was produced, with Malick Sidibé in Mali and Kelkoo and Khorshed Gandhy in India, for example.

In his catchily titled book *Small is Beautiful* (1973), the British economist E. F. Schumacher suggests a decentralised economic model. Applied to dealership practice, this manifests as a dispersed art market, with art galleries across the world being valued. At the heart of this lie our cultural stewards, focussed on their local art scenes. This reverence for the local is reflected by our first dealer, Herwarth Walden, who called himself Walden after Henry David Thoreau's landmark text, *Walden* (1854)[2], which recounts the author's retreat to the forest, where he lived more deeply by connecting to his surroundings. Walden's focus as a dealer on the domestic, German strand of Expressionism reflects the same preoccupation with his immediate context.

Lucy Lippard reflects, 'Travel is the only context in which some people ever look around. If we spent half the energy looking at our own neighborhoods, we'd probably learn twice as much.'[3]

Our cultural stewards were all concerned with their surroundings. Edith Halpert began her career in New York during a period when the city's art market was in decline. She was intent on finding an authentic American art which reflected American concerns and had American subject matter. She found this in Stuart Davis and the Harlem Renaissance artist Jacob Lawrence. Later, when New York became the focal point of the art world, her perspective, especially her interest in subject matter, was at odds with Greenberg's narrative, and for a long time her contribution was sidelined.

Schumacher poignantly said, 'The beginning of wisdom is the admission of one's own lack of knowledge.'[4] The sentence has a direct bearing on how we might address world cultures, foreign to our own. Wisdom here lies in recognising our lack of knowledge. It is this insufficiency that makes the cultural steward invaluable. Typically, these figures share their artists' cultural heritage and have knowledge of the local art scene. One essay here discusses how the Mexican dealer Lola Álvarez Bravo brought this depth of understanding to her solo retrospective for Frida Kahlo.

These dealers were all ahead of the curve. Kekoo and Khorshed Gandhy were attuned to the burgeoning art scene that followed India's independence. At that time, there were few opportunities for contemporary Indian artists, and Kekoo found ingenious places to exhibit the new art, including a cinema. Often, the exhibition spaces took a very different form to the branded galleries spoken about earlier. Sidibé drew production closer to the axis of life by operating from a high street unit. His hybrid studio/gallery became a meeting point for his community who sat outside, drinking tea, surrounded by the metal stands exhibiting Sidibé's photographs of the very people who gathered there. It was an intense and vibrant local exchange. As Schumacher said, 'There is a wisdom in smallness.'[5]

Herwarth Walden

(1879–1941)

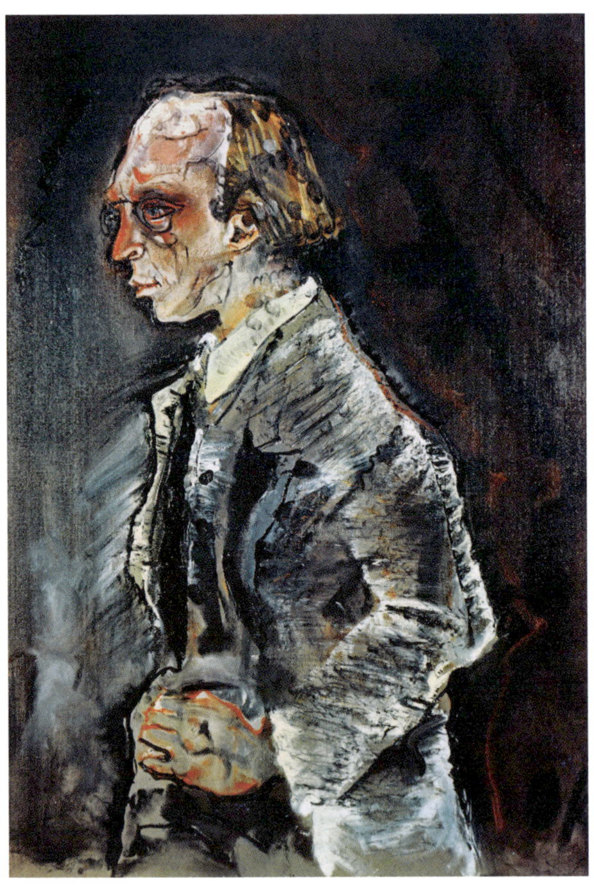

Oskar Kokoschka, *Herwarth Walden*, 1910,
oil on canvas, 100 × 68 cm (39 ⅜ × 26 ¾ in.),
Staatsgalerie, Stuttgart.

Reacting against the stagnancy of Wilhelmine society, Herwarth Walden would strive to vivify German culture, and champion German Expressionist art. Unkempt, gaunt and bespectacled, he was an unlikely hero, and this is captured in a portrait of the dealer painted in 1910 by Oskar Kokoschka (1886–1980). However, Kokoschka's frenzy of raw brushstrokes communicates something else about the dealer: his life force. Walden's passion bordered on the theatrical. Writing to the artist Wassily Kandinsky (1866–1944), he becomes extremely emotional about his art: 'Something like *Composition 2*, for instance, has never been created before. What life! What strength! What art! I am devastated.'[1] In a similar vein, he told Gabriele Münter (1877–1962) that her yellow was the most perfect yellow expressed in art and, unable to stop himself, he decided her very personality was a warm yellow.[2] His fervour was to prove contagious.

Born in Berlin, Walden was from an upper-middle class Jewish family. His birth name was Georg Lewin. The pseudonym was suggested by his wife, the German Expressionist poet, Else Lasker-Schüler (1869–1945). The aspirational name referenced *Walden* (1854, also called *Life in the Woods*), the key text of the American transcendental writer, Henry David Thoreau (1817–1862). Walden's first interest was music, and after studying composition and piano in Berlin and Paris, he pursued a career as a concert pianist. However, he became increasingly involved with the visual arts and in 1910 launched *Der Sturm*, a weekly cultural magazine. It ran from 1910, and combined literary articles, art reviews, poetry and showcased artworks. The title of the magazine (in English, 'the storm') marked Walden's intention to catalyse change in the German art world. His cultural storm was to prove unrelenting. He followed with a cartel of *Sturm* enterprises, including a gallery, a bookshop, an art school, a theatrical journal and even *Sturm* literary nights; all had the common aim of reinvigorating German culture, and connecting it with the Expressionist movement.

Walden's crusade was partly a reaction to the oppressive politicisation of German culture in the years leading up to World War I. Emperor Wilhelm II (1859–1941) had calcified progress in the arts; in his public lecture 'True Art' (1901), he decried modern art as evidence of a degenerate society and called on 'the German people alone to protect, nurture and carry on these great ideals of the classical past'.[3] Walden's first endeavour, his magazine, *Der Sturm*, positioned itself very carefully. While offering an alternative to this conservatism, it was careful not to alienate its middle-class readers;

its agenda was never to radicalise, but to open up the ethical and aesthetic values of modern art.

Nevertheless, the newspaper format, with black-and-white graphics set on cheap broadsheet, conferred an urgency, a sense that the latest news was being delivered. And this was how it was consumed by its readers; artists would gather at Café des Westens on Berlin's Kurfürstendamm to discuss the most recent edition. Every issue had a graphic artwork on the front page and a tear-out centrefold artwork for people to hang on their walls. Kokoschka created posters advertising the magazine that hung around the city.

From early on, Walden was intent on bringing attention to German Expressionism. Many members of Die Brücke, a group who could be considered the first generation of German Expressionists, had relocated to Berlin, and the magazine constantly featured their graphic works. The front page of the January 1912 issue carried a woodcut by Ernst Ludwig Kirchner (1880–1938). His hand-carved woodcuts had a rawness that made them the perfect vehicle for intense expression, and Kirchner heightened their pitch with dramatic contrasts and angular forms.

Walden's attempt to highlight a German tradition of Expressionism was supported by a new cultural discourse. The German aesthetician Wilhelm Worringer (1881–1965) had recently published *Formprobleme der Gotik* (1911; in English, *Form in Gothic*) which explored expressiveness as a Gothic outlook. In 1914, writer and critic Paul Fechter (1880–1958) developed Worringer's argument presenting German Expressionism as a progression of Fauvism, asserting, 'the tempo of the process was accelerated, the French lead was offset and, as things stand today, the leadership has shifted more and more to the German side again.'[4]

Significantly, the magazine would also feature international art; in the pre-war years the focus was mainly Italian Futurism and French Expressionism. This internationalism anticipated Walden's vision for Galerie Der Sturm which opened in 1912. For his inaugural show, Walden picked up the exhibition from the Moderne Galerie Thannhauser in Munich of works by Der Blaue Reiter. It was a bold move; in Munich the show had caused outrage; Thannhauser would wipe spit off the paintings in the evenings.[5]

Der Blaue Reiter included Franz Marc (1880–1916) and Münter. Initially based in Munich, it was considered a German group even though several of its artists were born in other countries. While the members had their own individual styles, there was a common vision. Their Expressionist idiom

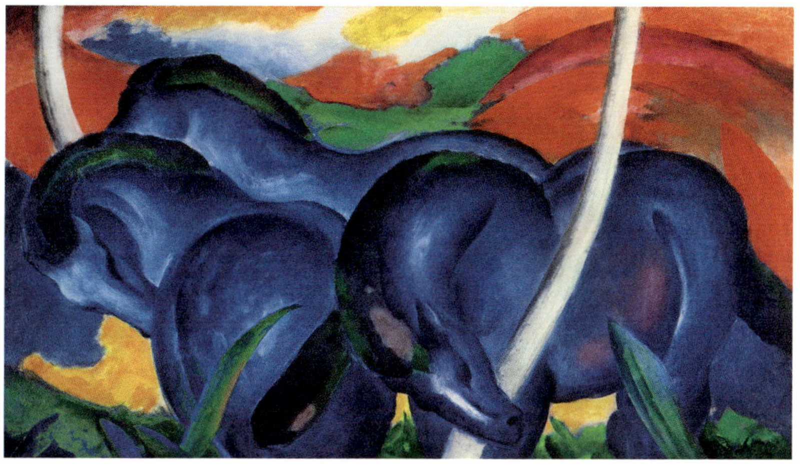

Fig. 22 Franz Marc, *The Large Blue Horses*, 1911, oil on canvas,
105.7 × 181.3 cm (41⅝ × 71⅜ in.), Walker Art Center, Minneapolis, MN, USA.

was more lyrical than the angst-ridden, angular Die Brücke works. Instead, they were exploring how stylisation of form and enhanced colour could bring a spiritual dimension to their work. Marc's *The Large Blue Horses* (1911, fig. 22)[6] demonstrates their ideals. For Marc, 'Blue is the masculine principle, astringent and spiritual.'[7] The repeated curving forms gather a rhythm and the deep resonant blue sounds out an elevating note.

Significantly, at this inaugural show, Walden showed Der Blaue Reiter artists alongside the French Fauve painters. The gesture stood firmly against the prevailing chauvinism. In 1911, conservative German artists and critics released their collaborative text *Ein Protest deutscher Künstler*, which rallied against the increasing number of shows of French art, believing them to contaminate the essence of German art. Perhaps the dealer was being strategic by including French art, and understood it would be folly to alienate collectors who'd been focussed on French painters. Either way, he would continue to show art from abroad, with his next exhibition dedicated to Italian Futurism.

His most international show was the First German Autumn Salon (1913), which deliberately referenced the Salon d'Automne held annually in Paris since 1903. Curated by Marc and fellow Der Blaue Reiter member August Macke (1887–1914), it included artists from the USA, Austria, France, Germany, Italy, the Netherlands, Russia and Switzerland. There was an entire section dedicated to Henri Rousseau (1844–1910), and the Italian

Futurist Filippo Tommaso Marinetti (1876–1944) read the Futurist manifesto at the opening. However, Walden's championing of internationalism was ambiguous here. Der Blaue Reiter artists were given centre stage, and in a sense, the more famous international figures became a legitimising framework for the new German art.

In 1912, Walden held a solo show with Der Blaue Reiter artist Kandinsky. The dealer felt a deep kinship with Kandinsky, who compared art to music and felt colour and form could directly evoke states of being, just as musical notes could. But for the Berlin critics, the show was a mash-up, with early folk landscapes mixed up with abstract compositions. They decried the lack of chronology and a unifying theme. By rejecting such curatorial frameworks, Kandinsky and Walden's intention was to stop the visitor from approaching the works analytically so they could experience them more fully. They could, for example, immerse themselves in Kandinsky's *Black Spot I* (1912) and its spiralling array of warm colours and suggestive forms, without thinking about its place in a chronology or its subject matter. For Kandinsky, 'there was no worse evil than art understanding'.[8] Art was of a higher order, a soulful encounter.

Walden would advance this idea of art being an autonomous field as art historian Kate Winskell explains: 'Der Sturm increasingly presented art not only as free from politics, but also immune to explanation, analysis, exegesis, its reception tantamount to an act of faith. The artwork was even seen as independent of the artist who produced it, the revelation of superior reality.'[9] This position would strangely work to Walden's advantage when World War I broke out. His business with now 'enemy' countries ceased, and he was forced to close his newly opened school in Paris. However, an opportunity opened. The art trade was booming in the neutral countries, yet these nations did not want to be seen to be taking sides in the war. Walden's position elevated art beyond national concerns, providing the reassurance these countries needed. As a result, he would secure numerous exhibitions.

It could be argued that Walden's opportunism sullied his apolitical claims for art. Winskell has delved deeper, charting his involvement with Zentralstelle für Auslandsdienst, a German government body infiltrating neutral Scandinavian countries with pro-German ideas. She also highlights Walden's editorial work for the Danish press *Nutiden*, which had German sympathies and received funding from the German government. And Walden involved art in this propaganda machinery.

In 1916, Walden would reassure a government officer that the Sturm exhibitions were serving national interests: 'During the war, "Der Sturm" [has] regularly organised exhibitions in Denmark, Sweden, Norway and Holland, partly in order to prove that we feel politically strong enough to organise exhibitions outside the Reich, partly in the interests of the import and propagation abroad of the best German art.'[10] His efforts were enthusiastically backed by the German Foreign Office who were keen to project an image of artistic tolerance that countered the boorish militarism with which the country was associated.

In 1918, Walden wanted to hold an exhibition in Copenhagen, however the Danes had become aware of the propaganda undercurrents to the Sturm activities and refused. Determined, Walden became more ambitious. He came up with a plan for the largest Expressionist show in Scandinavia since the beginning of the war. Its international aspect was to act as a veil, hiding the intention of foregrounding German art, and projecting Germany's progressiveness in cultural matters. A government official describes how the exhibition was promoted to the German Chancellor:

> Herr Walden has... suggested organising... an exhibition of international character that would prove to the Danes that in the field of art we consider ourselves free from political sympathies and antipathies. Herr Walden wants to compose the exhibition of works by German artists and by artists grouped from enemy countries, but grouped in such a way that the German works will stand out as the most significant component.[11]

The controversial nature of this is underlined by the fact that Wilhelm von Bode, the Director-General of Berlin museums and galleries, refused to lend works to propaganda-driven exhibitions abroad during the war.

By the time the exhibition opened in Copenhagen on 30 November 1918, the war had ended, and Wilhelm II had abdicated. Walden's activities during World War I originated with his enthusiasm to make German culture relevant again. During the war, he undeniably came to contradict himself. While advocating art's radical independence, he used this status to dissociate his business from the wartime politics to gain financial advantages for himself. Although this could easily be seen as a cynical manoeuvre, his representation of German Expressionist art undeniably created a valuable legacy.

Edith Halpert

(1900–1970)

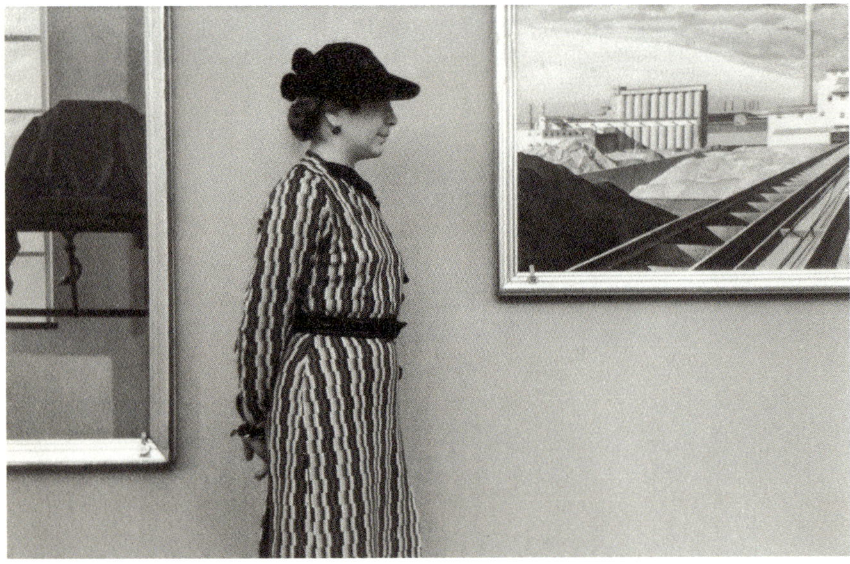

Halpert in a striped dress made from fabric designed by Charles Sheeler, taken at the exhibition Charles Sheeler/Charles Burchfield at the Society of Arts and Crafts in Detroit, January, 1935. Photographer unknown.

When Edith Halpert opened the Downtown Gallery in New York in 1926, she was intent on 'representing the best tendencies in contemporary American art', with no 'special prejudice for any school'.[1] It was a visionary move: at the time, there was little interest in modern art, let alone the contemporary American scene. The Metropolitan Museum of Art paid no attention to either. Institutional support only came later, with the opening of the Museum of Modern Art in 1929 (although its initial focus was on European modernism) and the Whitney Museum of American Art in 1931. In the commercial sphere, the art dealer representing modern art was Alfred Stieglitz, but his gallery was somewhat intimidating. Halpert was determined to reach the public and convince them of the significance of American art.

Halpert's family originally came from Odessa (then Russia, now Ukraine). As a young child, she witnessed terrible discrimination against Jews, which likely fuelled her strong ethical drive later in life. In 1906, when she was six years old, her family emigrated to New York, and her mother ran a stationery shop in Harlem. Her mother struggled to keep the business afloat, and Halpert helped out from a young age. She came up with a precocious sales strategy of blowing up bags of peanuts to make them look like they held more nuts. Her new product outperformed those of her rivals, and taught her the importance of marketing. As historian A. Deirdre Robson reflects, Halpert came to represent the 'New Woman' – independent, educated and someone who expected to earn their own way.[2] After her first clerical job, she worked for Bloomingdales, and later wrote advertising copy for Macy's department store. Prior to opening her gallery, she was a consultant at the investment bank S. W. Straus & Co. where she excelled, and her high earnings financed her new gallery. Her business savviness challenges the retrograde narratives, which present the first women art dealers as naive in financial matters.[3]

In November 1926, Halpert opened her gallery on 113 West 13th Street in Greenwich Village, New York. The location put her at the heart of the contemporary art scene as many artists had their studios there. The exhibition rooms were on the ground floor of a three-storey brownstone building, which Halpert had bought outright, and she rented out the unused space to fund the business. Initially, she named it 'Our Gallery', explaining, 'I wanted to make this gallery an intimate thing… so that anybody could come in at any time, day and evening, and so on.'[4] After opening, Halpert sent letters to local residents welcoming them to the new Downtown Gallery.

Halpert was focussed on artists who were dealing with American themes and ideals. One of her core artists was Stuart Davis (1892–1964) whose work combined a Cubist-inspired style with a populist subject matter that spoke to the American experience. Halpert celebrated how 'he removes the subject from the realm of the commonplace and gives a spirit of adventure to the American scene.'[5] In February 1932, she opened his solo exhibition, *The American Scene: Recent Paintings, New York and Gloucester*. The title reinforced the connection with nation and place. Davis's painting, *House and Street* (1931) introduced the clashing, bright colours of American merchandise to fine art. Evoking the cityscape of New York, the painting places the viewer at the shadowed window of a railway carriage looking out at the elevated line between Front Street and Coenties Slip. The inclusion of the word 'FRONT' helps identify the site, as does the snaking curve of the railway track. With regard to the scenes of Gloucester, Massachusetts, one painting was so successful in evoking its maritime harbour, a visitor said they could detect the local smell of 'glue and fishcakes'.[6]

Halpert had a progressively diverse roster, and artists who originated from different countries were very much included in the fold. In the early years, she represented the émigré artists Bernard Karfiol (1886–1952), Yasuo Kuniyoshi (1889–1953) and Ben Shahn (1898–1969). Later, in 1941, she held a landmark group show of Black American artists, in a time when racial segregation was in force in the United States. The exhibition featured works by nineteenth-century artists like Robert S. Duncanson (1821/22–1872) and Henry Ossawa Tanner (1859–1937), as well as contemporary names. To fit everything in, *The Migration Series* (1940–41) by Jacob Lawrence (1917–2000) was hung in Halpert's study. The dealer worked hard to convince MoMA to buy half of the 60-part series and her success was significant, as it placed work by an artist of colour in a public museum. After the show, Lawrence and Horace Pippin (1888–1946) joined the gallery.

Halpert also represented many women including Georgia O'Keeffe. Always a strong advocate for the artists she worked with, she spoke out against the overly sexualised reading of O'Keeffe's paintings and tried to reframe them in a different light. And when Kuniyoshi, a Japanese immigrant, was declared an enemy of the state during World War II, Halpert launched an exhibition of his work in support. On occasion, Halpert's outspoken opinions created controversy – something she never shied away from. In 1932, when the bronze sculpture of a nude dancer by William

Zorach (1889–1966) was considered improper and removed from the Radio City Music Hall, she leapt to the artist's defence, and provocatively exhibited his original plaster cast in the front window of her gallery. Her strategy was highly successful: people flocked to see it, and after *The New York Times* declared it 'one of the most significant pieces of plastic art ever produced in America',[7] the censored bronze was put back on show. The event brought instant fame to the artist while also gaining attention for Halpert's gallery.

In terms of selling her vision, Halpert held 12 exhibitions a year which included solo, Christmas and end-of-season exhibitions. Robson emphasises how 'it was the solo shows of the core gallery artists (about one-third to one-half the annual schedule) that were central to the Downtown Gallery becoming *the* place to see the "best" living American artists.'[8] Halpert never put pressure on her artists, and didn't demand an annual show from them, as many dealers often did. Between 1930 and 1961, Shahn had 11 shows with her. Occasionally, she also offered financial support if artists were struggling. When Davis's first solo exhibitions resulted in no sales, she gave him a monthly stipend, making it possible for him to continue his experiments in art.

Meanwhile she worked hard cultivating relationships with collectors and curators. She successfully placed many of them in the Whitney Museum of American Art and other key public museums. She became an influential advisor to many art patrons, including Duncan Phillips, founder of the Phillips Collection in Washington, DC, America's first museum of modern art. A friend of art patron and collector Abby Rockefeller, Halpert also supported Rockefeller's ambitious plan to open a new museum, which became the Museum of Modern Art. Of the 2,000 works Rockefeller eventually donated to MoMA, over 500 came from Halpert's gallery.

Halpert's vision for American art involved a radical democratisation of art collecting. She despised the prevailing elitism, and how 'Museums and galleries have prospered on snob appeal, the galleries basing their sales psychology on snobbism, high prices, rare items.'[9] Bringing her retail experience to bear, she took the exceptional step of diversifying her 'product line'. As well as her core roster, she represented artists considered to be second tier, who were more affordable to the middle class. She also sold smaller works that had cheaper price points like prints and drawings. In addition, she ventured into design, and marketed, for example, Kuniyoshi-designed wallpaper and textiles by Charles Sheeler (1883–1965). There is a photograph of Halpert wearing a dress made from Sheeler's iconic fabric. She was also one of the first dealers to show folk art and this diverse range of objects, which included metalwork, embroidery and furniture, was again more affordable. She saw no conflict between folk art and the contemporary art she sold, and indeed there were similarities in their use of primary colours and flattened forms.

Bringing her experience in retail, she used mass marketing techniques to reach a wider demographic, observing, 'You had to attract them with ideas.'[10] Her exhibition *Art for the 67%: Mr & Mrs* (1952) advertised that she was selling affordable art to ordinary people. The Christmas shows were always marketed well in advance and invitations were brilliantly conceived with witty visuals encouraging people to switch their boring gifts for original art. Another winning strategy was her end-of-season sales, catchily marketed as $100 exhibitions, which drew the crowds with the promise of a bargain. To reach the ordinary American, she also brought in interest-free payment plans, which the dealer reflected later 'was unheard of'.[11] Introducing this retail scheme (associated with buying fridges and washing machines) to the rarefied art trade was a provocative move. However, Halpert was extremely successful at reaching her intended audience – over half her sales were to new buyers.

A central part of Halpert's marketing lay in the gallery itself. The first, located downtown, was a welcoming space, which she curated to look like a home, allowing her audience to imagine how the art would look in their own sitting rooms. The rooms had old fireplaces, and there were bookcases and chairs. She further developed her curation style after visiting the Bauhaus in Dessau, Germany, and seeing the radical integration of industrial, decorative and fine arts there. Inspired by this, in 1930 she added a new architect-designed 'daylight gallery'. Effectively doubling her exhibition space, its austere design, with grey fabric walls and industrial-looking tubular chairs, suited the modern art on display. Marguerite Zorach (1887–1968) made a coloured concrete floor, and light streamed down from the overhead windows and lit the artworks. In interview, Halpert reflected on how the space itself became an attraction: 'It was a beautiful gallery, and every artist in America wanted to be there... I turned down all sorts of top people whose work I didn't like. There wasn't any gallery that compared with it.'[12]

In 1940, Halpert decided to move uptown. Initially at 43 East 51st Street, the gallery later moved to 32 East 57th Street. In the first building, she brought together her different interests, and told an interesting narrative through the space. Downstairs was a room of folk art, which attracted the visitor off the street, and offered a quick, affordable purchase. More significantly, this room and the nineteenth-century room beside it mapped an independent origin for American art, untethered from European tradition. After encountering this national history, the visitor could then ascend the stairs and experience Halpert's prized American contemporary artists on the floor above.

During her lifetime, Halpert amassed a large personal art collection, which included works by over 50 contemporary American artists. When she died in 1970, it was sold by Sotheby Parke-Bernet for $3.6 million (approximately $30 million today). At the time, the auction house attributed the high prices achieved to the 'Halpert effect' – with her name adding value. Halpert had been instrumental in mapping an independent history of American art, and contributing to America's contemporary art scene being increasingly valued. Embracing the country's diversity, her inclusivity is poignantly relevant today as our museums attempt to address the scope of their collections.

Manuel and Lola Álvarez Bravo

(1902–2002) and (1903–1993)

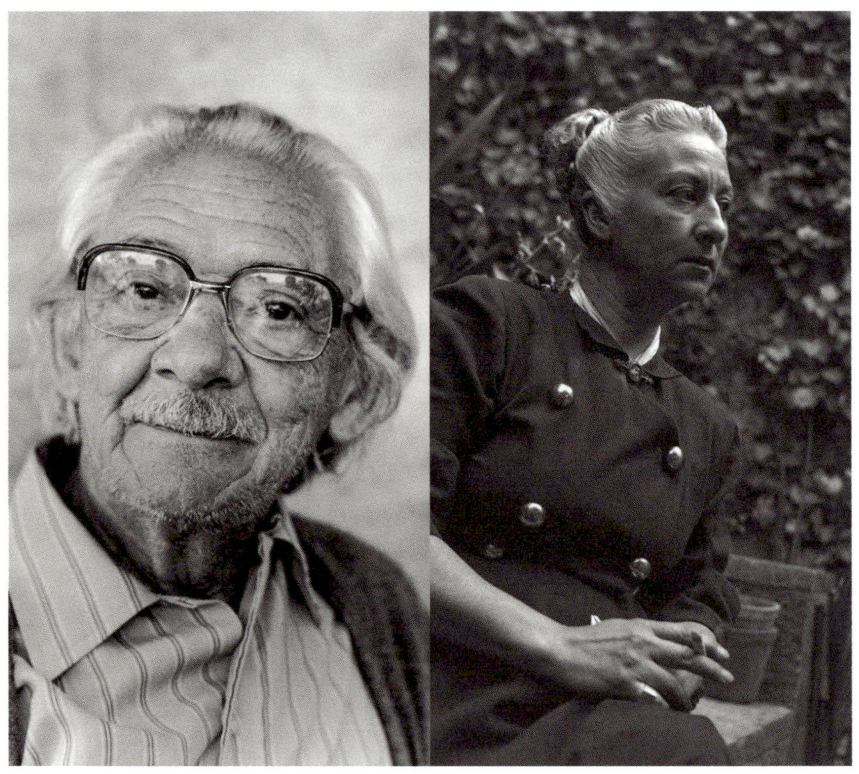

Jean Dieuzaide, *Manuel Álvarez Bravo during the Rencontres Internationales de la Photographie in Arles, France*, 1979 (left). Tomás Montero Torres *Lola Álvarez Bravo*, c. 1953 (right).

Lola and Manuel Álvarez Bravo are amongst the most important figures in Latin American photography. The couple were married for nine years, and when they were living in Mexico City, they converted a room in their home into a gallery. In this small space, they curated shows of contemporary Mexican artists, whom they knew personally, and with whom they shared a cultural heritage. The project was short-lived but, 20 years later, Lola would open another gallery where she continued to support Mexican artists and would show their work with the same sensitivity.

Lola and Manuel knew each other from childhood. Born in 1903, Lola had a somewhat extraordinary childhood. It is understood that her mother abandoned the family. Her father, a furniture importer, moved with Lola and her brother to Mexico City where they lived in a 28-room mansion, which had its own ballroom. Growing up during the tumultuous years of the Mexican Revolution (1910–20), Lola got to know Manuel, who lived nearby and was a friend of her brother's. Manuel's life was very different; his family were poor, and they lived in a small flat in an old colonial building near the city's cathedral. When Lola was 13 years old, her father died, and she and her brother went to live with her father's brother-in-law who happened to live in the same building as Manuel. He and Lola became friends; they would meet on the roof, and eventually they became romantically involved. Meanwhile, as a teenager, Manuel taught himself photography and would scour art magazines like *Mexican Folkways* to learn about the international scene. In 1925 Manuel and Lola married, and Lola started taking photographs herself, as well as assisting her husband. It would be many years before her own work was recognised.

In 1927, the couple opened an informal gallery in their own home in the Tacubaya neighbourhood of Mexico City. Frustratingly little is known about their gallery space other than that they painted it white. It is not even evident if it had a name. Their motivation to create this alternative venue indicates a dissatisfaction with the existing art scene. The cultural landscape in post-revolutionary Mexico was highly politicised. Many of the artists had been involved in the revolution, some fighting for the cause, while others, like the polemical caricaturist José Guadalupe Posada (1852–1913), used their work to criticise the affectations of the ruling class. When the revolution ended in 1920, after ten years of fighting, the government played an active role in ridding Mexico of its colonial past while also setting parameters for art production.

The first President Álvaro Obregón (1880–1928) appointed José Vasconcelos (1882–1959) as Secretary of Public Education. Vasconcelos strongly believed that art had a civic duty and he worked tirelessly to rehabilitate Mexican culture and connect with its ancient, pre-colonial past. At the time, Mexico had an 80 per cent illiteracy rate, and visual culture was the only viable way of communicating with a mass audience. His most famous initiative was the state-led mural scheme. Recognising the medium had a capacity to reach the wider public, he employed artists to decorate public buildings with images that celebrated Mexican culture, and reinforced socialist agendas. The murals by Diego Rivera (1886–1957) are didactic and typically celebrate revolutionary figures and workers. Mural painting came to dominate the artistic scene, and this continued through the 1930s when the government would scorn easel painting as bourgeois.

The Álvarez Bravos' gallery has remained in the shadow of the mural tradition, and is rarely discussed in art historical texts. Yet, it offered a crucial exhibition venue at a time when artists had no obvious outlets through which to sell their works. Rufino Tamayo (1899–1991), who showed at the gallery, recounted, 'At that time the only exhibition halls were within the walls of the academy, but I refused to exhibit my works there.'[1] The couple did show many of the famous mural artists, but these artists were now liberated from the didactic agendas of state-led murals. Tamayo had grown to dislike the heavy ideology; the historian MacKinley Helm explains: 'He was critical of Rivera for ignoring the interior culture of Mexico, the tradition handed down from ancient times, in favour of a superficial and exterior view of the national scene.'[2] The gallery was essentially a free space away from the official public works. Situated in their home, the setting was intimate, and the works displayed there were more personal.

The couple were now in contact with modernist photographers Edward Weston (1886–1958) and Tina Modotti (1896–1942) who had recently moved to Mexico, and were running an open studio in their neighbourhood, selling their works from there. Indeed, the Álvarez Bravos may well have modelled the gallery on their business. Modotti had introduced them to Mexican avant-garde painters including Tamayo, David Alfaro Siqueiros (1896–1974), José Clemente Orozco (1883–1949) and Frida Kahlo (1907–1954). Their small gallery showed work by all these artists as well as photography. Significantly, their roster of artists remained committed to expressing Mexican identity, without, however, the dogmatism of the government endorsed art. A spirit of experimentation followed as their artists took influences from Indigenous Mexican art traditions and drew on European styles.

Manuel's photography reveals the new artistic ideals that the gallery was supporting. His photo *Una Escalera Grande* (1930–32) identifies a Mexican sensibility in the poetry of everyday life. A Mexican woman walks in the shade, carrying a water pitcher on her shoulder. Mexico's intense sunlight dramatises the scene, with the contrast of the shadowed area playing against the bleached, sun-lit foreground. Meanwhile, the work shows the influence of modernist photography, especially in the strong compositional structure, with the verticality of the figure echoing the line of the ladder.

It is not known how long the gallery lasted, but it supported this period of experimentation. Tamayo would follow a similar path to Manuel, finding an abstract beauty in Mexican subjects, and later he would become known for his paintings of watermelons, which communicated a 'Mexicanidad', the red, white and green fruit being the colours of the country's flag.

In 1934, Lola and Manuel would separate (divorcing in 1948), and both continued their experiments in photography. Meanwhile, the art scene became more international; Paul Strand travelled through the country in the early 1930s, and Sergei Eisenstein (1898–1948) came to start filming *Que Viva México!* in 1930. Arguably, the most impactful visitor for painters was André Breton who visited for four months in 1938.

The Surrealist leader declared Mexico to be 'the surrealist place par excellence.'[3] In 1939, he dedicated the entire last issue of *Minotaure* to Mexican art.[4] Fascinated by Pre-Columbian art, the Mayan sites and festivals, Breton was also drawn to the work of Kahlo whom he offered an exhibition in Paris. Lola would also stage a solo show for Kahlo at her new Galería de Arte Contemporáneo in 1953. Although their exhibitions were 15 years apart, it is worth comparing them as they poignantly reveal their distinct curation, and, moreover, the value of Lola's local and personal knowledge of Kahlo for giving context to her work.

Breton described Kahlo's art 'as a ribbon around a bomb'.[5] He placed her within the canon of Surrealism even though she refused the label. The exhibition he promised her was held at Gálerie Renou et Colle in Paris on the eve of World War II. Breton's treatment of Kahlo leading up to the exhibition was downright shoddy. When she arrived in Paris, he hadn't collected her canvases from customs, nor had he secured a gallery – in fact, it was Marcel

Duchamp who found the space. Even more upsetting was the hang, and how Breton presented Kahlo's work in terms of the Surrealist agenda. Reflecting his approach to exhibitions at Gradiva gallery, he deliberately juxtaposed clashing artistic styles, and showed Kahlo's work alongside Manuel's photography, Pre-Columbian artefacts and novelties from Mexican markets which included children's toys and sugar cane skulls. It was the inclusion of the latter that particularly upset Kahlo who considered them to be junk. Breton's purpose was to convey 'a convulsive beauty'[6] by setting the crude market goods against the paintings. By presenting Kahlo's work in this way, he distorted her vision to prioritise his Surrealist fantasy.

Lola opened Galería de Arte Contemporáneo in 1951. The space had the homeliness of her earlier gallery with Manuel in Tacubaya, but with a new cosmopolitanism. It was like a modernist living room, with its Michael van Beuren sofa, organic shaped coffee table, flowers and potted plants. Like Edith Halpert's gallery, the domestic surroundings allowed the buyer to imagine what the works would look like in their own home. The journalist Rosa Castro described the experience, '[the] paintings and sculptures beautify a peaceful and friendly ambiance, where it is a pleasurable sight to go through its rooms, its hallways and its gardens, in which a mood of balance, quietness, and peacefulness can be felt.'[7] It was professionally run with monthly exhibitions, and Lola only showed Mexican art, and mainly paintings. Many of the artists were from her first gallery in Tacubaya, with important new additions, including the British-born artist Leonora Carrington (1917–2011), who was living in Mexico. Occasionally, Lola held themed shows. At the closing of *From Carnivals to Judas Figures in Mexican Painting* (1952), they burned figures in front of the gallery.

Lola's curation of Kahlo's solo show was informed by her intimate understanding of the artist. They were great friends, and the dealer understood the deeply autobiographical nature of Kahlo's work – hence her decision to stage a retrospective, and show works that spanned her lifetime. It would be the first solo exhibition of Kahlo's work in Mexico. Lola had photographed Kahlo many times and, after Kahlo's death, she wrote an essay about these photographs[8] and describes her favourite in detail. It shows the artist looking into a mirror, and essentially captures her twice. For Lola, the photo resonated with Kahlo's dual character – how she presented as a successful artist and a passionate individual, but was also a woman who had suffered tremendous physical pain and gone through endless surgeries. Lola likened her photo to Kahlo's own portrait, *The Two Fridas* (1939), which also communicates the sense of a divided self.

The opening night of the exhibition was a stage for these two Fridas: the gallery hung with vibrant self-portraits while the tortured Kahlo was also on show. Because of her declining health, the artist was brought into the gallery on a stretcher. Bejewelled and wearing a Tehuana dress, she famously presided over the evening from her own bed. The evening was a celebration of Mexican culture. The folk singer Concha Michel sang; the Mexican poet Carlos Pellicer read a poem; and major artists including María Izquierdo (1902–1955) were there. As reporters and photographers gathered (although only one photograph of the night exists), friends and artists lined up to wish Kahlo well; it was clear she would die soon. This extraordinary event, in combination with Lola's respectful curation, reinforces the limitations of Breton's exhibition which created a caricature of Mexican culture.

Between them, Lola and Manuel supported a generation of artists who were freeing themselves from state-led mural schemes and were looking at alternative ways of celebrating their culture. It was an intense period of experimentation which produced new trends in Mexican art. While Manuel and Lola were open to an international dialogue, it was their sensitivity to the local history, and their personal relationships with the artists that set their galleries apart.

Kekoo and Khorshed Gandhy

(1920–2012) and (1923–2013)

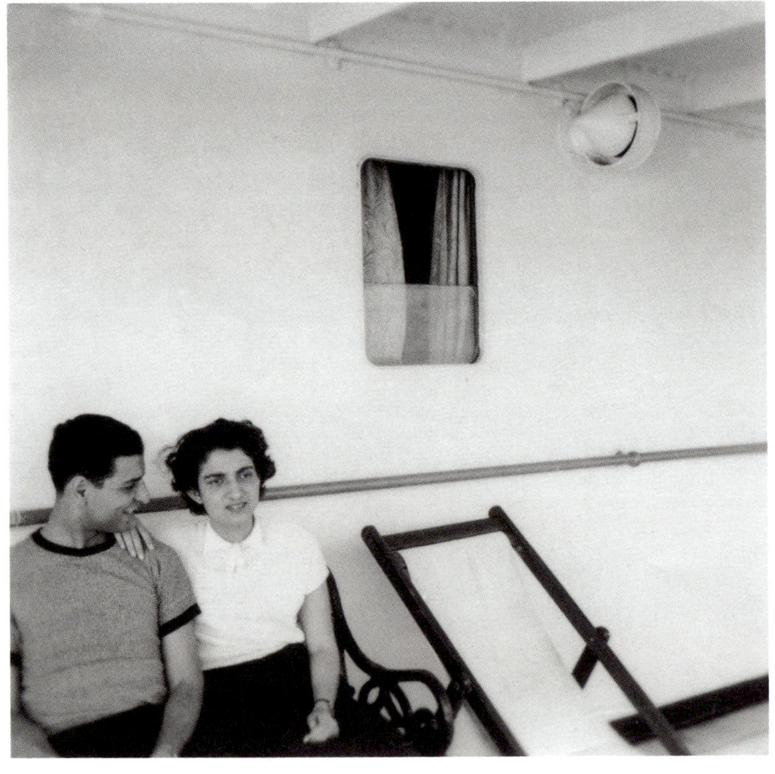

Kekoo and Khorshed Gandhy, photograph taken on their honeymoon trip to Kashmir after their wedding on 16 April 1944. Photographer unknown.

The story of Kekoo and Khorshed Gandhy's involvement in the burgeoning contemporary art scene of Mumbai, India (then known as Bombay) falls into two halves. In the early years, Kekoo ran an ad hoc enterprise, displaying local art in his frame shop. Later, Khorshed became involved when he opened Gallery Chemould in 1963. However, it is important to start at the beginning of this story.

There's undeniable magic to Kekoo's entrance into the art world. By his own admission, he knew very little about art before he became involved with local artists. Yet his journey to becoming a dealer seemed effortless, which has led him to be characterised as 'the accidental gallerist'.[1] Opening his picture frame factory was the first step. And the frame itself was symbolic of his mission. Challenging the art world's focus on European modernism, Kekoo was intent on bringing Indian art into the 'frame'. His daughter Behroze tells of his ardent belief that India had a story to tell,[2] and Kekoo indeed played a central role in the cultural renaissance that followed India's independence in 1947.

Born in Bombay, Kekoo was from a Parsi merchant family who traded in tobacco. He left to study at Pembroke College in Cambridge. However, when he came home for the summer in 1939, World War II broke out, and he remained in India, never returning to complete the course. Kekoo considered this a lucky moment – a release from family expectations. Later in the year, he had a chance encounter that brought about the framing business. Driving on the beach, he came upon a young Belgian man by the name of Roger van Damme, whose car was stuck in the sand. Kekoo went to help and explains what unfolded:

> [van Damme] had heard a news story back home about the many gods and goddesses that Indians kept in their homes. He knew that India would be a captive market to sell frames. Our acquaintance led to the establishment of the Chemould framing factory in 1940. He gave me know-how, we got the finance together and my brother Rusi and I set up the factory.[3]

This event was characteristic of Kekoo, who was always open to people. According to his daughter Shireen, 'He was utterly guileless. I love how he gave the same attention to politicians and dignitaries, as well as the common man who he constantly cared and fought for.'[4] Kekoo's magnetism was a gravitating force that drew people together. Early on, he became very involved with Italian prisoners of war who were working for the MURART programme and were involved in painting murals. He invited them to his home where they took over his kitchen every Sunday, and cooked risotto. As his factory business flourished, in 1947 he opened a shop on Princess Street, Bombay. He called it Chemould Frames, and it was here that he began exhibiting art.

Kekoo credits the arrival of émigrés during World War II as the catalyst which energised the Indian art scene. He explains that 'in those days, Indian artists had no means of going abroad or of following trends in Europe. Of course, there were magazines, but the unexpected arrival of all these Europeans – most of them Jews fleeing from Austria – really started the Progressive movement off.'[5] The Austrian artist Walter Langhammer (1905–1977) settled with his wife in Bombay where they held weekly salons at their home. European modern art was discussed, especially the work of Pablo Picasso and Oskar Kokoschka who was Langhammer's old art teacher. Crucially, Langhammer was focussed on the possibility of a new Indian modern art; he believed, 'India had a great store of inspiration to draw from and the colours and light of India would make the difference.'[6] Another key figure was the German Rudolf von Leyden (1908–1983) who became an art critic for the *Times of India*, in which he championed Indian modern art.

It was through Langhammer that Kekoo became acquainted with the Progressive Artists' Group whose founding members were K. H. Ara (1914–1985), M. F. Husain (1915–2011), S. H. Raza (1922–2016) and F. N. Souza (1924–2002). All of them were reacting against the established traditions, as Husain explains: 'We came out to fight against two prevalent schools of thought of these days [...] the Royal Academy, which was British-oriented, and the revivalist school in Mumbai, which was not a progressive movement.'[7]

Freedom of expression was paramount to Kekoo. The Progressives had no group style, and Kekoo embraced their wide-ranging approaches which included abstraction, narrative and representation. The artists followed different faiths, and were Muslim, Hindu and Catholic. By supporting this multi-religious group, he reflected the position of Prime Minister Jawaharlal Nehru (1889–1964) who advocated for a secular India, united in its diversity. Kekoo openly acknowledged, 'We hero worshipped Nehru.'[8]

With few opportunities for contemporary Indian artists, Kekoo became a crucial link between artist and public. As well as showing works at his frame shop, he worked with the Bombay Art Society, and set up exhibitions in alternative spaces, hanging works in the corridors of the Taj Mahal Palace hotel. And when the new Metro Cinema opened, he had dedicated wall space on the first floor.[9]

Kekoo's rallying spirit comes across in his account of his first solo show of Husain's work: 'I looked out of the window and saw my wife's uncle, the founder-owner of *Parsiana* magazine, passing by. I just pulled him in and said we needed a crowd. The poor man had no idea what was going on. But Husain sold so well that we were flooded with work from artists all over India.'[10] Through his long career, Kekoo worked hard to create interest in his artists. He would later open a second frame shop in Calcutta where he also exhibited works. When he became more established, he travelled abroad for extended periods to find galleries to show his artists,[11] and he held regular exhibitions at the Vadehra Art Gallery in Delhi. In the 1970s, he was involved in founding the present-day National Gallery of Modern Art, Mumbai, a landmark event in the history of Indian art.

There is little archival evidence on the early exhibitions. Husain's painting *Untitled (Doll's Wedding)* (c. late 1950s) was likely exhibited at Chemould Frames at some point. It resonates with the Progressives' ambition to foster an Indian art, free from colonial traditions. The work has the vibrancy of traditional Indian weddings: the vivid red background is a colour that Indian brides often wear, and the citrus yellows and greens bring the energy of a celebration. The artist was also drawing on India's rich visual traditions, and the depicted figures have a craft-like quality; the artist explained, 'My paintings, drawings and the recent paperwork have been directly influenced by my experience of traditional Indian dolls, paper toys, shapes galore.'[12]

Some of Kekoo's artists shared a fascination for Indian myths and scripture. And exhibitions at Chemould Frames became a melting pot of cross-cultural dialogues in an independent India. The religious scriptures were often given a perennial spiritual context, which on occasion created controversy. Kekoo himself was involved in new-age spiritual thinking. In 1952, he visited Switzerland, and chanced upon the headquarters of the Christian Moral Re-Armament movement near Montreux. The group's core belief was that spiritual enlightenment came from within an individual. What Kekoo took from this was that his life journey had an ethical purpose. Later, he consulted with Indian guru Swami Muktananda (1908–1982), and often took artists with him to visit his spiritual ashram.

The Progressives disbanded by 1956; many had relocated – Raza to Paris and Souza to London. Art historian Zehra Jumabhoy has emphasised how their departure, far from negating their nationalist intentions, reinforced the ideals of the new independent India, 'These artists felt that *because* they were now citizens of a Free Nation, a vibrant free India, they too had a right to a place in the international dialogue of the Modern.'[13] Kekoo would continue to represent many of them. And India remained a central part of their story – in France, Raza would say, 'what I paint I get from India'.[14] In the 1980s, he worked on his iconic series, *Bindu*, which features an emanating circle that references the Hindu idea of there being a single point of creation. Undoubtedly, this work would have resonated with Kekoo who searched for spiritual meaning in his own life.

In 1963, Kekoo opened Chemould Gallery on the first floor of Jehangir Art Gallery, Bombay. A step-up from the makeshift exhibition space in his frame shop (which he continued to run), it was one of the first galleries in India dedicated to modern and contemporary art. Kekoo's wife, Khorshed, now took an active role in the gallery.[15] They brought new artists into their roster, including the figurative artist Bhupen Khakhar (1934–2003). When Kekoo arranged an exhibition of Khakhar's work at Cottage Industries (a gallery and framing business in Delhi), the manager was deeply concerned by the homoerotic content. Although Kekoo had to compromise, the exhibition did open, and this reflects his steadfast inclusivity, and commitment to freedom of speech.

Another important artist they took on was Tyeb Mehta (1925–2009). Later, Mehta would recognise the Gandhys' role: 'By ensuring a fixed income in the early years without pressurising me, Chemould helped me to remain independent and work my own way.'[16] His art satisfied Kekoo's quest for a modern Indian art. His recurring image of a fallen figure has an elemental power and draws on his memory of witnessing a man being beaten to death during the violence between religious communities that broke out following the partition of India and Pakistan in 1947. The flat, clashing colours, and the energising diagonal axis were inspired by Indian miniature paintings. Mehta also used the ancient Indian practice of creating a sequence of multiple images to animate the work. Eventually, Mehta moved to another dealer who offered him a more lucrative arrangement, but Kekoo continued to rate Mehta most highly and owned one of his fallen figure paintings.

Meanwhile Khorshed had developed an interest in the tribal art of the Warli from Maharashtra in western India. Dating back to the 10th century, these ritual images were painted on the earth-red walls of the mud huts with a white paint made from rice flour. Khorshed visited a Warli village where artists had started working on paper. She especially admired a work by Jivya Soma Mashe (1934–2018), and she encouraged him to create works that explored the tribes' myths and legends. She also offered him a solo show at Gallery Chemould, which opened in 1975. According to Khorshed, 'people were clamouring for the paintings',[17] but she chose to sell only two works, and donated the rest to the National Crafts Museum in Delhi. Ultimately, her desire was to spread the importance of this art form, and she explained, 'I couldn't sell off these paintings; then they will be gone, and no one will know the stories.'[18] Following the exhibition, Khorshed set up the publishing imprint Chemould Publications, and released a book dedicated to Warli art.

In 2022, Mehta's painting *Untitled (Bull on Rickshaw)* (1999) sold via the Indian auction house Saffronart, for $5,596,000. Kekoo and Khorshed Gandhy had played a crucial role in Indian contemporary art being valued so highly. Part of the reason for their success was that their vision for art aligned with the values of the newly independent India. As Kekoo reflected: 'It's a matter of good fortune. I just happened to sow seeds and some fell on fertile ground.'[19]

Malick Sidibé

(1936–2016)

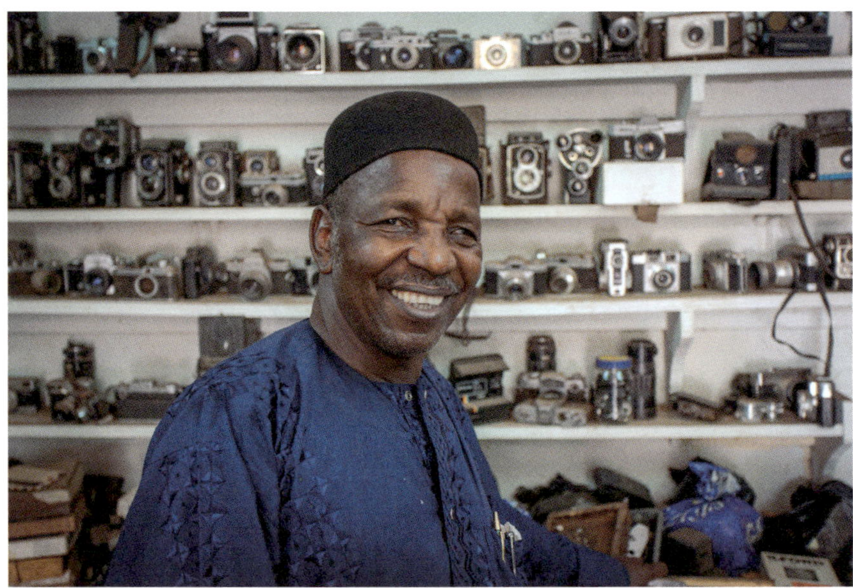

Horst Friedrichs, *Malick Sidibé in his studio in Bamako, Mali, c. 2006.*

Malick Sidibé's photography is world-renowned. In 2007, he was the first photographer and first African artist to receive the Golden Lion for Lifetime Achievement award at the Venice Biennale; four years earlier he had been the recipient of the prestigious Hasselblad Award. Sidibé welcomed this international recognition. It was late in coming: in Mali where he was based, his photography of Bamako's youth culture had been appreciated for over 40 years. As filmmaker and writer Manthia Diawara explains, 'For the youth in Bamako, Malick Sidibé was the James Brown of photography.'[1] Though his work now has a global profile, something that is rarely discussed is the role of his studio. Functioning as an exhibition space, it was a destination, first drawing locals, especially the youth who wanted to see photos of themselves, and later attracting an international audience.

Sidibé grew up in the rural village of Soldoba, which was then part of the French colony of Sudan. His father was a peasant farmer, and from six years old Sidibé was herding animals. When the village chief offered to send one of his children to school, Sidibé's father chose him. He was an incredibly bright child: top of his class, and an excellent draughtsman. In 1952, he moved to Mali's capital, Bamako, to study jewellery at the École des Artisans Soudanais (now the Institut National des Arts).[2] Following his graduation, the French photographer Gérard Guillat-Guignard hired him to paint his studio and store. In 1956 he bought his first camera, a Brownie Flash, and Guillat-Guignard asked him to photograph his West African clientele. A year later, Sidibé struck out as an independent photographer.

In 1962 he opened Studio Malick at 30th Street, in the neighbourhood of Bagadadji in Bamako. The concrete building had no windows, and its door opened onto a busy street. Inside, the main space was the storeroom for Sidibé's vast collection of cameras and meticulously archived photos, and there was a small backroom set up for studio portraits. The 'gallery' happened outside on the street where the photographs were pinned on a board. There were chairs for people to sit and gather, and Sidibé sold directly to buyers. There is a parallel with William Hogarth who represented himself, and set up his own shop where he sold directly to the buyer. However, it is crucial to look beyond this Eurocentric perspective to appreciate how Sidibé's enterprise worked within the local ecology. What stands out is the collective nature of the experience. Sidibé was part of the social scene he was photographing and, moreover, the sales, at least initially, were to local people.

The early years of his career coincided with a period of massive cultural change. After gaining independence in 1960, President Modibo Keïta (1915–1977) introduced education policies to teach the youth about Mali's precolonial history and traditional culture. Photography played a critical role in terms of Malian identity, although, its practice often ran counter to Keïta's ideals. A modern medium from the West, it was concerned with picturing the living, the now. From the previous generation, Seydou Keïta (c. 1921–2001) (a relative of President Keïta) had created aspirational studio photos of the middle class. This was not to be Sidibé's audience. He was attracted to the flourishing youthful countercultural scene which was determined to break with tradition.

It is important to keep in mind there were few opportunities for artists to exhibit in Mali. Also, Sidibé was not marketing his work as 'art' but as studio photography and reportage – the framing of it as art came later when it was discovered by a Western audience. In terms of reaching his demographic, the studio had a youthful edge. There was a neon sign that hung outside and advertised the business as a hip place. Also, the studio had attractive mod cons and as Sidibé explains, 'to be photographed where there was electricity, people enjoyed that. Electricity was something of a luxury.'[3] Most importantly, as a young man, he shared his subjects' outlook, and lifestyle. A charismatic figure, one interviewer tells how, 'Right away, his presence fills the room, captivating us. He's the kind of person that doesn't leave you indifferent.'[4]

In his reportage photography, Sidibé abandoned the studio. He was one of the first photographers in Bamako to use a 35mm camera: its light weight and cheaper film were liberating. It allowed him to follow his young audience as they partied at hip clubs like Las Vegas, and hung out at the beach. On Saturday nights, he would leave the studio at around 11pm, attend four or five parties, and return home around 5am. Hardly sleeping, he would then process 400 to 500 shots, and by Monday, or Tuesday at the latest, the proofs would be on view outside his shop.

The display of photos transformed his workplace into an exhibition site and public spectacle. The artist describes the interest: 'all the young people would come to see photos of the parties.'[5] In terms of their value, curator and writer, Michelle Lamuniere recounts, 'A matte print 9 × 13 cm cost 200 CFA francs, and a glossy print 150 francs – about ten times the cost of a soft drink.'[6] The small photos could be exchanged with friends or pasted into albums. Sometimes, the lack of sales grated on Sidibé who needed to turn a profit. For the young, it was all about the social exchange – the pinned-up proofs worked like Instagram today, marking their presence at some cool event, and parading their fashions and dance partners. Sidibé describes how, 'Lots of people would come and point themselves out. "Look at me there! I danced with so-and-so! Can you see me there?"'[7]

Diawara lived a few blocks away from Sidibé's studio and, years later, looking through a book of his photos, he reminisced:

> They are the gateway to everything that was fashionable then...
> marked by dress style (from B-boys to hippies), music appreciation
> (from Latin beat to James Brown), movies (from Westerns to *Easy
> Rider*), hair style (from Patrice Lumumba and Marlon Brando to
> the Afro), and dance moves (from the Twist to the Camel Walk).[8]

But Diawara also warned against reading them purely in terms of personal memory, and emphasised Sidibé's fundamental role in shaping and expanding Bamako's youth culture.

President Keïta had quickly brought in the military to support his repressive policies which restricted social behaviour, and, for example, imposed curfews on the young. In this sense, the youth's late-night parties were an act of defiance; for Sidibé, 'Music was a true revolution in Mali.'[9] By photographing his subjects dancing, their bodies moving, he highlighted their agency. In his work, *Regardez-moi! (Look at Me!)* (1962), the central male figure, who is dancing the limbo, lurches forward into our space, inviting us to join him, and share his zeal and sense of freedom.

Sidibé's photographs – and his exhibiting of them – became a crucial visual platform that was publicising the transgressive values of the youth. The artist talks about how the music brought the freedom to mix with the opposite sex, and he reflects on his role in publicising this:

> I have to tell you, music liberated African youth from the taboo
> of being with a woman. They were able to get close to each other,
> which is why I was always invited to these parties. I had to go in
> order to record these moments, when a young man could dance
> with a young woman close up. We were not used to it.[10]

His pictures of couples have extraordinary tenderness and joy. His iconic photo, *Nuit de Noël (Happy Club)* (1963) shows a brother and sister dancing. Dressed in their finery, they stare down at their feet, perhaps making sure they are in sync. Theorist Roland Barthes puts forward the idea that the emotional power of a photograph is often held in a detail, explaining, 'A photograph's punctum is that accident which pricks me (but also bruises me, is poignant to me).'[11] The girl's bare feet are the telling detail. In this state of undress, they anticipate the African pride message of the iconic song *Gentleman* (1973) by Fela Kuti (1938–1997):

> Africa hot, I like am so I know what to wear but my friends don't
> know Him put him socks, him put him shoe...

As Sidibé acquired this currency with the young, he ventured into more formal portraits. These happened in a backroom studio where he staged a set, and had a supply of patterned backdrops and floors to switch out. Relying heavily on this setting to establish his composition, he energised his work by introducing clashing patterns of checks and stripes. His clients clearly valued the artistry as Sidibé highlighted, 'people come to me because they know that I will compose it properly and make sure that it's right.'[12]

Reinvigorating the studio portrait, the atmosphere at Sidibé's studio was relaxed, and his clients felt comfortable to express themselves. They'd dress up and show off a new hairstyle, and would often pose with a significant item: a fancy watch, a stereo, a motorbike. Some people brought their goats to the studio. The photographs are assertions of their independence, and often open the door on a Pan-African diaspora. In Sidibé's photo *James Brown Fans* (1965), two girls hold up a record by the Black American musician James Brown. They appear to almost be dancing with their idol.

Typically, the portraits were bought by the person being photographed, but significantly, they were also exhibited outside for people to see. Over the years, Sidibé's production cycle and the audience changed. In the early reportage and portraits, it was an intensely local circuit as the young were both subjects and buyers. The photographs acted as an intensifier to that sense of the local. With the advent of automatic processing and colour photography, however, the youth turned to these modern and more immediate formats. Because of this, the studio's currency dissipated to a degree, and more changes were to come.

In the early 1990s, Sidibé's work was discovered by the French photographer Françoise Huguier (b. 1942) and the curator André Magnin (b. 1952) on a trip to Mali. Magnin went on to organise a solo exhibition for Sidibé at the Fondation Cartier in Paris in 1995, following which he began to attract global attention. His studio was visited by an international audience, as Sidibé explained: 'People came from Zurich, from New York, from Paris, from all over the world.'[13] They saw the photographs hanging outside, and Sidibé would often give them precious negatives to take home. In 2002, he was picked up by the New York dealer Jack Shainman who gave him numerous solo shows.

Around this time, a friend visited Sidibé, and reflected how, 'He was a little saddened because he said to me, "They bought everything. They bought everything. Even the albums that I had; they are all gone now." Once the Americans discovered him, they just went and cleaned up the place.'[14]

These comments poignantly reflect the complexity of Sidibé's international success. Undeniably, he took enormous pride in being recognised as an artist globally. In his homeland, he was revered, and children from remote villages were named after him. However, there was a loss, and this is bound to the role of the studio, and how it brought this intense locality to the production. In 2008, a documentary about Sidibé brought together some of the youths he photographed at the Las Vegas club. By this stage, they were old, and the film shows them outside the studio, chatting as they look through photo albums. As the documentary unfolds, they decide to recreate a Las Vegas party, and seem convinced it will be their best party ever. In the end, it is a bittersweet event – as they discover their dancing does not have its youthful fervour. This scene resonates with how Sidibé's photographs, and his studio, were bound into a unique cultural moment of Mali's history.

Courting Controversy

Introduction

Controversy is an ambivalent term. Historically, in art dealership, it has been associated with dishonest practices, including selling forged artworks, falsifying provenance and manipulating prices, all of which challenge the integrity of the art market and deceive unsuspecting collectors. However, since the mid-nineteenth century, controversy has also held a positive value. Provocation in art has become a hallmark of progressiveness. The Salon des Refusés was first set up in Paris to provide a venue for artists to show work that had been rejected by the Academy, and it soon became the epicentre for avant-garde activity and the place to buy controversial art. And in the modern period, dealers have capitalised on the frisson of selling cutting-edge art.

This chapter mainly examines the uglier side of controversy, and highlights problematic dealers. Historically, these figures have been treated too leniently – their positive contributions have been emphasised, and the contentious aspects of their dealership have been obscured. An argument often made is that it is anachronistic to apply contemporary standards to the past, but this reasoning quickly falls apart.

Take, for example, Paul Guillaume, whose exploitation of colonial routes has recently been brought to light,[1] but whose activities need to be unpacked further, particularly his writing. The very title of his book *Primitive Negro Sculpture* (c. 1926) includes deeply problematic slurs. Such terms were used in this period, but there were also rare, progressive voices. Félix Fénéon published an article in the Bernheim-Jeune gallery magazine which questioned this language, 'L'Art nègre, another scandalous word. We apologise for using it. But it has no equivalent. Arts from remote countries? Current language does not suffer the use of such long phrases. Indigenous would be too cowardly, exotic too louche. Who will assist us?'[2]

The final question highlights the limitations of these early, sparse critiques, as today there is an obvious answer to who can and should 'assist': the cultural descendants of this art, the Black artists and critics who were wrongfully excluded from this earlier discourse.

Sigmund Freud uses the metaphor of the archaeological dig to describe the process of therapy, and the 'excavation' of trauma – and this is precisely what needs to happen here. The past needs to be unearthed in order that the problems can be processed, and for there to be clarity. This task is difficult because the dealers' business structures were often labyrinthian. It requires forensic probing to fathom their activities. In the case of Nazi collaborator, Hildebrand Gurlitt, there is an urgency for this to happen so the crucial task of restitution can take place, and looted works can be returned to their rightful owners.

This chapter ends with an example of positive controversy, exploring Stephen Radich's provocative decision to exhibit anti-Vietnam War art and his refusal to settle the legal dispute that followed, instead using it as a platform to argue for the freedom of speech. This case points to how controversy can be a beneficial force. Supporting disruptive art can bring attention to injustices, and in our troubled world this is much needed.

Paul Guillaume

(1891–1934)

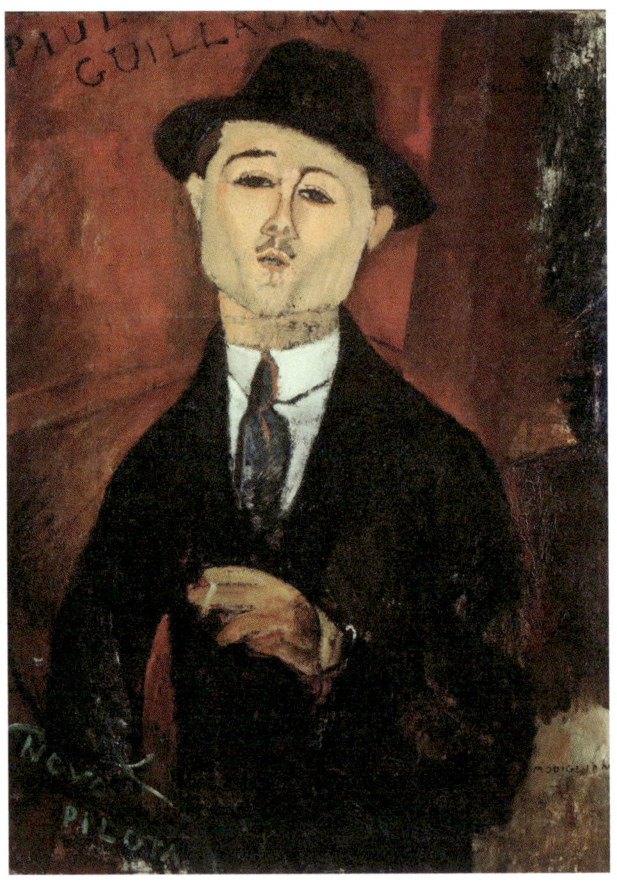

Amedeo Modigliani, *Paul Guillaume, Novo Pilota*,
1915, oil on canvas, 105 × 75 cm (41⅜ × 29½ in.),
Musée de l'Orangerie, Paris.

The French art dealer Paul Guillaume was painted numerous times by Amedeo Modigliani (1884–1920); the well-known portrait *Paul Guillaume, Novo Pilota* (1915) shows the dealer as a fashionable, dandy figure. Sporting a trilby and tie, he smokes a cigarette, and stares out towards the viewer. A telling detail is in the inscription 'Novo Pilota', which translates to 'new pilot'. Modigliani considered Guillaume to represent the vanguard of art dealing. He was one of the first dealers to show African art, and Modigliani shared his interest. In the portrait, the sitter's facial features have the angular forms of African masks – a presentation the French dealer would have appreciated. Guillaume was not modest. He saw himself as an intrepid 'discoverer' who was uncovering an ancient African art that would inspire modern artists. However, the narrative was fraught with inaccuracies, and its premise was highly problematic.

Born in Jura, in eastern France, Guillaume came from a modest background – his father was a messenger at a bank, and it is not clear whether his mother worked. He was ambitious and drawn to money – his first job was working in an upmarket car dealership in Paris. He discovered an African statuette in a shipment of rubber delivered to the garage, which he displayed in the shop window. This attracted the attention of the poet Guillaume Apollinaire and the two men became friends. Apollinaire introduced him to his avant-garde circle which included many artists who were already looking to African art for inspiration. Guillaume saw an opportunity, and started selling African art alongside work by these contemporary artists.

In February 1914, he opened the Galerie Paul Guillaume at 6 rue de Miromesnil in the centre of Paris. It would prove to be terrible timing as World War I soon broke out and he was forced to close. Enterprisingly, he found an alternative market in America and gave the Mexican artist and writer Marius de Zayas (1880–1961) a trunk full of African sculptures to show at Alfred Stieglitz's 291 gallery. By 1916, the art market was recovering in Paris, and Guillaume started trading again from his apartment-cum-gallery at 16 avenue de Villiers in the 17th arrondissement, and when the war ended, he opened luxurious premises on rue La Boétie, where the prestigious galleries were located. Revealingly, Guillaume took advantage of Daniel-Henry Kahnweiler being declared an enemy of the state and bought up key works from his sequestered art collection including Picasso's painting, *Ma Jolie* (1911–12). He started showing key modernists including Modigliani, André Derain, Matisse and Francis Picabia (1879–1953). Meanwhile, he was also becoming heavily involved with the art collector Albert C. Barnes and was helping build his famous art collection in Philadelphia, a significant part of which was African art.

Guillaume was relying on established colonial trading routes to source African art. Since the 1870s the French had been expropriating thousands of African and Oceanic objects from its colonies and placing them in ethnographic museums or selling them through curio-antiquities dealers. Guillaume exploited this circuit, and placed ads in colonial newspapers, appealing to seafarers to source works for him. He also cultivated relations with the colonial administrator, Astride Courtois.

The dealer had developed his ideas about African art through collecting and reading, and by visiting the Trocadéro ethnographic museum where Picasso famously had his epiphany in front of some African masks. Guillaume came to dislike the display at the Trocadéro where the objects were presented as ethnographic artefacts. Instead, he was intent on 'elevating' the artefacts to the status of art. Following traditional practices in Western Europe and America, he placed the sculptures on pedestals which were made by the master craftsman Kichizo Inagaki who had worked with Auguste Rodin. The pedestals had an austere, geometric form and foregrounded the formal beauty of the African artworks. In the gallery, Guillaume then set the pieces against coloured backgrounds, which isolated them further.

Guillaume brought the same meticulous presentation to his publications. With art historian Thomas Munro (1897–1974), he co-wrote the book *Primitive Negro Sculpture* (1926), which included photographs of Barnes's collection of African sculptures. It is an incredibly luxurious publication: great attention is given to the illustrations. With an entire page for each piece, the sculptures are set against a white background, and are typically shown on pedestals. The black and white photography further enhances the aesthetic presentation and the text consistently emphasises that the value of the artworks lies in their formal qualities. Guillaume especially rated works from Gabon, Sudan and Congo. In the case of a relinquary figure by a Kota artist from Gabon (fig. 23), the writers focus on the rhythm of the curved forms established by 'the tremendous domed forehead', 'cheek glides' and the 'branching curves of nose and eyebrows'.[1]

Guillaume later developed his story of how African art influenced modern art. He held shows that juxtaposed African pieces with modernist works, and foregrounded formal similarities. One of the earliest exhibitions was held at a studio in Paris in 1916, where 25 African works from Guillaume's

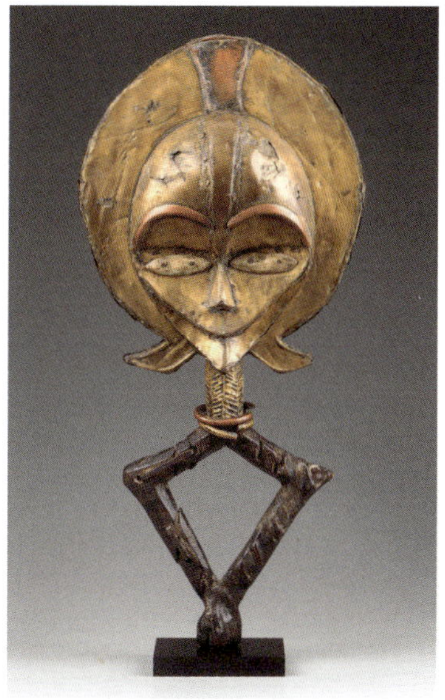

Fig. 23 Kota artist, reliquary figure (mbulu ngulu), late nineteenth to early twentieth century, wood, copper, brass, bone, 59.7 cm (23 ½ in.), Museum of Fine Arts Boston.

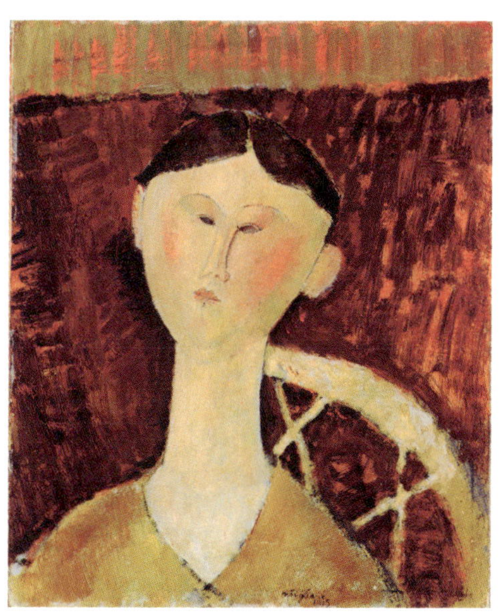

Fig. 24 Amedeo Modigliani, *Portrait of Mrs Hastings*, 1915, oil on cardboard, 55.5 × 45.4 cm (21⅞ × 17⅞ in.), Art Gallery of Ontario, Toronto.

personal collection were displayed alongside paintings by Picasso, Matisse and Modigliani. By this point Guillaume was representing Modigliani, and was paying for his studio at the Bateau-Lavoir. Guillaume had convinced him to spend more time painting and the results were clearly satisfying him; one critic notes, 'In Modigliani's work, he recognised the fine stylizations of the Côte d'Ivoire.'[2] The artist was undeniably taking inspiration from African sculpture. His *Portrait of Mrs Hastings* (1915, fig. 24), for example, resonates quite clearly with a Gabon reliquary piece. Hastings's face has the moonlike form of the African sculpture, and her ovoid eyes and vertical strip of nose are also similar in their stylisation.

Significantly, the Black writer and philosopher Alain Locke (1885–1954), who was a key player in the Harlem Renaissance, initially supported how the artistic value of African sculpture was being recognised by Guillaume and Barnes.[3] However, Locke later came to blows with Barnes when Locke organised the *Blondiau-Theatre Arts Collection of Primitive African Art* exhibition at The New Art Circle in New York. The show took an alternative position and emphasised the importance of craft and sought to engage with African history. Barnes criticised the show, and Munro stepped in, adding that the exhibited works didn't deserve to be considered 'African', 'primitive' or even art. Locke's rebuff would expose the distorted narrative that Guillaume (and Munro) had been putting forward for years:

> Mr Munro's arbitrary distinction between art and handicraft is a vicious misinterpretation of African art. The distinction did not exist in the culture itself, and recognition of that fact is basic in the competent study and appreciation of African art... Certainly it is at least as legitimate a modern use of African art to promote it as key to African culture... as to promote it as a side exhibit to modernist painting and to use it as a stalking-horse of a particular school of aesthetics.[4]

The cultural role of the artefacts was consistently ignored by Guillaume. Most were reliquary and ceremonial objects, and often functioned as part of an ensemble of symbolic objects, with many used in ritual performances. Guillaume glibly dismissed this aspect, commenting, 'Delightful as these reveries may be, they are a sort of pleasure quite distinct from the enjoyment of the object's merit as a work of art.'[5] And the problems go well beyond this. In a chapter in *Primitive Negro Sculpture*, Guillaume attempts to define 'The Negro Mind' and succumbs to offensive racist stereotyping. He makes the evaluation, 'One general fact does emerge, unquestionably: they developed no durable intellectual culture, no technique of applied science or logic of abstract thinking.'[6] In other places, he presents 'passivity', 'lack of initiative' and 'intellectual backwardness' as 'native traits'[7] amongst contemporary Africans.

As mentioned, Guillaume insistently focussed on the plastic qualities of the African artefacts, and 'their effects of line, plane, mass and colour.'[8] A formalist viewpoint carries with it the idea that art is divorced from life, and free from politics, and this position has excused his art analysis from scrutiny. But Guillaume's insistence on the artfulness of African artefacts served an agenda. As the writer Ijeoma Oluo warns, 'appropriation, more often than not, disproportionally benefits the dominant culture that is borrowing from marginalized cultures, and can even harm marginalized cultures.'[9] Guillaume argued that the African artists advancing this abstract language came from a forgotten, ancient past. From this specious position, he adopted his messianic role as discoverer, and positioned the European artists as the gifted interpreters. It is a highly problematic standpoint and one that denied agency to contemporary African artists. It was this that prompted Locke's demand for 'a modern use of African art [which] promote[s] it as key to African culture'.[10]

For Guillaume, the artistic value of these artefacts was tied to their age. The dealer would boast that his collection of African art was tens of thousands of years old. On one occasion, he claimed, 'archaeologists do not hesitate to date certain ancient pieces to a period that long predates the Christian era.'[11] These dates were wildly out, and as art historian John Monroe explains, 'Guillaume's early dates were always controversial... the vast majority of African wood sculptures then available in Europe were made in the late nineteenth and early twentieth century.'[12] It's a staggering revelation. When dated accurately, the African artefacts are often contemporary with modernist artworks, completely dismantling Guillaume's argument.

Guillaume blindly persisted. He would emphasise the patina on sculptures as evidence of them being old, and critics supported him. When the Gabon reliquary piece (fig. 25), now part of the Metropolitan Museum of Art

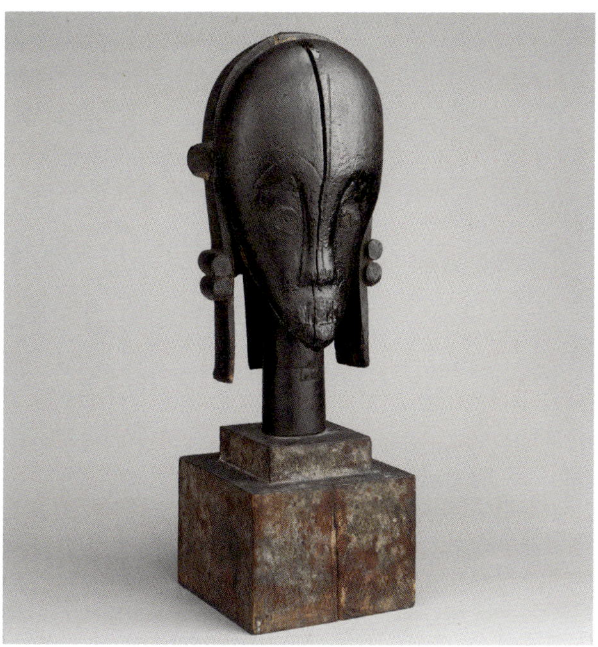

Fig. 25 Fang-Betsi artist, Sculptural Bust from a Reliquary Ensemble (The Great Bieri), Gabon, nineteenth century, wood, metal, palm oil, 46.5 × 24.8 × 16.8 cm (18 5/16 × 9 3/4 × 6 5/8 in.), The Metropolitan Museum of Art, New York.

(and dated to the nineteenth or twentieth century) was shown at Guillaume's gallery, Marcel Astruc, in an article in *Vogue,* isolated the wear on 'the ravaged mouth' and argued that it endowed a 'royal dignity' to the face.[13] The damage was in fact recent, and likely the result of ritual use.

While Guillaume valued the formal beauty of African art, his underlying story was inaccurate, and rife with racist ideology, and one cannot ignore this. As the writer Chinua Achebe emphasises, 'We cannot trample upon the humanity of others without devaluing our own. The Igbo, always practical, put it concretely in their proverb *"Onye ji onye n'ani ji onwe ya"*: "He who will hold another down in the mud must stay in the mud to keep him down."'[14]

Surprisingly, Guillaume's highly problematic book spun new, and positive narratives. It circulated widely, and was read by African and African diasporic artists, who upturned its original narrative. In 1936, the South African artist Ernest Mancoba (1904–2002) discovered the book in a library in Cape Town, and saw the illustrations, and the fragmented African artefacts, and the power of them prompted him to look at his own cultural heritage.

Dikran Kelekian

(1868–1951)

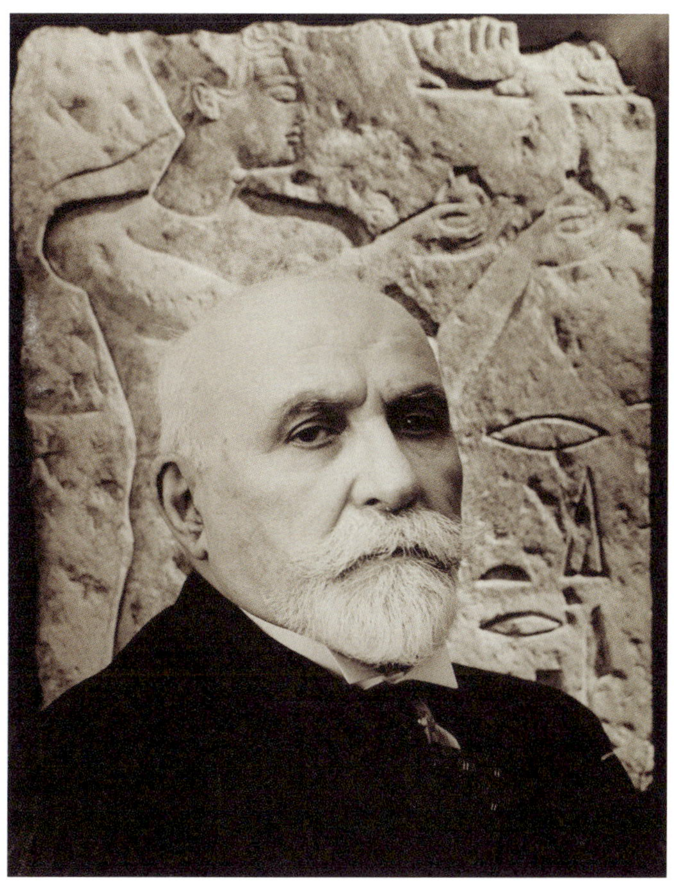

John Schiff, *Portrait of Dikran Kelekian*,
date unknown. Leo Baeck Institute at
the Center for Jewish History, New York.

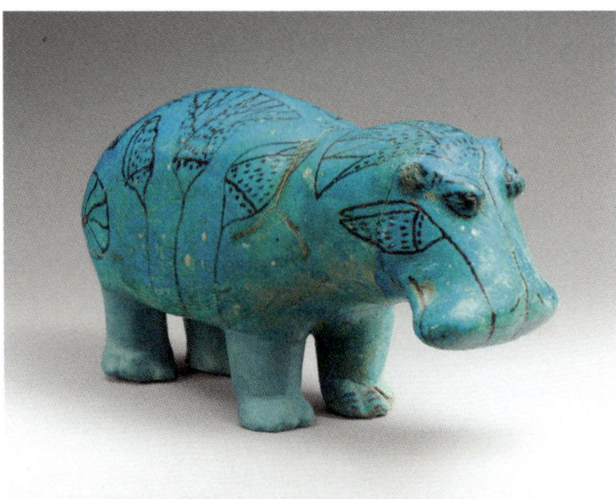

Fig. 26 Middle Kingdom, Egypt, 12th Dynasty, Hippopotamus
('William'), c. 1961–1878 BCE, faience, 11.2 × 7.5 × 20 cm
(4 ½ × 3 × 7 ⅞ in.), The Metropolitan Museum of Art, New York.

The charismatic art dealer Dikran Kelekian sold the Metropolitan Museum of Art one of their most treasured items. The ancient Egyptian hippo has become a mascot of the museum, and is affectionately known as William (fig. 26). While Kelekian sold many ancient Egyptian artworks, he became world-famous for his trade in Islamic carpets and ceramics. At the time, Islamic art was considered little more than bric-a-brac and Kelekian was to seize on cultural trends and weave his own narratives, bringing character to his dealership, and ultimately stoking his buyers' interest. However, controversially, his stories often reflected problematic Orientalist views.

Born in Kayseri, Turkey, Kelekian was the son of an Armenian banker. He was educated at an American school in Constantinople (today Istanbul) where he studied the history of the Ancient Near East, and he completed his education in Paris. After working with his uncle who sold 'oriental curiosities and diverse antiquities',[1] he established his own antiquities shop in Paris in 1891, and a year later, with his brother Kevork, opened another premises in Constantinople.

Though luxury goods from the Islamic world had been traded widely in Europe and were beloved by the elites during the Middle Ages and Renaissance, from the eighteenth century onwards new approaches within art history meant works from the Islamic world were less valued, and thus not included in the international art trade. They were deemed too recent to be valuable as archaeological artefacts in the way ancient objects from the Middle East were. But they also didn't present as fine art because their most popular mediums – ceramics, glassware, textiles – were now considered minor arts in Europe. Challenging this negative opinion, Kelekian would reframe the perception of these objects. With a vacuum in expertise in the West, and no existing concept of Islamic art history,[2] Kelekian generated interest by selling a fantasy of the Orient.

According to the Palestinian-American writer Edward Said (1935–2003), 'The Orient was almost a European invention, and had been since antiquity a place of romance, exotic beings, haunting memories and landscapes, remarkable experiences.'[3] The painting *The Carpet Merchant* (*c.* 1887, fig. 27) by Jean-Léon Gérôme (1824–1904) points to how Orientalism impacted

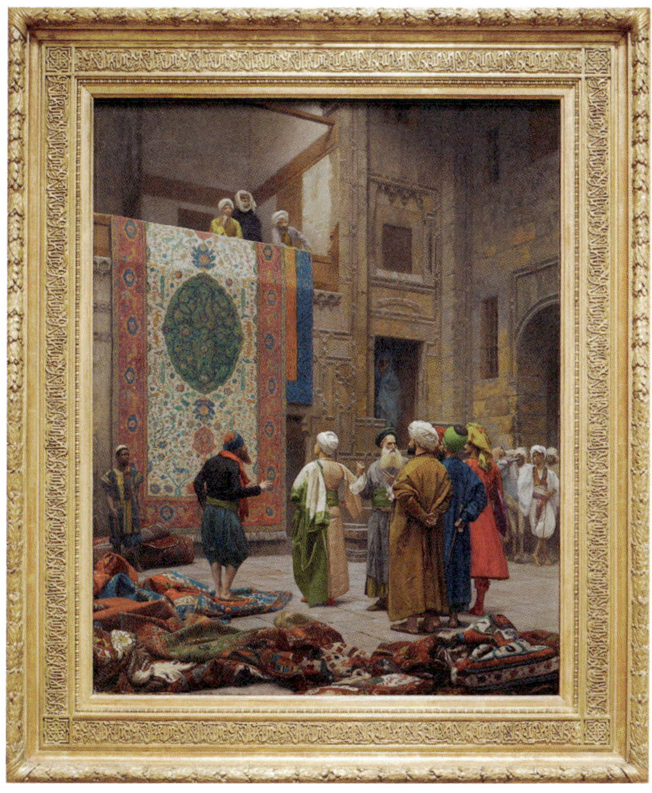

Fig. 27 Jean-Léon Gérôme, *The Carpet Merchant*, c. 1887, oil on canvas, 86 × 68.7 cm (33 ⅞ × 27 in.), Minneapolis Institute of Art, MN, USA.

the display and selling of art. It shows the court of the rug market in Cairo, which the artist had visited in 1885. At the centre of the work is a carpet which hangs down from the balcony, displaying its opulent patterns. The sumptuous spectacle becomes all-consuming as the merchants are dressed in colours that complement the hues of the carpet. An interesting detail is the chaotic pile of carpets on the left, intended to capture the informality of the street bazaar. The implication is that it is only when the carpet is hung, and framed within Gérôme's composition, that it acquires the status of art. The colonialist message is that the ruling nations are the rational counterforce to the unbounded sensualism of the Orient.

Kelekian's involvement in the world fairs put him at the centre of these Orientalist narratives. In 1893, he travelled to the United States to attend the Chicago World Fair where they set up model villages from across the world for Americans to roam like tourists and discover 'exotic' cultures. Kelekian was responsible for a booth in the Turkish village where there was a plethora of bazaars. What is interesting is how he raised his prices to emphasise the quality of his works. An article appeared in *The Chicago Daily Tribune* (most likely penned by Kelekian himself), which highlighted 'a most excellent collection of Oriental fine goods owned by Mr Dikran G. Kelekian at Booth No. 14, Turkish Village'.[4] The report mentioned a sale of an Oriental rug at $5,000, a staggering cost compared to the $1 bargain deals on offer at the other bazaars.[5] To support his exorbitant prices, Kelekian produced a catalogue, and the descriptions of the pieces are rife with superlatives, with him claiming items to be the 'most beautiful', 'most ancient' and 'rarest piece'.[6]

At the fair, Kelekian was awarded several blue ribbons for his displays. These weren't particularly noteworthy commendations – tens of thousands were handed out. However, the master salesman had more made to give out to customers. And further accolades followed. In 1900, he was awarded the honorific title of Khan by the Shah of Persia for his services to Persian culture, and made the Consul of Persia in New York. Kelekian also served as the general commissar of the Persian Empire at the World Fair in St Louis in 1904, where the performative dealer wore full military costume, complete with a fez, a medal for the Order of the Lion and the Sun and a ceremonial sword. It is unlikely that he was oblivious to the advantages of wearing the national costume, and how it served to legitimise his business as a purveyor of Persian artefacts. He was sure to include his honorary titles in the catalogue, and appeared as Dikran Khan Kelekian, Commissioner General for Persia.

At the St Louis World Fair, he displayed over 100 objects which were exhibited as an eclectic mix with Persian goods shown beside pieces from different countries, and objects from centuries apart shown alongside one another. The principle of the display was to mimic a Persian bazaar. The problem with his method was it reduced them to exotica. Added to this, the catalogue erroneously listed many entries as Persian when they were not. It is not entirely clear whether this was a mistake or strategy – if the latter it could be that Kelekian simply wanted to appear to have more Persian items, which at the time were the most highly valued artistic objects from the Middle East, perhaps, in part, due to Kelekian's own activities.

Following his success at the Chicago Fair, Kelekian opened a shop in New York, Le Musée de Bosphore. The name reinforced the idea that only the highest-quality, museum-worthy objects were on sale, and by using the French word for museum added a further degree of sophistication. As with the Chicago Fair, he set high price points; for example, an Arabian lamp was listed for $1,200.

Kelekian published a small catalogue when the shop opened. Its introductory text conjured up contemporary travelogues with the writer contrasting the busy streets of New York to the interior of the gallery where one was transported '[to] the rough streets of Cairo and Damascus [...] Greek and Persian bazaars [... and] the Sultan's palace'.[7] The curation had the sensuous exoticism of Gérôme's painting of a bazaar, and reinforced the stereotyping of the Middle East as 'other'. There are descriptions of carpets piled high, and again the displays had the same mix of objects without any historical context. The press reinforced this troubling narrative with the periodical *The Collector* describing the gallery as 'a palace transported on an enchanted carpet from the lands of legends'.[8]

Kelekian soon was lauded as the world specialist on Persian art, and indeed Islamic art more generally. In 1901, an article on Persian textiles in *The Art Amateur* had singled out the dealer, saying, 'no one has done more than the recipient to make known to the West, the beauties of Persian art.'[9] He was present at several important early excavations of sites in the Islamic world, including Rayy in present-day Iran, and Raqqa in Syria. Although it seems his involvement was accepted by the authorities, he certainly took full advantage and sourced the finest pieces for bargain prices. He also purchased some high-profile collections; in 1898 he bought the Charles A. Dana Collection of Oriental Ceramics in New York at auction, on which he

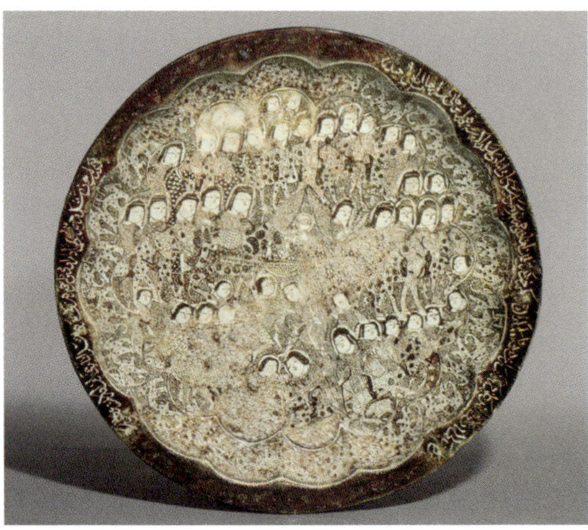

Fig. 28 Dish depicting a wedding procession,
first quarter 13th century, attributed to
Iran, Kashan, diam. 41 cm (16⅛ in.), The
Metropolitan Museum of Art, New York.

supposedly made $20,000 profit. Significantly, he wrote to the Metropolitan Museum of Art informing them how he was 'painfully surprised'[10] at the lack of interest in the auction and convinced the museum to exhibit the ceramics. Through such exhibitions, Kelekian became a tastemaker, bringing attention to Persian ceramics, and reinforcing their importance.

Today, the Metropolitan Museum of Art possesses one of the largest collections of Islamic art in the world, and Kelekian was involved with a large proportion of the items, through selling the pieces either directly to the museum or to collectors who later donated their works. The ceramics, a particular speciality of his, are now recognised to be of the highest artistic quality. One such example is an early thirteenth century dish (fig. 28) which depicts a wedding procession. In this modestly scaled object, 44 figures are clustered together around a central veiled figure – probably the bride. There's great attention to the intricately patterned costumes which are synthesised to create a decorative harmony.

Three years before his exhibition of Persian ceramics, Kelekian had convinced the President of the Metropolitan Museum of Art, Henry G. Marquand, to show 84 textile works in a dedicated room. Kelekian played a part in securing a mid-seventeenth century opulent floral carpet for their permanent collection (fig. 29). The piece has a central flowering poppy,

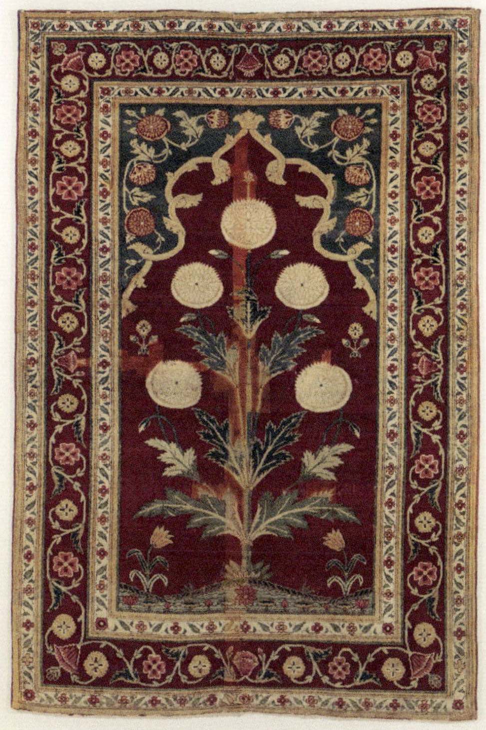

Fig. 29 Carpet with niche and flower design, mid-seventeenth century, made in Kashmir, India or Lahore, Pakistan, cotton (warp and weft), silk (weft), wool (pile); asymmetrically knotted pile, 154.9 × 102.8 cm (61 × 40 ½ in.), The Metropolitan Museum of Art, New York.

which was a popular motif in Mughal emperor Shah Jahan's reign. The flower is depicted within a niche, which was a highly unusual design in textiles, and suggests that this piece was originally hung vertically. These two pieces in the museum's collection alone reflect the diversity in Islamic art, which up until this point Kelekian's Oriental fantasy had obscured.

Between 1909 and 1910, Kelekian's approach changed significantly. Around this time, he was asked to lend works to the landmark exhibition *Masterpieces of Muhammadan Art* which opened in Munich in 1910. With almost 3,600 items, the curation by Friedrich Sarre (1865–1945) and Hugo von Tschudi (1851–1911) marked a turning point in the display of Islamic art. Sarre stated it 'was a war against the popular understanding of Oriental art, against fairy-tale splendour and bazaar commodities'.[11] Rejecting the abundance of the bazaar, the hang was deliberately sparse, and the walls were painted white. There was also far greater attention given to context, with the objects placed by region and divided by medium. Historian David Roxburgh discusses the presentation:

> This was hardly a neutral context free from ideological frameworks, as scholars have amply shown, but the conceptions that guided the museological modality had the intention of distancing the experience of artworks from other contexts, foregrounding the historical approach to things while maintaining aesthetic experience.[12]

Mirroring the direction of the Munich exhibition, Kelekian's new approach was reflected in his book, *The Kelekian Collection of Persian and Analogous Potteries 1885–1910* (1910). Gone are the fantasy narratives and the hyperbolic language of the catalogue for his shop. Instead, there is an attempt to contextualise the works; plate descriptions detail where the object was found, its date and a brief description of the work. Echoing the curation of the Munich exhibition, the design is minimal: the photographed object is set on a white background, and the description sits on the opposite page. One cannot be certain it was the exhibition in Germany that prompted this shift, but whatever the case, Kelekian required an updated narrative to keep abreast of the times. Modern artists had become interested in Islamic art, and Kelekian was selling work to many of them, including Henri Matisse who'd visited the Munich exhibition.

Kelekian now marketed the relevance of Islamic art (using the generic misnomer 'Persian') to the modern age: 'The Persian art is nearer to the spirit of the time in which we live. It is more human than its predecessors...'[13] He had also started selling modern art. Indeed, he would be awarded the French Legion of Honor for organising some of the first exhibitions of modern art.[14]

In 1951, Kelekian's life ended dramatically when he fell from the 21st floor of the Hotel St Moritz in New York. The hippo in the collection of the Metropolitan Museum has a symbolic relevance to the dealer's life story: decorated with lilies, symbols in Egyptian culture of regeneration, Kelekian had continually reinvented himself. He had managed to achieve commercial success for himself while also bringing Islamic art to the attention of leading institutions. However, this cannot hide his penchant for problematic Orientalist storytelling and how these narratives decontextualised Islamic art.

The Wildenstein Family

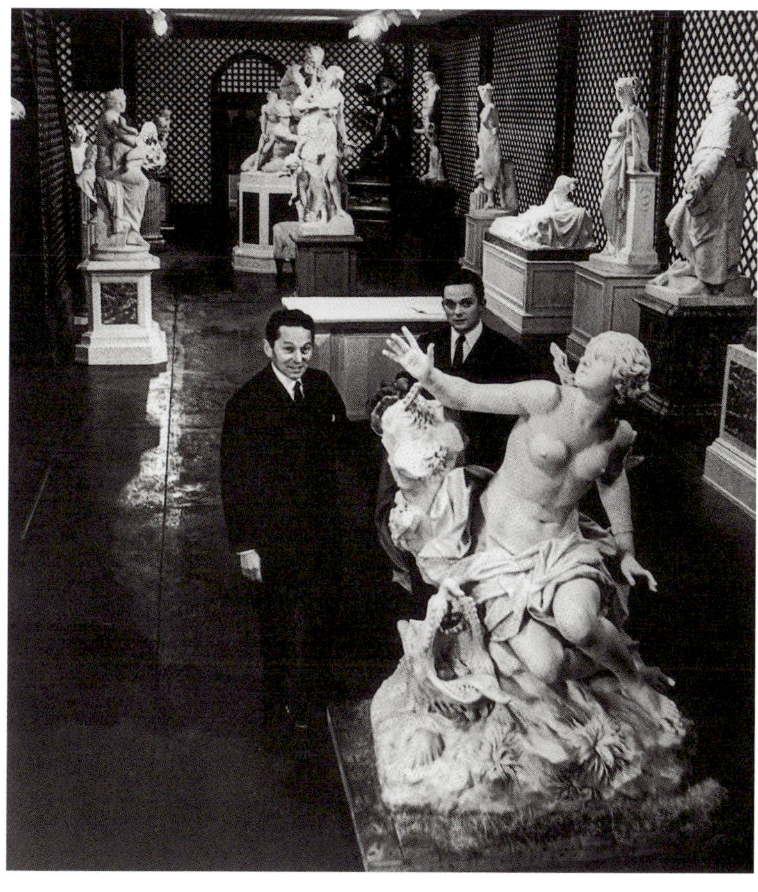

Daniel Wildenstein, left, and his son, Alec, look over the
sculpture garden housed in an old firehouse in New York
City, 8 December 1965. Photographer unknown.

Originating in France, the Wildenstein art dynasty has been a formidable force in the art market for four generations. Nathan (1851–1934), his son Georges (1892–1963) and grandson Daniel (1917–2001) established their billion-dollar empire, and in 2001 great-grandson Guy (b. 1945) took over the helm. Their immense wealth and power have been bound up with their control of knowledge, both suppressing information and masterminding its production. Secrecy has been paramount as Daniel explained in an interview in 1999: 'Now, I must tell you that, in my family, we have elevated discretion to the rank of silence. We do not speak. We do not tell. We do not talk about one another.'[1] Their dealership is like a black box whose operations are hidden. This opacity has covered the darker side of business, which has involved the obfuscation of their wealth, tax evasion and possible Nazi links. Daniel wrote the family biography, *Marchands d'Art* (1999) partly to address such controversies, but in the process, he let slip the deep-set generational conflict.

The story begins with Nathan who, in 1870, fled his Alsatian village during the Franco-Prussian War. His family considered his departure to be an act of betrayal; Nathan never saw his parents or siblings again.[2] Arriving in Paris, he worked as a tailor's assistant before he moved into art dealing. Nathan proved to be a charismatic dealer who had an instinct for the market. His grandson Daniel later recounted, 'He had always been an exceptional salesman. He would be the only one in the family. My father was not good; me neither; my children no more... He knew how to operate, detect tastes, desires...'[3]

Nathan bought the most imposing building on rue La Boétie, and had the architect, Walter-André Destailleur (1867–1940), create a lavish, neo-classical setting. And the dealer played up to his surroundings, dressing in finely tailored suits, enlivened by his signature floral waistcoats. His dealership followed the path of the nineteenth-century connoisseur dealers like Duveen and Jacques Seligmann and centred on buying up highly prized art collections.[4] He partnered with the art dealers Ernest and René Gimpel, with whom he established Gimpel & Wildenstein in New York in 1903. He also opened branches in London and Buenos Aires. Unlike his successors, Nathan's career was not entangled in controversy; however, some of the family's later troubles seem as if they could be traced back to his complex and sometimes conflicting personality traits.

Daniel said of his grandfather, after leaving Alsace, 'There was a sort of secret shame in him.'[5] Nathan fabricated a story that he was the only child born of a Sephardic rabbi who died before he was born. He insistently retold

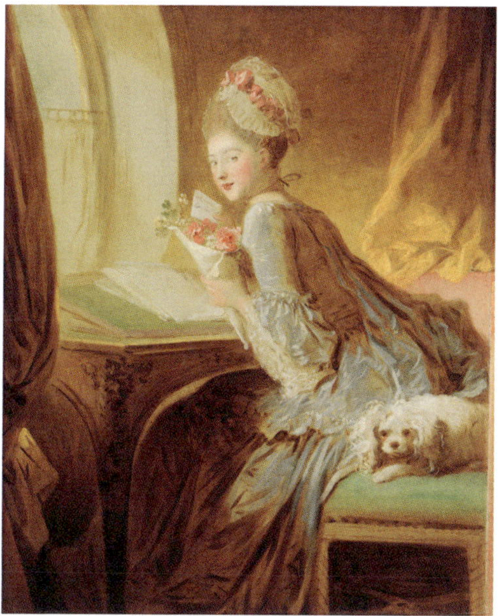

Fig. 30 Jean-Honoré Fragonard, *The Love Letter*,
early 1770s, oil on canvas, 83.2 × 67 cm (32¾ × 26⅜ in.),
The Metropolitan Museum of Art, New York.

this to his wife for years to come.[6] There was also a profound disconnection between his personal ethos and his business. He was a staunch supporter of the French Revolution and the new republic, believing it had liberated Jewish people by recognising them as French citizens. Daniel recounts him saying, 'We were nothing… and France in 1789 made us full human beings.'[7] Yet contravening the very tenets of the Revolution, his specialism was eighteenth-century Rococo art. He sold *The Love Letter* (early 1770s, fig. 30) by Jean-Honoré Fragonard (1732–1806), which shows an aristocrat in her lavish boudoir. Holding flowers, and wearing a highly fashionable 'robe à la française', her decadence and frivolity are exactly what turned the French public against the ruling classes, and precipitated the Revolution in 1789.

When Georges entered the business, Nathan had a mythical authority with his imposing gallery and the prestige of being associated with Old Master art. Georges's relationship with his father was complicated – his mother had made him spy on his father as a child, and report back on his infidelities. Daniel recounts, 'One could speak of a profound break, complete, between my father and my grandfather. A rupture of taste, of style, a cultural rupture in all areas of life.'[8] Defining himself in opposition, Georges would slight his father, saying his dress was 'a bit too elegant'.[9] He preferred to wear a simple black suit. Also, while Nathan had dismissed Cubism as ridiculous, Georges would partner up with Paul Rosenberg (1881–1959) and represent Picasso. Nathan funded Georges's gallery, located on the same street as his own, yet he never fully embraced Picasso or modern art generally. Georges had a red telephone with two lines – one reached Rosenberg, the other Picasso. Controlling information became crucial. Indeed, as French philosopher and historian Michel Foucault recognised, knowledge was a way of exercising power.[10]

Unlike his father, who left school at 14, Georges had received an excellent education and had studied Art History at La Sorbonne. He took over the business when Nathan died in 1934. An obsessive character, he was intent on building and controlling knowledge. He bought over 10,000 books a year, and created an enormous library. He started writing artists' catalogues raisonnés, and his son Daniel continued this legacy, producing the definitive catalogues of Claude Monet, Édouard Manet and Paul Gauguin. It was the ultimate tactic of control as they decided what was included in an artist's oeuvre, and their attributions could substantially influence the value of an artwork. However, in time, their scholarship would be challenged. In 1965, Georges's catalogue raisonné of Gauguin (1964) was publicly denounced in the *Times Literary Supplement* by the art historian Douglas Cooper: 'Gauguin's oeuvre has been shorn of some authentic works and adulterated with others that do not belong.'[11] Unabashed, the Wildensteins' response was to hire Cooper to work on the next edition.[12] Before the Sotheby's auction of Mildred Allen's estate in 1997, experts contested Daniel's attribution of *La Liseuse* to Manet.[13] Daniel's son Alec[14] blithely dismissed the query: 'We happen to make the book on Manet. I think we know a bit more about Manet than either Sotheby's or Christie's.'[15]

Georges and Daniel came to run the business like a military campaign. They documented the location of every desirable artwork and employed agents around the world to inform them of any potential sales coming to market. Writer Philip Hook reflects, 'As a covert information-gathering organisation, it could probably have taught valuable lessons to many countries' intelligence services.'[16] Undeniably, their knowledge affected the art market. By cloaking their buyers in the same secrecy, they prevented other dealers from knowing who their clients were. In 1955, they were investigated for tapping the telephone lines of the New York dealer M. Knoedler & Co. Somewhat ironically, in what became a characteristic move, the great information gatherers denied any knowledge. Daniel writes in the biography, 'The judge recognised, thank God, we were complete strangers to the story.'[17] An employee was singled out, and the family apologised, and said the culprit would not be receiving a Christmas bonus.

An especially troubled area is Georges's possible involvement with the Nazis. It is known that Georges met Nazi art dealer Karl Haberstock (1878–1956) in November 1940. When Haberstock was interrogated after the war in 1945, he said Georges had been 'very eager to do business' and a willing collaborator.[18] The family have denied involvement and, again, pointed the finger at an errant employee, saying the manager of their Paris gallery, Roger Dequoy, was involved in some shady deals which they knew nothing about at the time.[19]

Legal cases however emerged. In 2001, the heirs of Alphonse Kann (1870–1948) took their case to trial. They claimed the Wildensteins wrongfully possessed eight illuminated manuscripts which had been looted from their relative during the World War II.[20] The Wildensteins insisted Georges had bought the manuscripts before the war.[21] In the end the Kanns lost the case on technical grounds. More damning evidence came to light when police raided the Wildenstein vaults in 2011,[22] and paintings were found that had Nazi swastikas on the frames.[23] Officers recovered lost works by renowned artists like Edgar Degas and Berthe Morisot (1841–1895), some of which had been reported stolen by a Jewish family during the war. Guy denied ever having seen the works in the vault.

Nathan had strongly believed that dealers should not be collectors. However, the succeeding generations scrambled to hold on to their dynasty, and their inventory is legendary. An article in *Vanity Fair* in 1998 reported that their collection at one point included 'some 400 Italian primitives, two Botticellis, eight paintings each by Rembrandt and Rubens, three Velazquezes, nine El Grecos, five Tintorettos, 79 Fragonards, and seven Watteaus, not to mention an enormous collection of Impressionist paintings'.[24] Daniel admitted, 'Me, I would like to have everything. A dealer wants to have everything. If not, he is not a dealer.'[25] He was insatiable, as was his father. And they both could be ruthless.

Daniel considered his 'biggest coup' to be the acquisition of 500 paintings by Pierre Bonnard.[26] When the artist died in 1947, he left his estate to be divided between three nieces. However, Daniel approached a relative of Bonnard's and offered him $1 million for his inheritance rights, and then supplied him with a team of lawyers to fight his case.[27] The outcome of the ten-year legal fight was that Daniel walked away with 500 Bonnards, and the nieces shared out 25. It was a staggering betrayal of the artist's wishes.

Daniel kept 180 of the paintings by Bonnard – 'the most beautiful ones'.[28] One exquisite work in this collection was *Nude Washing Feet in a Bathtub* (1924) which shows Bonnard's wife, Marthe, washing her feet in a bath. It reveals a tender beauty to ordinary, daily life, something the Wildensteins had long been disconnected from.

The latest part of the Wildensteins' story has unfolded like a Greek tragedy; greed spurring betrayals, and ultimately leading to downfall. After Daniel's death in 2001, Alec and Guy successfully convinced their stepmother, Sylvia Wildenstein (1933–2010), that their father had died in financial ruin, and the only chance of her avoiding ruinous debt was for her to sign legal documents that annulled her inheritance. Clearly this was preposterous (Daniel's estimated wealth was between $5 and $10 billion), but Sylvia unknowingly signed, and then watched as a mover entered her home, and took a Bonnard painting off the wall. For eight years, she built a case to sue, but died in 2010.[29]

However, her situation brought attention to the Wildenstein's potentially illegal finances, and Sylvia's evidence was used to build a case.[30] In 2017 Guy was charged with tax fraud and money laundering charges stemming from allegations that he had hidden high-value art and other assets in a web of foreign trusts and shell companies. The prosecutor emphasised that the corruption was deep-rooted throughout the generations, arguing it constituted 'the longest and most sophisticated tax fraud in modern French history'.[31] In the end the judge decided trusts were a grey area, and found Guy not guilty. However, his ruling was overturned by a French appeals court in 2021.

A second trial concluded on 5 March 2024 when Guy was found guilty of tax fraud and money laundering. He was sentenced to four years' imprisonment, though he will only serve half the time, and this will be under house arrest. It was reported in *Apollo* magazine that he will also pay a $1.1 million fine, and is expected to repay hundreds of millions in tax arrears.[32] Meanwhile, some works of art sit in their lead-lined family vaults, others in a bunker at a free port in Geneva. The latter allows them to avoid import duties and capital gains on artworks, and is a legitimate tax loophole regularly exploited by blue chip dealers. However, it comes at a cost. Thus squirrelled away, the invisibility of the works goes against the spirit in which art is made – for it to be seen, if not in the public realm, then at least privately.

Hildebrand Gurlitt

(1895–1956)

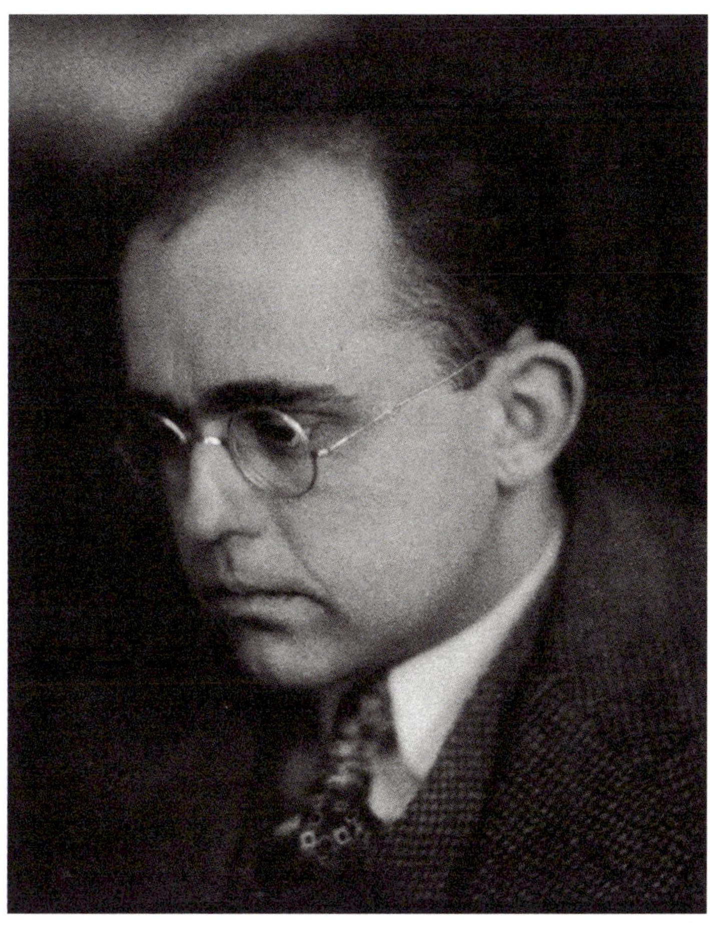

Fritz Alter sen., *Hildebrand Gurlitt*,
c. 1925, bromoil print, Kunst-
sammlungen Zwickau, Germany.

In 2012, Cornelius Gurlitt (1932–2014) was on a train from Switzerland when customs officers made a routine check and discovered he was carrying €9,000 in cash. Though within the legal limit, the nervous 80 year old aroused suspicion. Further investigations revealed Cornelius had no bank account, no employment record and no tax records. When police raided his flat in Munich, Germany, an art collection of over 1,400 works was discovered, with art by Paul Klee (1879–1940), Henri Matisse and Ernst Ludwig Kirchner. More artworks were found at a second property in Salzburg, Austria. Cornelius had lived his life as a recluse, disconnecting his television in the late 1960s to seal out any intrusion from the outside world. Attention soon turned to his father, the art historian Dr Hildebrand Gurlitt, who had been the director of the Association for Rhineland and Westphalia in Düsseldorf until his death. The focus became his forgotten role as art dealer to the Nazis.

Born in Dresden, in 1895, Hildebrand Gurlitt came from a cultured family. His father Cornelius (1850–1938) was a professor of architecture at the Royal Saxon Technical Institute, and introduced Gurlitt to modern art. When Gurlitt was 11 years old, he visited a small exhibition of works by the artists' group Die Brücke, and their audacious colours made a lasting impression on him. Gurlitt had two siblings and was particularly close to his sister Cornelia (1890–1919) who became an Expressionist painter, and was studying in Paris when World War I broke out. During the war, Gurlitt served in the Saxon Infantry Regiment no. 100.

As with so many, Gurlitt was deeply traumatised by war. Injured several times, he was also treated for shellshock. He tried desperately to make sense of the experience, and read Friedrich Nietzsche and Fyodor Dostoevsky. Like his father, he believed in a Pan-Germanism, and was influenced by Nietzsche's idea that conflict was necessary to achieve a better world. However, as war raged on, and German defeat became inevitable, Gurlitt had a spiritual crisis. In his diary, he writes, 'To be afraid and not run away is not cowardly.'[1] A muddled version of a line from Dostoevsky's novel *The Idiot* (1869),[2] it shows a bleak attempt at mustering a sense of purpose. He was tormented by his own passivity.

Shortly after the war ended, Cornelia, who was pregnant, committed suicide, leaving all her Expressionist art to Gurlitt. The tragedy seemed to galvanise his commitment to art. He studied art history in Berlin, Munich and Frankfurt, and after gaining his doctorate, he became the director of König-Albert-Museum in Zwickau in 1925. He showed great vision in the role, modernising the building, holding exhibitions of Expressionist art and producing catalogues with cutting-edge graphics. But his pioneering stance made him a victim of discrimination: criticised for exhibiting 'trash',[3] he was pushed out of his job by far-right conservatives. The same happened at his next post at the Kunstverein in Hamburg where Nazis had gained a stronghold. Following this dismissal, he removed the flagpole from the museum's façade in order to ensure that the Nazi flag could not be raised. It is hard to know whether this was bitterness, albeit justified, or a rare political stance from him.

Gurlitt stayed in Hamburg, and opened the commercial gallery, Kunstkabinett. With the Nazis now in power, Gurlitt was considered 'a second-degree half-caste' on the basis that his paternal grandmother was Jewish. Clearly fearful, he registered the business in his wife's name, and ran a clandestine operation. The gallery was in his apartment block, had no shop window and visitors had to ring a bell. Hidden away, he would continue to show Expressionist art and had exhibitions for newly emerging artists like Max Beckmann (1884–1950).

Adolf Hitler considered art to be the bedrock of culture, and after gaining power he sought to control its production. In 1933, anyone involved in the art business had to be a member of the Chamber of Culture, and the following year, Jews were excluded from joining. Because the so-called 'second-degree Jews', like Gurlitt, were still allowed to trade, Gurlitt benefitted from there being less competition. Also, there was a rush of artworks coming to the market since Jewish families were selling theirs because they had lost their jobs or were trying to raise funds to pay the costly emigration tax.

Gurlitt's position became increasingly ambivalent. He was painfully aware of the ongoing discrimination against Jews (his own father and brother had lost their jobs),[4] but by the end of 1938 he was acquiring works from persecuted Jewish collectors including Ernst Julius Wolffson and Adolph Menzel at massively deflated prices. To justify his actions, he might have argued that the sales allowed these people to escape.

To strengthen their control, the Nazis were using art as a tool to manipulate the psychology of the nation. Hitler deemed modern art degenerate, and had all such works purged from German museums. In 1937 the Nazis held their infamous *Entartete Kunst (Degenerate Art)* exhibition in Munich. The message was that modern art's bright colours and distorted forms were evidence of a debased modern psyche, and to reinforce this, canvases were hung lopsided, and the walls were graffitied with disparaging remarks. Following the exhibition, the Nazis started upon a course of burning degenerate art.

In 1938, the art dealer Karl Haberstock proposed to senior Nazi politicians that they halt burnings, and instead sell the works to collectors abroad to secure foreign currency. Gurlitt got wind of the plan and approached the Nazi propaganda minister to offer his services. He was one of four art dealers to attend the state-organised auction of degenerate art in Lucerne, Switzerland on 30 June 1939 – and he was the chief buyer.[5] After the war, the Allies did not prosecute dealers involved in the trade of degenerate art because in their eyes, the Germans were stealing from themselves by selling off their own national art collections.[6]

There is an argument that Gurlitt was saving these works from destruction. He was also buying degenerate works for himself. In 1940, he purchased a graphic study of two nude figures by Kirchner, which he originally bought for the König-Albert-Museum from where it had been confiscated by the Nazis. The work has a startling vivacity: the human figures are marked out in coloured chalk lines, and the expanse of white background confers a radiance. The optimism of this work hides the fate of its creator. Persecuted as a Jew, and labelled a degenerate artist, Kirchner had fled to Switzerland where, tormented by paranoid thoughts that the Nazis were going to capture him, he committed suicide. It remains unclear why Gurlitt started on this path of collaborating with the Nazis when he would have seen such suffering around him.

When the trade of degenerate art came to an end in 1940, Gurlitt tried to ingratiate himself with the Nazis. A customary practice in the Nazi party was to laud their senior politicians by giving them lavish presents. Aware of this, Gurlitt reached out and suggested a Christmas gift for Hermann Göring (1893–1946): 'There is an exceptional stained-glass window with eight images from the Lorenzen Kirche near St Marien in Mürtzel I can recommend.'[7] It was deemed suitable, and he sold the piece to the Nazis for 25,000 Reichsmarks (RM). Gurlitt's dealership had entered its darkest hour.

Soon after, the dealer began sourcing art for the Linz Commission,[8] which was responsible for acquiring works for Hitler's Führermuseum. By 1943 Gurlitt was the main art buyer in Paris. Exploiting his connections, he was highly successful. Between 1941 and October 1944, he sold over 300 paintings, sculptures, drawings, fine textiles and rugs to the Commission.[9]

All the time, he was supporting Hitler's vision, and sourcing whatever Hermann Voss, the leader of the Special Commission, requested.[10] Putting aside his preference for Expressionist art, Gurlitt bought Old Master drawings, and in the process made a fortune. On 28 June 1944, he spent 3 million RM on artworks for the Linz Commission, and he received 156,500 RM in commission on this. It is worth noting the average annual income in Germany at this time was around 2,300 RM.[11]

Most problematic was the provenance of these works, which in all probability were looted from persecuted groups. Of course, the Nazis were uninterested in this. Soon after invading France, the *Einsatzstab Reichsleiter Rosenberg* or *ERR* (Reichsleiter Rosenberg Taskforce) had targeted high-profile Jewish art dealers and collectors including Germain Seligman, Paul Rosenberg and the Rothschild family, and confiscated their art collections. Protected by the Nazi machinery, Gurlitt's sales avoided public examination as the bills were settled by the Linz Commission. It still remains difficult to ascertain the exact items he sold, let alone their provenance.

After the war, Gurlitt would be interrogated by the Bamberg-Land tribunal. He presented himself as a victim of the regime, pointing to how he'd been forced out of museum jobs, and how he himself was a quarter Jewish. He was absolved of any crime on this occasion. However, his case was reopened when a colleague informed on his potential profiteering.[12] The second case against him was closed in 1948. Gurlitt was still legally obliged to inform the government of any works that were either looted or had been previously owned by a Jew. He never came forward with any information. Within his collection there were two categories of artworks: those bought legitimately, and those with a troubled provenance. By lending the legitimate works to exhibitions around the world, Gurlitt re-established himself on the international art scene.

On his death his children, Cornelius and Renate, inherited his collection. In a letter, Renate poignantly asks her brother:

> Do you ever enjoy what you have of it in Salzburg? For I sometimes
> think, his most personal and most valuable legacy has turned
> into the darkest burden. I tremble with fear every time I think of
> it. What we have is locked away in the graphic cabinet or behind
> pinned-up curtains – no one sees it, no one enjoys it. When we
> think of it, we think of tax inspections, war, dangers, family rows.[13]

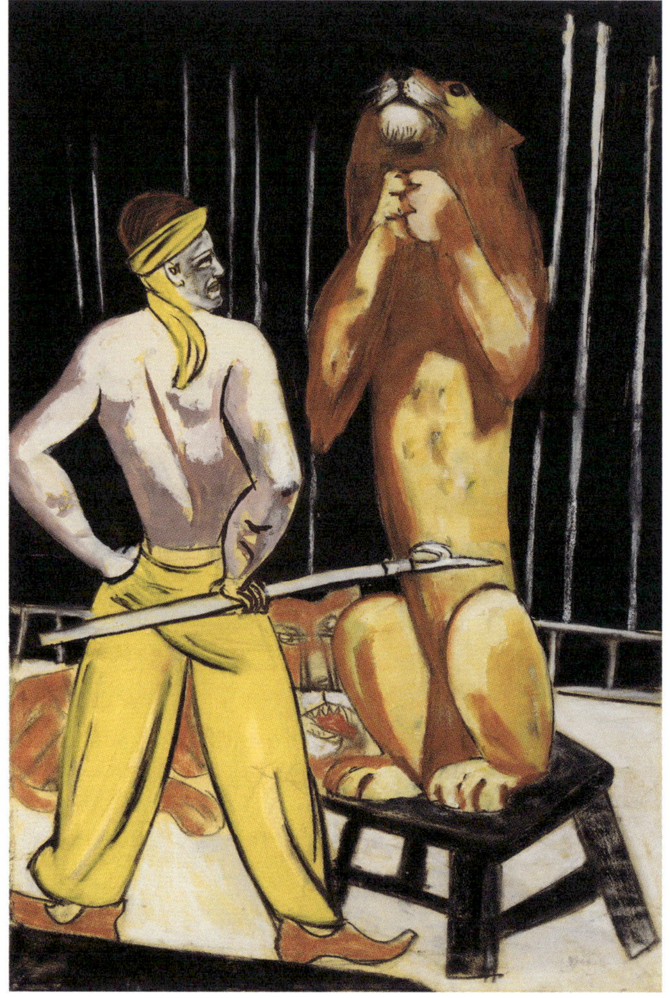

Fig. 31 Max Beckmann, *Löwenbändiger – Zirkus (Lion Tamer – Circus)*,
1930, gouache and pastel on woven paper, 90 × 59.3 cm (35⅜ × 23⅜ in.).

One of the works recovered in the raid of Cornelius Gurlitt's flat in 2012 was *Femme assise* (1921) by Henri Matisse, which had been taken from Rosenberg. It was returned to the Rosenberg family in 2015. In fact, the process of retribution began before the discovery of Gurlitt's hidden art collection. When Cornelius put the gouache *Lion Tamer – Circus* (1930, fig. 31) by Beckmann up for sale with a Cologne auction house in 2011, the work was flagged as originally belonging to the Jewish art dealer Alfred Flechtheim (1878–1937). Cornelius agreed to share the proceeds of the sale with the Flechtheim family whose lawyer released the statement, 'Mr Gurlitt was willing to accept the fact that Mr Flechtheim was a persecuted Jew who had lost his collection under duress.'[14]

As the President of the World Jewish Congress Ronald Lauder explains, 'the artworks stolen from the Jews are the last prisoners of World War II. You have to be aware that every work stolen from a Jew involved at least one death.'[15] However, the process of retribution is complicated. Families are not always aware of what was in their predecessor's art collection. Sometimes memories are sparked when works appeared in exhibitions, but then families are often thwarted by the statute which requires a claim to be made within 30 years of the artwork being lost.

In 2014, Cornelius Gurlitt instructed his legal team, 'should there be reasonable suspicion about individual works having been looted, please return them to Jewish owners.'[16] He also made an agreement with the German government to waive the statutory time restriction on a claim. It was an attempt at atonement. On his death, he left his collection to the Kunstmuseum Bern where research continues into the provenance of many works.

Stephen Radich

(1922–2007)

Controversy around art is not always negative. In fact, it is integral to political art. In December 1966, Stephen Radich opened a solo show of sculptures by Marc Morrel (b. 1937) which featured American flags, and were statements against the Vietnam War. The exhibit soon caught the attention of the police and Radich was arrested. Convicted the following year for casting contempt on the American flag, he was ordered to pay a $500 fine or serve 60 days in prison. The dealer took his case to the Supreme Court where the votes were split, leading him to launch a second appeal. In 1974, a federal judge finally overturned the case. Over those eight years the battle had become a cause célèbre in New York. Protesting against Radich's conviction, artists held *The People's Flag Show* (1970) at the Judson Memorial Church on Washington Square. Despite significant attention at the time, Radich has been lost to history, and is never mentioned in literature on art dealerships which is problematic in itself, and opens up questions around how we define a successful dealer.

Radich grew up in Mountain View, California. His parents had emigrated from what was then Yugoslavia, and his father ran a fruit farm and grew peaches, apricots and prunes. Radich left home to study at an advertising school, however, his course was interrupted when World War II broke out. He served four years in the Navy. For part of this, he was stationed on a military boat which was tasked with delivering President Roosevelt to different conferences – an unusual duty that perhaps reinforced the dealer's political interests, and his attention to freedom of speech. After the war, Radich studied art history and philosophy at Columbia University in New York. In the 1950s he worked for several commercial galleries in the city including Curt Valentin Gallery and Martha Jackson Gallery before opening the Stephen Radich Gallery at 818 Madison Avenue in 1960. Placing himself at the centre of avant-garde art, in the first year he offered an exhibition to the then relatively unknown artist, Yayoi Kusama (b. 1929).

In her autobiography, Kusama details, 'In May 1960... I signed an exclusive contract with Stephen Radich Gallery in Manhattan. The year later I held my fifth US solo exhibition, and the largest yet, at the Radich Gallery. I presented monochrome works that included collages, watercolours, and oils of enormous size – nets on canvases measuring 10, 20 and even 35ft.'[1] The works on show challenged the hegemony of Abstract Expressionism and its macho, demonstrative mark-making. Kusama's brushwork was instead meticulous; her repeated arcs and loops had the optical dazzle of Pointillism, but on a massive scale, which brought an obsessive, pulsating energy. The economy of means – the reduced colour and repetitive form – looked forward to Minimalism.

Six years later, Radich opened the infamous exhibition of Morrel's work. The artist was an ex-marine, who was just back from the Vietnam War, and was highly critical of America's role in the war. One of the centrepieces was an octopus with an American flag wrapped around its torso. Bedecked in an army helmet and a gas mask, the creature's tentacles extended malignantly outwards, signifying America's invasive involvement with Vietnam. Its radicalness can be understood in terms of French philosopher Georges Bataille's concept of the *informe*, a formlessness that is earthy and coarse. The octopus, lacking a backbone, is an amorphous creature, and in the exhibit, it was strewn across the floor.

In terms of desecrating the American flag – the issue which caused such public offence – Morrel did not sabotage the flag in any way. However, he subverted the symbolic association of a flag with an elevated height (something that is physically enacted when a flag is hoisted up a flagpole). In the octopus exhibit, the flag was at ground level, and worn by a creature from the sea depths. In a second work, the American flag was stuffed to create a corpse-like form, which was then hung by a noose.

Radich could have paid the fine, and the situation would have dissipated. However, he chose to uphold the freedom of expression in art, believing the legal decision 'could affect the future of art galleries, a very important industry in New York, whose right to show new work without interference from police could be severely threatened'.[2] At the trial, he argued that the exhibit was not about desecrating the American flag, but was a political gesture against the Vietnam War. He explained how this message was reinforced during the show by playing anti-war music in the gallery. *The New York Times* art critic Hilton Kramer was asked to give evidence at the trial – he attested Morrel had produced legitimate works of art, albeit feeble ones.[3] Notoriously conservative, Kramer's caustic slight shows a reluctance within the established art world to engage with political art.

However, anti-war events were happening within the counterculture scene. An early activist piece was *Peace Tower*; in February 1966, its frame was erected in a vacant lot at the corner of Sunset Boulevard in Los Angeles, and 400 identical-sized works from artists around the world were then stuck on. Contributors included Eva Hesse (1936–1970), Robert Motherwell and Alice Neel (1900–1984). The following year, the Artists and Writers Protest movement launched the multi-disciplinary event, the Angry Arts Week. Artists, including many famous names, contributed 150 different works which were brought together in a large collage. Leon Golub (1922–2004) outlined how the piece resisted the trend for 'perfectibility' in fine art, and was deliberately 'gross, vulgar, clumsy, ugly'.[4] These terms could equally well be used to describe Radich's octopus. This points to the way in which protest art inevitably involves an attack on artistic conventions – especially beauty – and suggests another reason why political work becomes marginalised.

The pastor at Judson Memorial Church, where *The People's Flag Show* was held following Radich's conviction, was the liberal Reverend Howard Moody (1921–2012). In his life, Moody would become known for championing of freedom speech and Civil Rights, supporting women to find safe abortions, and running an AIDS clinic. At the exhibition's opening, Moody gave the sermon, 'Symbols and Fetishes: a Left-handed Salute to the Flag', and some artists burnt a flag with some rotten meat and old bones. The dancer and choreographer Yvonne Rainer (b. 1934) performed with a group of dancers, who wore flags as bibs, but were otherwise naked. Radich attended and gave a short speech; the event celebrated his role in challenging the repressive laws concerning flag discretion.

The artist and activist Faith Ringgold (1930–2024) made the poster for the exhibition (fig. 32). In an act of defiance, she reinterpreted the key elements of the American flag: replacing the rectangle of stars with information about the exhibition, and in the place of stripes, text questioning what the flag meant to American people. Hostility towards the American flag had intensified following the assassination of President John F. Kennedy on 22 November 1963 and Martin Luther King, Jr on 4 April 1968. The murder of King especially made Black Americans distrustful of any notion of a collective nationhood. Ringgold explains:

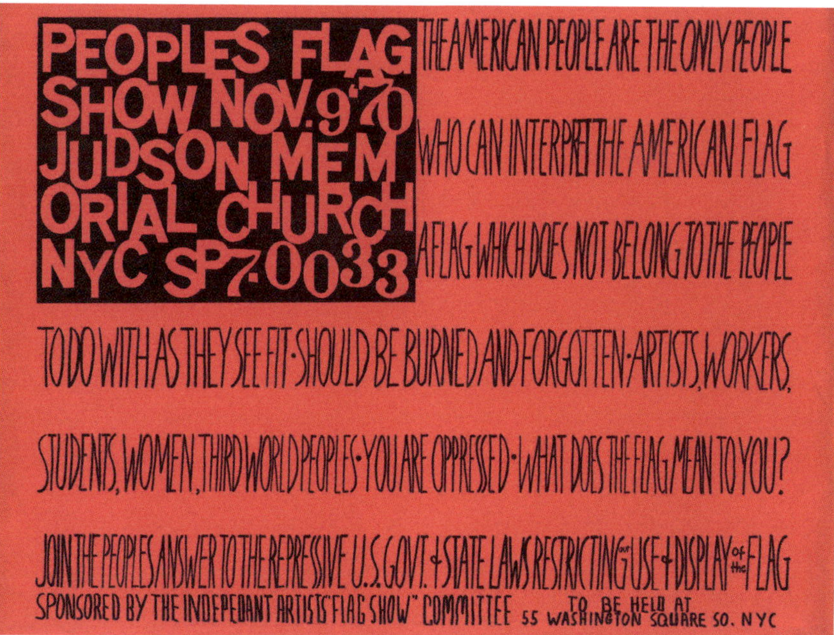

Fig. 32 Faith Ringgold, *The People's Flag Show*, 1970, offset lithograph,
45.7 × 61 cm (18 × 24 in.), Museum of Modern Art, New York.

There was a lot of false holiness attributed to the American flag.
You weren't supposed to do anything with it, and if you did you
were arrested. We thought of our American flag as a symbol of
freedom but we were losing our freedoms in the sixties. All the
blood laying all over the sidewalk. Nothing about it in the papers.
I mean silence, like it didn't happen.[5]

On the penultimate day of the exhibition, Ringgold, Jean Toche (1932–
2018) and Jon Hendricks (b. 1939) were arrested for flag desecration. They
became known as the Judson Three, and their trial also received huge
public attention.

Radich's stance resonated with far broader cultural dissent. In the
summer of 1969, Jimi Hendrix (1942–1970) had given his iconic performance
of 'The Star Spangled Banner' live at Woodstock. Evoking the American flag
in the title, the piece was a radical interpretation of the national anthem on
electric guitar with distorting feedback. The startled audience vowed that

they heard within Hendrix's rendition the sounds of planes crashing, bombs dropping and screaming. The association of Radich with this countercultural scene made him more threatening to conservative groups. Significantly, the Art Dealers Association of America, keen to dissociate the business of fine art from dissenting protest, refused to support Radich.

The question remains why Radich's exhibit was singled out. Whether knowingly or not, it transgressed boundaries. Countercultural activity in the 1960s was generally event based, and often outside in the streets, and there was a reassuring transience to the happenings. The *Peace Tower*, mentioned earlier, was a temporary structure and, tellingly, was brought down sooner than intended as the landlord buckled to local pressure. When Radich brought this contentious political art into the gallery, it was destabilising. There was a sense that the legitimising framework of fine art sanctified the political message. At the trial of the Judson Three, it was questioned whether fine art should be treated as communication, and have the protection of the First Amendment. Interestingly, sculpture was also singled out to be especially inflammatory by Assistant District Attorney Gerald Slater, who reasoned, '[Sculpture] can be touched, it can be seen, and it is more likely to arouse public wrath.'[6]

Renowned artists were supporting the anti-Vietnam War movement, but their contributions were one-off gestures, and typically they didn't work within their usual mediums. Instead they borrowed modes of communication like posters and letters from popular countercultural practice. For example, in 1969, Jasper Johns worked with the dealer Leo Castelli to release *Flag (Moratorium)*, a limited-edition poster of the American flag, to raise money for the anti-war movement. In this piece, the colours of the American flag are transformed to a lurid orange and sickly green, and there is a single bullet that punctures the work. Perhaps because the poster had a more ephemeral status, it went under the radar of the conservative authorities.

In her key text *A Different War: Vietnam in Art* (1990), Lucy Lippard argues that the art establishment avoided engaging with these controversial gestures:

> Art in 1967 was safely ensconced in its own world, primarily
> concerned with its own physical properties… Even realist art
> rarely touched on social issues, and when it did, it was rarely
> shown or written about. The older New York artists harbored
> taboos against social content inherited from the days of Stalinism

and McCarthyism, and the younger artists were unaware that art could be politically effective. They had been trained to understand that all political art was corny and old-fashioned – barely art in the highest sense – and few had the political sophistication to combat these dominant views.[7]

Lippard's argument has ramifications today, especially these last sentences which speak of the discomfort towards political art which undeniably still exists. This may, in part, explain why Stephen Radich has been forgotten, and not credited as being a significant dealer who stood up for freedom of expression.

Chapter 6

The Personality Dealer

Introduction

The last line in Tom Wolfe's essay 'The "Me" Decade' (1976) is the perfect introduction to this final chapter: 'And this one has the mightiest, holiest roll of all, the beat that goes... *Me... Me... Me... Me...*'[1] The personality dealer is all about 'me'. These extraordinary figures attracted people like fireflies to their light.

Several writers shared Wolfe's opinion that the 1970s was the decade of self-absorption. In *The Culture of Narcissism* (1978), Christopher Lasch describes how the phenomenon gained currency in the United States:

> After the political turmoil of the sixties, Americans have retreated to purely personal preoccupations... Harmless in themselves, these pursuits, elevated to a program and wrapped in rhetoric of authenticity and awareness, signify a retreat from politics and a repudiation of the recent past.[2]

This fascination with the self dates back to the French Revolution when the established powers were overthrown, and individualism was heralded. When Lasch explores this history, he emphasises how the erosion of communal values, like the family and state, left people insecure. He argues that they circumvented this anxiety by identifying their 'grandiose self' in the celebrity figure. The personality dealer functions as this star individual who radiates charisma and magnificence. In addition, their occasionally controversial lifestyles satisfied the public's salacious curiosity about the private lives of famous people.

The personalities of these dealers were immediately apparent from their unique looks. The photographer Berenice Abbott photographed Julien Levy when he first arrived in Paris to explore the art world. Her black and white photo shows him with a bald head, staring wistfully into the distance. Before he'd left America, Levy had shaved his hair off. A transgressive act in the 1930s, it set him apart. This singularity was crucial. The anarchist dealer Félix Fénéon had his 'diabolic goatee'.[3] And then, of course, there was Peggy Guggenheim with her iconic butterfly sunglasses, designed for her by the artist Edward Melcarth (1914–1973).

As with the idealist dealers, this section could have had many other fascinating inclusions like, for instance, the New York dealer Alexander Iolas (1908–1987) who was known for being candidly forthright. When he first saw René Magritte's painting *Personal Values* (1952), with its oversized objects crowding out its setting, he felt sick. He wrote and told the artist, 'I am so depressed that I cannot yet get used to it. It may be a masterpiece, but every time I look at it I feel ill... It leaves me helpless, it puzzles me, it makes me feel confused and I don't know if I like it.'[4]

Magritte was not offended, but in terms of artist-dealer relations, it was a transgression. Professionalism was put aside as the dealer's ego took over, and his characterful reaction coloured everything. It is radically different to the idealist, so sensitively attuned to their artist and their vision. The personality dealer liked to be centre stage.

This chapter follows the history of the cult of the self, and starts with the nineteenth-century dealer, Fénéon, whose anarchist views were based on the values of the French Revolution and aligned with a radical form of individualism. It then looks at the twentieth-century dealers who display the more self-absorbed narcissism identified by Wolfe, who isolates qualities in the 'me decade' which have a direct bearing on our dealers' lifestyles. For example, he points to how sex became revered as a state of self-expression and liberation, and this chimes with our glamorous dealers whose sexual persona is often part of their identity and allure.[5] He also pinpoints a current of mysticism, and our last dealer, Robert Fraser, followed this path. After his hedonistic London lifestyle collapsed, Fraser went to India where he meditated in caves and consulted with gurus – all part of the mix that made this personality dealer extraordinary.

What is exciting is how individuality manifests in their art dealing practices. By nature these people were not followers of received ideas. Led by their imagination and flair, they came up with innovative schemes. In terms of gallery space alone, our twentieth-century dealers all wanted something different to the conventional 'white cube' space – Levy hated its rigid straight lines and designed a gallery with glamorous curved walls, while George Maciunas was more extreme and came up with a way of selling art without needing a physical space at all. In all cases, our personality dealers created unique experiences.

Félix Fénéon

(1861–1944)

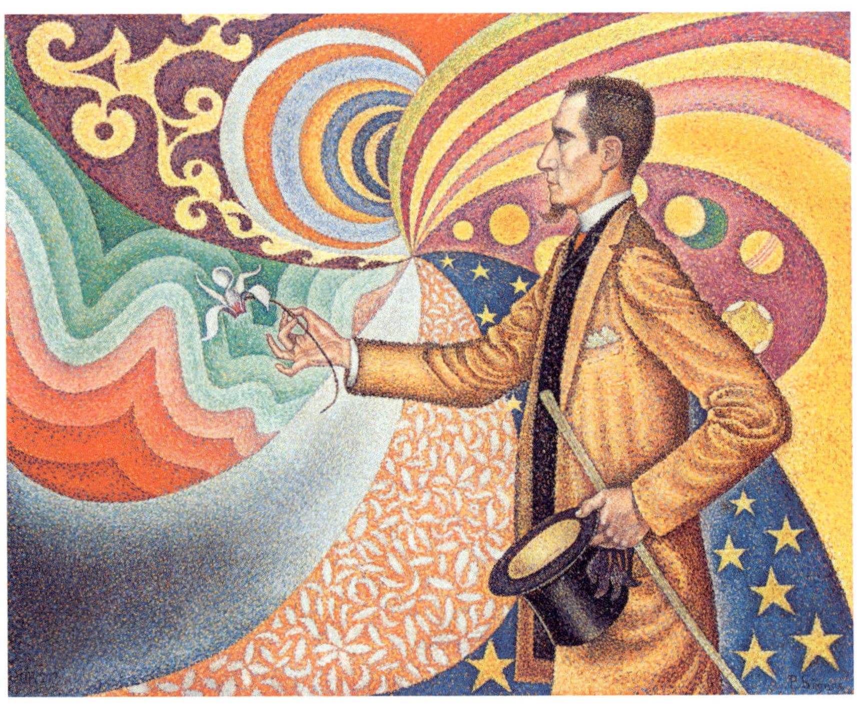

Paul Signac, *Opus 217. Against the Enamel of a Background Rhythmic with Beats and Angles, Tones and Tints, Portrait of Félix Fénéon in 1890*, 1890, oil on canvas, 73.5 × 92.5 cm (29 × 36 ½ in.), Museum of Modern Art, New York.

In the portrait of Félix Fénéon painted in 1890 by Paul Signac (1863–1935), the subject looks more like a magician than an art dealer as he presents a cyclamen flower which he seems to have conjured from the top hat tucked under his arm. Fénéon never liked the portrait, probably because Signac had depicted him in profile when he'd asked for a frontal portrait. The side viewpoint is, however, telling, for the dealer appears distant and doesn't connect with the viewer. The novelist Remy de Gourmont (1858–1915) evoked his 'air d'un Mephistopheles americain'.[1] Indeed, Fénéon was frustratingly difficult to pin down. In his political writing, he used multiple pseudonyms, including the female names Thérèse, Lucie and Ophélix. Adding to his elusiveness, he played different roles, and as well as being an art dealer for Bernheim-Jeune Galerie in Paris, he was a critic, an anarchist, an art collector and a suspected bomber. Fénéon's unique art dealership was influenced by his varied pursuits and colourful nature.

Born in Turin, Italy, Fénéon grew up in Burgundy, France. At the age of 18, he served his obligatory military service and then sat a competitive exam to work for the Ministry of War. After placing first, he was offered the position and moved to Paris. He worked there for 13 years and was clearly valued, becoming chief clerk. Meanwhile he plunged himself into the avant-garde scene and started attending the Tuesday salons held by the poet Stéphane Mallarmé (1842–1898). Mallarmé was advocating that the purpose of language and art was to reveal the essence of things. He believed strongly that the creator must be anonymous, explaining, 'The pure work implies the disappearance of the poet as a speaker, yielding his initiative to words.'[2]

In the 1880s Fénéon co-founded three short-lived art journals, and was responsible for saving Arthur Rimbaud's poetry collection *Illuminations* (1886) from obscurity by publishing the poems in instalments in the magazine *La Vogue* in 1886. Included in the collection is the poem 'Barbarian', notable for its stark juxtapositions, exemplified by the line: 'The pennant of bloody meat against the silk of arctic seas and flowers.'[3] This anarchic literary context shaped Fénéon's mindset. His early art reviews attack academic art – on one occasion, he caustically dismisses the academic painter William-Adolphe Bouguereau (1825–1905), and his frivolous nudes, with their 'little nude asses'.[4] He was intent on discovering a modern art form that had the vivacity of the poetry he was reading. Mallarmé had found this in the Impressionists, but Fénéon disliked how the Impressionist pictures only captured a fugitive moment and were so sketchily executed. He was looking for something more permanent.

Following Mallarmé's position, Fénéon fostered an anonymity, rarely signing his art reviews, or sometimes adding only his initials. He saw himself as a channel between art and public. In his criticism, he didn't explore the creator's personality, or delve into their biography. Instead, he focussed purely on formal expression. It was a radical new position for art criticism, and an important precursor to modernist art criticism of the latter part of the twentieth century. Possessing an incredible way with words, his writing is exceptionally lively. His friend, the writer Téodor de Wyzewa (1862–1917), noted at the time that Fénéon engaged in a 'grammatical hylozoism' whereby he conferred the artistic forms with a living entity. To quote Wyzewa, 'He always sees the sky incurving itself, the brushstrokes scattering THEMSELVES, the little boats inverting their own image in the water.'[5]

In 1884, Fénéon discovered the painting *Bathers at Asnières* (1884) by Georges Seurat (1859–1891) at the Salon d'automne, hidden away in the café. The extraordinary stillness of the work imbues it with a timelessness, embodying the permanence Fénéon had been searching for. The painting unveiled a new reality.

Fénéon was particularly interested in Seurat's technique of applying the paint in small dots of pure, vibrant colour. He would champion the method, and coin the term 'Neo-Impressionism'. The aesthetic ratified his anarchist sympathies. Echoing his belief in a radical individualism, each coloured dot had autonomy, and when seen at a slight distance, they came together, and suggested a unified image. As art historian Patricia Leighton explains, they guided 'the viewer towards an equivalent social harmony'.[6] Fénéon always had this highly individual appreciation, and artists had to match his criteria for him to write about them. Later he would be just as uncompromising in his dealership, during which he was prepared to sacrifice profit to exhibit artists that shared his vision.

While playing civil servant in his day job, Fénéon was penning political articles for the anarchist newspaper *L'En-Dehors*. Amidst a highly repressive government, anarchism emerged as a potent and widespread ideology, attracting numerous artists and writers to its cause.[7] However, Fénéon became more extremist, later advocating violence as a more effective way to bring about change.[8] On 26 April 1894, he was arrested on suspicion of planting a bomb at Restaurant Foyot. In the explosion, the writer Laurent Tailhade

(1854–1919) was blinded in one eye. It is also highly likely that Fénéon had collaborated on an earlier bombing, on that occasion providing the bomber, Émile Henry, with one of his mother's dresses as a disguise.

After being arrested for the Foyot bombing, Fénéon spent three months in prison, and was tried in the infamous 'Trial of the Thirty'. When interrogated, he blithely goaded the judge with his wordplay. For example, when it was put to him that he had been spotted talking to a known anarchist behind a gas lamp, he replied coolly: 'Can you tell me, Monsieur le Président, which side of a gas lamp is its behind?'[9] His disarming wit worked, as he was acquitted. He was fired from his post at the Ministry, but in 1896 a friend secured him a job at the leading avant-garde literary art journal, *La Revue Blanche*, which put Fénéon in contact with a new generation of artists including the Nabis – one of whom, Félix Vallotton (1865–1925), was producing powerful graphic works. It is likely Vallotton introduced Fénéon to Galerie Bernheim-Jeune.

It seems an unlikely marriage: an anarchist bomber and a respected art dynasty. Fénéon's own circle was confounded, with Signac declaring, 'Felix has joined monkey-nut Bernheim... I don't see our friend winning out over the boorishness of those industrialists.'[10] However, Signac would change his mind quickly when Fénéon produced sales. For the gallery, hiring Fénéon was a risky but ingenious decision. Founded in 1863 by Alexandre Bernheim, the gallery had sold Impressionist art, but this movement had lost its avant-garde edge. Alexandre's sons Gaston (1870–1953) and Josse (1870–1941) wanted to reinvigorate things, and Fénéon had connections with the younger generation. Moreover, his history as a bomber and anarchist writer brought a desirable frisson of danger. Essentially, he was the perfect figurehead to attract the avant-garde and revitalise the gallery's image.

In 1906 Fénéon was put in charge of their new contemporary art gallery at 15 rue Richepanse.[11] Initially, he showcased work by his Neo-Impressionist friends, holding shows for Signac, Maximilien Luce (1858–1941) and Henri-Edmond Cross (1856–1910). And Neo-Impressionism had a lasting influence on his dealership, shaping his taste for bold colour and dynamic forms. Soon he turned to the radical Fauves who had shocked the art world with their audacious colours.[12] When Henri Matisse showed his portrait of his wife, *Woman in a Hat*, at the 1905 Salon d'Automne, it had been ridiculed, and people had turned up to laugh at it. Even today, the clashing colours are brutal: Madame Matisse's face is bisected by a lurid green line, with harsh dabs of colour on either side. In 1907 Fénéon offered Matisse representation.

The prestige of being represented by Galerie Bernheim-Jeune was attractive to the artist, who had a young family and was seeking stability. In 1910 it hosted his first solo exhibition.

Fénéon had an ingenious way of promoting Matisse. Reflecting his own chameleon-like personality, the dealer marketed different 'Matisses'. To the American audience, he sent mostly the artist's graphic work while he sold his interiors and still lifes in Germany. The writer Gertrude Stein's opinion was that 'the influence of a man called Fénéon... changed the fortunes of Matisse. He now had an established position.'[13]

Fénéon approached other Fauves – the once suspected bomber was disruptive and prepared to poach artists from other dealers. He convinced Albert Marquet (1875–1947) to leave Galerie Druet, and Kees van Dongen (1877–1968) transferred from Daniel-Henry Kahnweiler. Significantly, his competitive strategy had a positive effect on the art market, and soon there emerged a fruitful rivalry between Kahnweiler representing Pablo Picasso and the Cubists, and Fénéon with his Fauves. It was a compelling narrative, and buyers joined camps, and became 'Picassoites and Matisseites'.[14]

Fénéon's personality created a unique customer experience – certainly, there was a very different atmosphere to the pampered luxury of other commercial galleries. It is worth remembering that his client base was middle class – the intended target of his bomb attack. This might explain why customers were treated with mild disdain. His sharpness complemented the avant-garde identity of the gallery, and made the customers work for his trust. Following his ideals, he fostered an anonymity in his transactions, and typically, he'd present clients with a work of art, and leave them alone in a room, rarely commenting. Ironically, his silence was a successful selling strategy, creating a sanctified atmosphere around the display of the artwork. Because of his wit Fénéon always had the upper hand. Once a customer, attempting to ridicule an Amedeo Modigliani nude, asked, 'Sir, tell me frankly, would you sleep with that woman there?' Fénéon had the perfect answer: 'Never with a woman who is three millimetres thick.'[15]

Another eccentricity was that he treated the artworks as living entities, just as he had done in his writing. This reverence for the artworks endeared him to many artists. Matisse told a story of some collectors trying to buy some paintings, and Fénéon dissuading them. Once the couple left, Matisse enquired why he'd done this, and Fénéon's response was, 'But my dear friend... you surely did not want your beautiful compositions to go *to live* with those stuffy people!'[16]

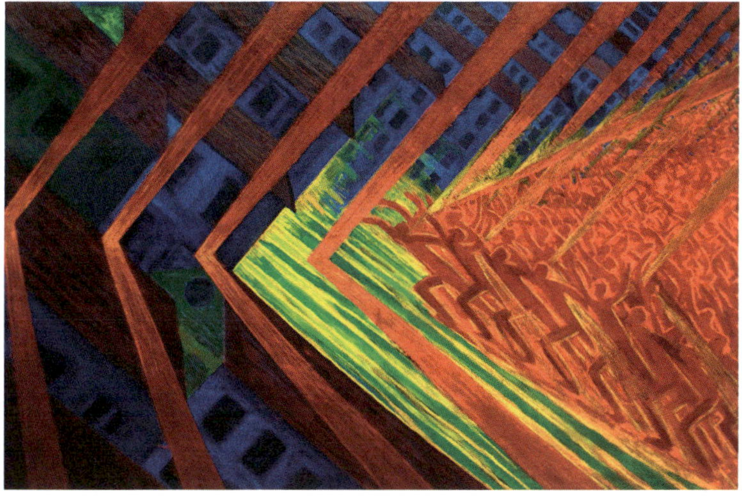

Fig. 33 Luigi Russolo, *The Revolt, c.* 1911, oil on canvas,
150.8 × 230.7 cm (59 ⅜ × 90 ⅞ in.), Kunstmuseum Den Haag.

In 1912, Fénéon embraced the Italian Futurists and gave them their first show in Paris. It was a meaningful exchange since they shared ideals. The painters were drawing inspiration from the dealer's favoured Neo-Impressionists and replicating their energising dots of raw colour while also pushing new boundaries. Resonating with Fénéon's politics, the art movement was also advocating for social revolution; *The Revolt* (*c.* 1911, fig. 33) by Luigi Russolo (1885–1947) shows an advancing crowd, united in action.

Returning to Signac's enigmatic portrait of Fénéon, the image of the dealer may tell very little about him. However, his personality is captured in the decorative background and the rhythmic swirls of anarchic coloured patterns that surround him. In all aspects of his life, Fénéon sought the energy and provocation so vibrantly manifested in these forms. He embodied the autonomy and self-contained nature of the Neo-Impressionist art he promoted. When he moved into art dealership, he made no compromises. Never interested in commercial success, he supported radical artists, and refused to pander to his bourgeois buyers, approaching them with the same wit and irreverence that characterised his art criticism and political writing. His dealership was a tool for extending his revolution. In his political life he had been an aesthete, once describing a bomb that killed six people, as a 'delightful kettle'.[17] His gallery went on to explode with colour.

Julien Levy

(1906–1981)

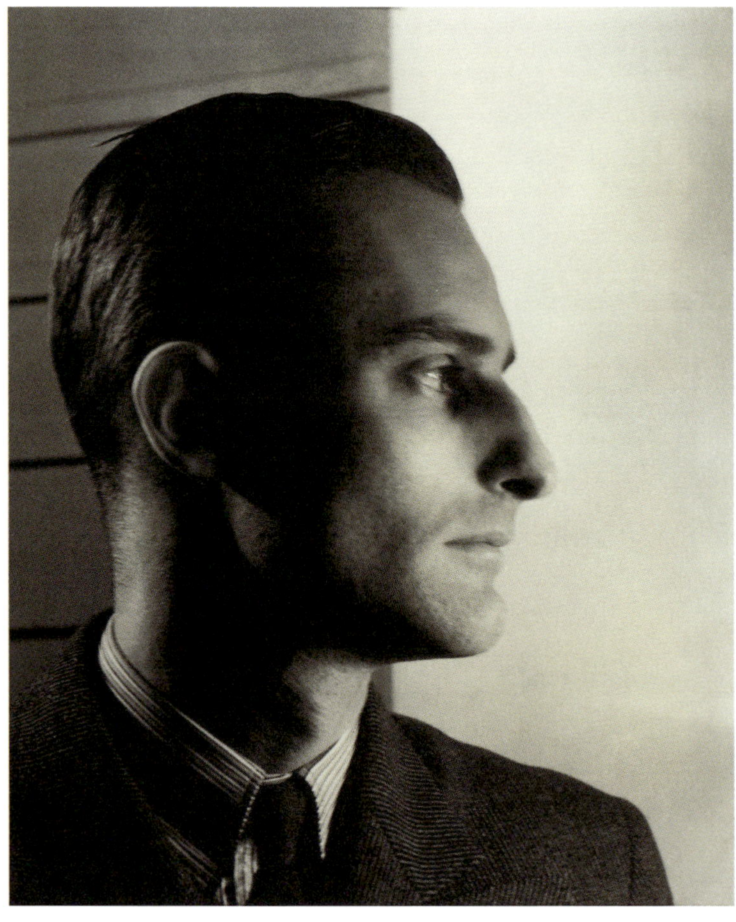

Jay Leyda, *Julien Levy*, c. 1930–39.
The Art Institute of Chicago.

Julien Levy advised the artist Alexander Calder (1898–1976), early in his career, to stop using motors in his mobiles and let them hang freely. Animated by natural forces, Calder's mobiles spiralled in wondrous patterns, their free-flowing movement reflecting Levy's character. The dealer rarely had a plan and was propelled by the promise of new experiences. His first wife, Joella, said he could not bear to leave a party early in case something exciting happened,[1] and the dealer himself explains:

> I really seemed to follow my nose and my nose led me into all kinds of things that eventually became more and more interesting for me, and fortunately kept me away from most of the kinds of things that your nose can get you involved in if you were absolutely without any discipline. I didn't have discipline, but I found my way somehow into the most extraordinary, lucky coincidences.[2]

His charmed existence was part of his attraction. For the artist Dorothea Tanning (1910–2012) 'his persona was a magnet of adjectives. They swarmed around him, clung to his profile (lovely to draw), hair (shiny and black), silhouette (slim, gracile), the ensemble elegant, suave, debonair, elusive....'[3] People were drawn to him, and his gallery became *the place* to see the most advanced contemporary art and be served cocktails. The glamorous dealer liked to boast, 'I invented the cocktail opening. That had never been done before.[4]

Born in 1906, Levy grew up in New York where his father was a successful real estate developer. He studied at Harvard University where his fluid lifestyle began. He failed his first year English exam because, according to him, he was too liberal with his commas. His mother intervened and got him transferred onto Paul Sach's pioneering museum course, which was looking beyond fine art, at cinema and photography – disciplines that would be central to Levy's dealership. Key art dealers came to speak there, and many of Levy's student cohort would play significant roles in the art world, including Alfred H. Barr Jr, the future director of the Museum of Modern Art in New York. Levy became fascinated by cinema, the slapstick of Buster Keaton and Hollywood stars. A few months before his course ended, he suddenly dropped out and headed off to Hollywood where he found work on a film set.

He eventually found his way back to New York where he met Marcel Duchamp. By his own admission, he was a hero worshipper. He had two 'godfathers', Duchamp and Alfred Stieglitz. Levy told Duchamp of his plans to make a film, and the artist convinced him to come with him to Paris, and meet Man Ray. In February 1927, before they set off, Levy shaved his hair off – he said Duchamp put him up to it.

His time in Paris was a heady mix of parties and café encounters. The first day there, he joined a gathering at Peggy Guggenheim's studio where he met the writer and artist Mina Loy (1882–1966) who ran an unusual lamp shop. Loy became his third 'godparent', and her aesthetic taste was an important influence. Her apartment was a poetic assortment of flea market finds, and her own artworks. Art and life merged in a place where birdcages were used as room dividers, and the silver paper pasted on the wall to hide cracks became exquisite patterning.[5] It was an introduction to a Surrealist sensibility – an art that challenged expectations and conjured marvellous fantasies.

At the same party, Levy met Loy's daughter, Joella. He fell madly in love with her, and they later married. He soon was part of the Surrealist scene, and friends with André Breton, Max Ernst and Man Ray. He explains how this played to his advantage: 'when it came to opening my own gallery [I] already knew the gang as far as modern art went.'[6] Levy loved the glamour of this scene, and when he recounts his wedding day in his autobiography, he relishes mentioning that he'd asked James Joyce and Constantin Brâncuși to be the witnesses. The latter came bearing the gift of the oval bronze, *The Newborn* (1920).

Levy never made the film in Paris. Over the years he had ideas for numerous projects that were never realised and he admitted to being pathologically lazy. But his artistic mind was not wasted – it shaped his dealership, and sharpened his appreciation for the most vital art. In Paris, he discovered the photographer Eugène Atget (1857–1927) and bought many works from him. Living in poverty, Atget had photographed an old Paris which was vanishing amid the modernisation of the city. The haunting psychology of his images chimed with the Surrealist aesthetic. *Boulevard de Strasbourg, Corsets, Paris* (1912, fig. 34) shows a ghostly window display with headless mannequins in tight corsets. When Atget died in 1927, Berenice Abbott (1898–1991) rescued his works, and sold part of the collection to Levy for $1,000. Levy held a solo exhibition of Atget's work at New York's Weyhe Gallery bookshop where he was working at the time, and this show set him on his path as an art dealer. He offered the collection to MoMA who declined; Levy was ahead of his time.

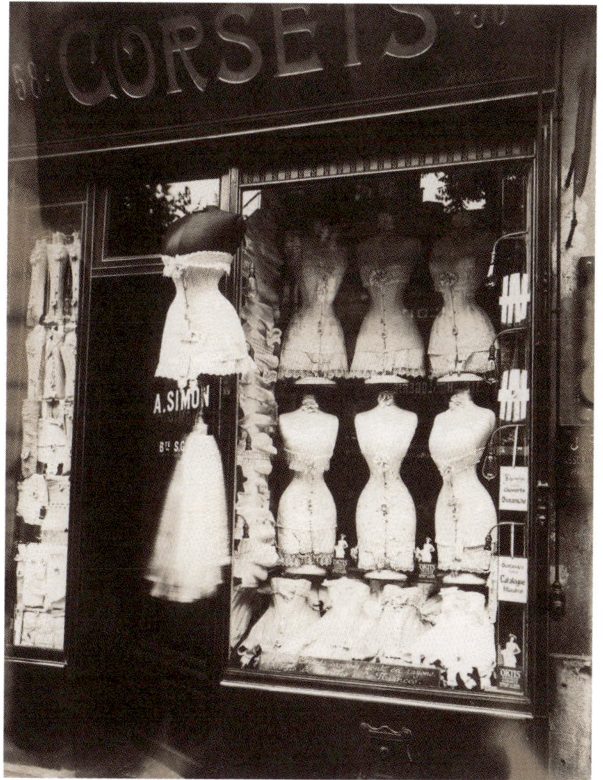

Fig. 34 Eugène Atget, *Boulevard de Strasbourg, Corsets, Paris*, 1912,
gelatin silver print from glass negative, 22.4 × 17.5 cm (8⅞ × 6⅞ in.).

In 1931, he opened Julien Levy Gallery. He wrote and told his mother, 'I have found a beautiful location, about 20 by 50 feet, with a good shop window, very *bon marché* because of the Depression.'[7] Over the course of his 17-year dealership, he had four galleries. His second space, at 15 East 57th Street, had a particularly innovative design which he conceived himself. An article in *Vogue* celebrated its glamorous look, 'The newly-planned walls are broken up artfully, dipping and waving and straightening out again. The rug is dark wine, the walls white, the effect, naked and modern.'[8] In terms of curation, the stark white space was radical, though it would soon become the classic design for commercial galleries and was to be picked up by Betty Parsons and Leo Castelli. The current taste was for sumptuous, wallpapered interiors, and interestingly, Levy kept an element of this. As well as the dark wine rug, there was also a scarlet room where more ephemeral items like theatre posters, costume designs and old books were exhibited. The bric-a-brac display suggested old curiosity shops, but also Loy's apartment.

One particularly noteworthy feature in the design was Levy's marvellous curving wall, which had 'the shape of a painter's palette'.[9] Levy explained later how he was keen to get away from 'the rigidity of the Bauhaus',[10] and its rectilinear form, insisting the curving wall was his invention and that it predated Frank Lloyd Wright's curved architectural forms.[11] The effect was transformative. When hung on the curved wall, the pictures were no longer presented in a regimented line, but were revealed as an unfolding experience. Curator Ingrid Schaffner describes the cinematic effect: 'Accelerated by the viewer's advance, the curve rapidly dissolved one image into another, like frames in a film screened through a projector.'[12] The reference to cinema brings to mind his time at Harvard where he'd become fascinated by early Hollywood films.

When he opened his first gallery on Madison Avenue, Levy's intention had been to focus on photography. He held a succession of photography exhibitions, and showed avant-garde films including Luis Buñuel (1900–1983) and Salvador Dalí's infamous *Un Chien Andalou* (1929), known for its nightmarish montage sequence of an eyeball being cut open. Levy considered that, 'the showing of this, more than anything else, established Dalí's reputation in this country.'[13] However, neither the film nor the photography exhibitions made any sales, prompting Levy to diversify. He would soon become known as New York's Surrealist dealer.

In 1932, Levy opened his exhibition *Surréalisme* which proved to be a critical sensation, with Dalí's *The Persistence of Memory* (1931), with its famous melting clocks, drawing most attention. Following this, Levy held solo exhibitions for the key Surrealists including Ernst, Dalí and Leonor Fini (1907–1996), and many of them had multiple shows at the gallery. These played a critical role in introducing this European tradition to America. However, Levy was also extending the parameters of the movement. In Europe, Breton controlled the identity of the group, even ejecting artists if they didn't meet his standards. Levy was more empathetic and could see the individual merits of an artist. In 1931, the reclusive Joseph Cornell came to his gallery to show Levy his collages. While the artist openly admitted the influence of Ernst, the dealer saw something else, something more innocent, more spiritual. The two of them talked about the artist's commitment to

Christian Science, and Levy mentioned that his mother-in-law and wife were also Christian Scientists. He recommended the artist work in three dimensions, and Cornell went on to create his shadow boxes. *Untitled (Tilly Losch)* (1935–38) was one of the first and it has the distinct Cornell other-worldly atmosphere with the dancer Tilly Losch floating above a glacial landscape. The act of arranging the elements in the boxes became a focal point for art as devotional practice. The contents were intensely cared for, and reflected the placement of objects at religious shrines, and the adornment of religious icons with gems and precious metals. Levy supported the new direction and held several solo shows with him.

Levy also played a significant role in expanding Surrealism beyond the gallery and into shop design and live events. He was instrumental in Dalí's commission for the Bonwit-Teller store in 1939 for which the artist designed two themed windows, one representing Day, and the other Night. These windows were an extraordinary sight: wax hands reached out from a bathtub lined with black lambskin, and taxidermy formed parts of a four-poster bed. And the Surreal drama escalated when Dalí discovered his display had been altered. Enraged, he climbed in, and thrust the bath through the window, sending glass shattering across the pavement. He was arrested two days before his solo exhibition opened at Levy's gallery, but the sensational press coverage worked to their favour. The same year, Dalí's *Dream of Venus* (1939) opened at the World Fair. The project was Levy's brainchild. He thought a Surrealist funhouse might make the movement more accessible to an American audience, and his own designs included a dream corridor, an audible staircase and rocking floorboards. However, to attract more visitors, Levy's concept was handed over to Dalí who realised an underwater fantasy. Visitors entered his sea castle via a fish head whereupon they discovered half-naked models, dressed as mermaids, swimming in an underwater parlour, complete with a roaring fire. The spectacle was pure Dalí.

Levy was equally thrilled by Dalí's surreal theatre as by Cornell's tender spirituality. While he gave artists opportunities, and offered advice that influenced their paths, his own life remained in flux. Unanchored, there was a fragility to him. His first wife, Joella, tired of his endless affairs and drinking, divorced him. In 1942, Levy left his gallery to serve in the military and by the time he returned in 1943, Peggy Guggenheim had replaced him as New York's Surrealist art dealer. He searched for new talent. Many years before, Arshile Gorky (*c.* 1904–1948) had shown him his drawings, but he had felt at the time they were too Picasso-like and had advised Gorky to find his voice. But Gorky had since flourished, and over the next few years Levy arranged several solo shows with him.

In 1948, the artist and dealer were in a car crash – Levy broke his collarbone. Gorky's injuries were much more serious, and he was in traction for weeks. This, combined with other struggles, overwhelmed Gorky and he killed himself. Levy had followed the rhythm of other people's lives, and this tragedy was his undoing. He kept his gallery open for a last season to hold a retrospective for the artist. The final chapter of his memoir is titled 'Goodbye my Loveds'[14] – the words Gorky chalked on the rafter of the barn before he died.

Peggy Guggenheim

(1898–1979)

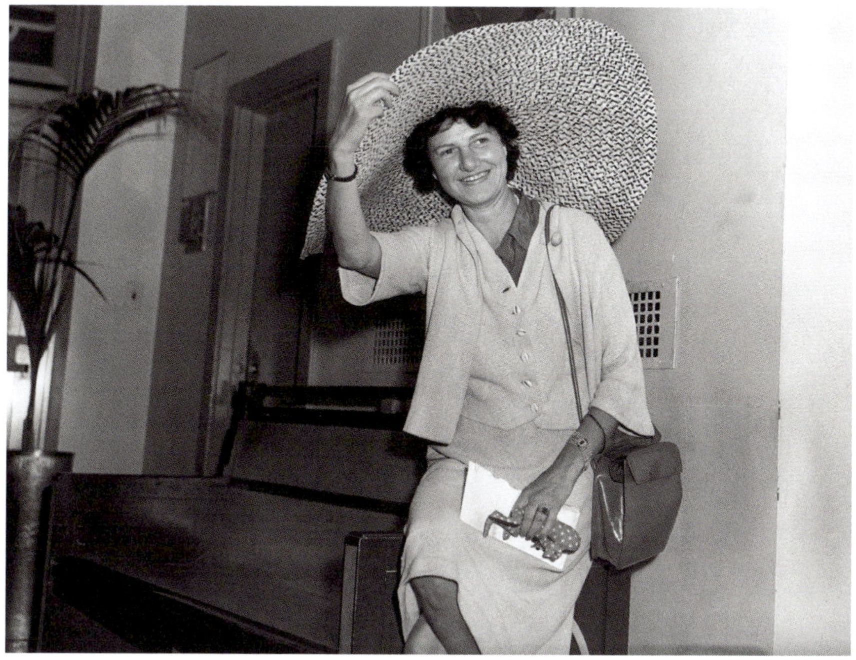

*Peggy Guggenheim arriving in New York
from France aboard the* Atlantic Clipper,
14 July 1941. Photographer unknown.

Peggy Guggenheim's Venetian palace sits on the Grand Canal and, when Guggenheim was alive, she had the bronze sculpture, *The Angel of the City* (1948) by Marino Marini (1901–1980), placed in full view of the passing boats. It's a life-affirming piece: the figure on horseback radiates pleasure with his outstretched arms, head back and erect phallus. Wickedly irreverent, Guggenheim relished telling interviewers his penis was detachable, and could be removed if a boat of nuns passed by.[1]

Guggenheim was a character. At the high point of her dealership, she released her infamous autobiography, in which she candidly recounted her sex life.[2] The critic Clement Greenberg said her contribution to art would take time to be fully appreciated, implying that the gossip had to dissipate first.[3] However, Guggenheim's life and career were entangled. For her, 'It was all about art and love.'[4] As a woman living before the sexual revolution of the 1960s, it was radical to live sensually. Indeed, the Marini figure embodies the natural, sensuous charm that drove Guggenheim.

The dealer described her childhood as 'excessively unhappy'.[5] Brought up by nannies, she only spent an hour with her mother every day while her father, whom she adored, was usually embroiled in a love affair. Precocious, Guggenheim was aware of his infidelities, and aged seven challenged him, 'Papa you must have a mistress as you stay out so many nights.'[6] Being educated at home intensified her claustrophobic existence and her memories have a lurid quality.[7] She remembered a bearskin rug with a lolling tongue and broken tooth which sometimes fell out.[8] The macabre beast suggested the Surreal artworks that she later sold in her galleries. On 14 April 1912, her father was on the *Titanic* when it took its maiden voyage and sank. At 14 years old, she was told her father had died nobly and, dressed in his evening wear, had gone to save others.[9]

There was a vulnerability to Guggenheim. She was insecure about her appearance, and compared herself with her sisters Benita and Hazel, who were very beautiful. She especially hated her nose, and was one of the first to try plastic surgery.[10] Interviewed about Guggenheim, the art historian John Richardson (1924–2019) said she lacked 'beauty' and 'art historical training', and had 'no innate taste' for art.[11] It is a pretty comprehensive damnation from someone she considered a friend, not to mention inaccurate. In 1919, Guggenheim received a considerable inheritance, but she went to work in Sunwise Turn bookshop in New York.[12] She was reading the great novelists, and art history texts by Bernard Berenson and was fortunate to be able to afford to travel, and explore art, following the well-trodden path of most male art dealers.

For Guggenheim, sex and art were always inextricably connected. Piquing gossip, she had affairs with many well-known figures including Samuel Beckett (1906–1989) and Max Ernst. The artist Marina Abramović (b. 1946) is unusual in recognising Guggenheim's progressiveness: 'She had a really good dose of sexual energy which was transmitted in her personal life and art. She definitely would take the man she wanted on her terms, so refreshing.'[13] Refusing the idea that women should be chaste, Guggenheim was open about her attraction to men and in interview talked with great rapture of Alberto Giacometti's large lion-like head and shaggy hair, and Ernst's 'beautiful body'.[14] Her appreciation of art was driven by this sensuality. Certainly, it motivated her first art purchase, the bronze *Head and Shell* (c. 1933) by Jean Arp (1886–1966); the dealer describes how, 'I fell so in love with it that I asked to take it in my hands. The instant I felt it, I wanted to own it.'[15]

In 1938, she embarked on her first art venture, and opened the Guggenheim Jeune gallery on Cork Street in London where she focussed mostly on Surrealism, holding landmark solo shows for Wolfgang Paalen and Yves Tanguy. Guggenheim's liberated lifestyle chimed with the Surrealists' revolt against bourgeois life, and their espousal of free love and erotic desire. The gallery opened with an exhibition of drawings by Jean Cocteau (1889–1963). Guggenheim had visited the artist in Paris, who received her in bed in an opiate haze. One work, a bedsheet with drawings inscribed, didn't make it through customs. Guggenheim explains, 'It was not the nudes but the pubic hairs which worried them.'[16]

From the start, Guggenheim was interested in making art accessible to the public and there's a wonderful story of a schoolteacher approaching her after seeing her Wassily Kandinsky show and asking to borrow some works to show to his pupils. Remarkably, he drove off with ten canvases, and returned the next day to say his class had loved seeing them.

While travelling, Guggenheim encountered radical curation styles. She discovered Tanguy's work at the Gradiva gallery where André Breton had created his Surreal fantasy. In 1938, the International Surrealist Exhibition opened in Paris, and here, visitors negotiated their way through darkened rooms by torchlight, and in one room, Marcel Duchamp had hung coal sacks from the ceiling. Guggenheim would implement similar ploys to involve the visitor in her later career.

When the exhibitions in her London gallery failed to translate into sales, Guggenheim decided to close, and focus instead on setting up a contemporary art museum in London. She approached Herbert Read (1893–1968) who resigned from his position at the *Burlington Magazine* to be the director. Read drew up a list of the most important artists to be included in their museum, but World War II broke out, and made their plan unviable. She moved to Paris, the epicentre of avant-garde art, taking Read's list with her, and her friend Duchamp offered advice, and put her in contact with artists.

In Paris, Guggenheim famously bought 'a picture a day'.[17] She purchased *Bird in Space* (1932–40) by Constantin Brâncuși. An extraordinarily beautiful work, it captures the graceful movement of a bird in flight in the sinuous line of the polished bronze. It represents Guggenheim's commitment to non-objective, abstract art. In Paris, artists heard Guggenheim was looking for new art and as the dealer explains: 'People telephoned me all day long and went to my house in the morning and brought me pictures in bed.'[18] She bought a canvas from Salvador Dalí while lying in bed.

By 1941 the Germans were advancing on Paris, and the city was not safe. Guggenheim was Jewish and in great danger but, as she explained, 'It wasn't in my nature to be afraid.'[19] During her time in France, Guggenheim had bought 50 works of art for $40,000 (a collection now worth millions) and she was now determined to find a safe place to store her works.[20] She approached the Louvre who said her collection, which included works by Pablo Picasso, Dalí and Paul Klee (1879–1940) was not noteworthy enough for them to help. She managed to have her artworks shipped as household goods, and then fled to the United States.

In October 1942, Guggenheim opened her gallery, *Art of This Century* at 30 West 57th Street in New York. Setting it apart, it had a museum element, with permanent galleries for her modern European collection. Complementing the recently opened Museum of Modern Art, it played a crucial role in introducing America to the latest developments, highlighting two trends: abstract art and Surrealism. With great panache, Guggenheim stated her allegiance to both at the opening of her gallery by wearing two earrings: one by the abstract artist Alexander Calder, and one by the Surrealist Tanguy.

Guggenheim approached the architect Frederick Kiesler (1890–1965) to design the gallery. He came up with four spaces, and while Kiesler had free rein, Guggenheim's priorities also informed the design. The Daylight gallery displayed the art for sale and was a conventional space with white walls. The subversive curation happened in the rooms that housed her collection. The Surrealist room recalled the fantastical exhibits at the International Surrealist exhibition and Breton's Gradiva gallery. Engendering the distorted perspective of a hall of mirrors, it had concave gum walls, and the curves continued in Kiesler's undulating furniture, and pedestals. A sense of the uncanny was brought into play with theatrical gags – the lights were sequenced to turn on and off, so every three seconds one half of the room was plunged into darkness while the other half lit up. Adding to the drama, the recording of a roaring train reverberated through the space.

The Non-Objective room was equally experimental. The paintings were attached to ultramarine canvas sheets, which hung from ropes from the ceiling, and appeared to float in space. Reflecting Guggenheim's own intimate relationship with art, the set-up involved the visitor. Instead of addressing the artwork at eye level, the work was brought closer and hung lower, making for a more bodily experience. They could also pull the canvas towards them. Kiesler and Guggenheim used very thin frames for the paintings, again encouraging intimacy with the work. In the Kinetic gallery, the visitor's sense of touch was engaged. To experience Duchamp's *Box in a Valise* (1935–41), they had to turn a wheel, which made the contents of the suitcase pop into view.

The design of the gallery had implications well beyond curation. It was suggesting ideas (like spectator involvement, and a temporal-based art) that were relevant to the next generation of artists. Guggenheim produced a highly original catalogue for her collection. She rejected the protocol of having critics and art historians explain the art, and instead asked artists who provided far more personal essays.

In terms of the commercial gallery, Guggenheim was one of the earliest supporters of the emerging American scene, and held the first solo shows with Mark Rothko, Robert Motherwell and Clyfford Still. She considered Jackson Pollock to be her greatest achievement. When he first submitted a work to her Spring Salon, she dismissed his work as unruly, but quickly changed her mind. As well as giving him a solo exhibition, she commissioned him to make *Mural* (1943) for her hallway. At about 2.4 by 6 metres (8 by 20 feet), it was on an unprecedented scale for the artist, and he struggled initially. However, the final work, with its immersive, calligraphic rhythms, anticipated his mature works, like *Autumn Rhythm (Number 30)*

(1950). Importantly, Guggenheim gave Pollock a monthly stipend and lent him money to buy a house in Long Island, away from New York's taverns. For a while, he was more stable and produced some of his best work.

In 1943, Guggenheim showed the first-ever exhibition dedicated to women artists. The intention of *Exhibition by 31 Women* was to disrupt the idea that women were simply muses for male artists. Méret Oppenheim exhibited her visceral fur-lined cup, *Object* (1936). All of the women had worked hard to be taken seriously, just like Guggenheim. It is worth remembering that when she had visited Picasso at his studio, he'd dismissed her with the comment, 'Madame, you will find the lingerie on the second floor.'[21] The exhibition received poor reviews, with critics questioning whether an exhibition on women's art was worthwhile, which reinforces Guggenheim's plucky resilience in the face of the prevailing chauvinism of the art world.

Guggenheim's unique vision for art was undeniably shaped by her personality: her vitality and sensualism. In 1976 she told an interviewer, 'I was the original liberated woman... I did everything, was everything; I was totally free financially, intellectually and sexually.'[22] Guggenheim was a life force, and old age didn't suit her, as she declared: 'It is horrible to get old. It's one of the worst things that can happen to you.'[23] And yet her provocation and sense of mischief live on through her art collection, especially in that ecstatic sculpture by Marino Marini.

George Maciunas

(1931–1978)

It is unlikely that George Maciunas would ever have called himself an art dealer. The self-appointed leader of the avant-garde art movement, Fluxus, he was outspoken about his dislike of professionalism in art, and denigrated art institutions. Intent on disrupting the gallery system, on one occasion he placed a large order of especially cumbersome office furniture to be sent to a gallery on an opening night, causing havoc and ruining their launch. However, Maciunas did sell art, and he started his own gallery. He was a mass of contradictions; Fluxus member Milan Knížák (b. 1940) describes him: 'Dreamer. Child. Utopian, Fascist, Christ, Democrat, Madman... He was beautiful, foolish, dogmatic, charming. Impossible.'[1] This extraordinary character was to challenge the traditional sales routes and set up innovative networks of distribution.

Born in Lithuania, Maciunas had a troubled childhood. He was a sickly child and, in 1933, he and his sister were taken to a sanatorium in Montreux where they lived for over a year, and were seldom visited by their parents. Later, when World War II broke out, his country was occupied by the Nazis, and violence became part of everyday life – once Maciunas was caught in enemy fire when he failed to make it to a bomb shelter in time. According to his mother, the worst time was when the Russians took back control towards the end of the war and began persecuting professional Lithuanians.[2] Maciunas's father had been working as an engineer for Siemens-Schukert's industrial plant, and the family worried that he would be criticised for collaborating with the Germans, and possibly shot. They fled their home, and for two years lived at a refugee camp before emigrating to America. Maciunas was 16 years old when they arrived, and his parents resumed their lives, and enjoyed a middle-class lifestyle, but Maciunas always struggled to find his place. Dominated by his authoritarian father, he looked for ways to exert control. As a young boy, he was obsessed with playing soldiers, and was always the Commanding General.

From his early years, he appears to have experienced shame around his gender. Maciunas was a talented piano player but gave it up because he considered it to be too 'feminine'.[3] This reflection does not sound like the thinking of a young child, and likely mirrors his parents' opinion. One wonders if his parents were aware of his gender fluidity. From nine years old, Maciunas sometimes dressed in girl's clothes, something he kept secret until the end of his life. As an adult, he typically wore a bowler hat and suit – a formality which served his commanding role as Fluxus leader. His desire for control also manifested itself in his compulsive organising and categorising of information. Diagrams were a life-long obsession. After studying art history and graphic design at university, he mapped out his personal history of art in a chart, which culminated in the Fluxus movement.

In 1961 Maciunas founded the AG Gallery in New York, with artist Almus Šalčius (1925–2000). Maciunas had been exploring the art scene at Chambers Street where Yoko Ono (b. 1933) and La Monte Young (b. 1935) were holding events in Ono's studio. Future Fluxus members Henry Flynt (b. 1940) and Philip Corner (b. 1933) were contributing and also holding events there. The Chambers Street group were exploring ideas around Zen Buddhism, absurdism and impermanence, and were experimenting with new media including film and performance.

Through his work at AG, Maciunas played a part in bringing this countercultural scene to a gallery context. Ono was shocked when Maciunas offered her an exhibition at the gallery, and later recalled: 'I said, Oh my god, this is the first time somebody wanted to do my show.'[4] Included in her exhibition was the piece *Painting to be Stepped On* (1960–61), which involved a cut piece of unstretched canvas laid out on the ground. Signage directed the visitor to walk across the canvas, and their participation was a vital element of the experience. Despite its radical intentions, the show received very little interest, as the artist tells it: 'I think the first opening, five people came. One was John Cage, one Isamu Noguchi.'[5]

Through the spring and summer of 1961, AG Gallery also held a series of music events with experimental musicians. One of the performances was Young's *Composition 1960 #7* (1960). The piece had a radically reduced score of only two notes: a B3 and F#4, and instructions stated the musical notes were 'To be held for a long time.' Choosing to bring a piece of music to the gallery was a controversial move for it had no obvious material form, or connection to the art world. However, Young's piece, and his entire oeuvre, is characterised by its investigation of the environmental and physical properties of sound. This immersive aspect would become central to Maciunas and his subsequent involvement in performance.

Maciunas designed the promotional material for these music events. The La Monte Young pamphlet has a visual austerity; the information is harmonised in a simple geometric layout, and set on a square page, with two vertical panels. The font is Sans Serif, and typed on the electric typewriter he used for all the Fluxus material. A vitality is created by the contrasting black and white background, and by including photography. Maciunas said he was simply interested in producing the cheapest product possible, however, his aesthetic had elegance, and brought a cohesive identity to Fluxus which involved artists with very different styles and outlooks. Essentially, Maciunas's design shaped a brand.

AG Gallery closed within a year. At the end, visitors had to use torches to see the works in the evenings because the electricity had been cut off. Chased by debt collectors, Maciunas fled the United States, and settled in Wiesbaden, Germany where he worked as a graphic designer for the US Airforce. Again, his extraordinary organisational skills came into full force as he pulled together numerous performance events there. Now working outside the gallery context, he hired concert halls to stage events. One of the most famous pieces was Corner's *Piano Activities* (1962) which was performed by several future Fluxus artists including Maciunas himself. Collectively, they destroyed a piano with hammers, saws and hatchets, in front of a live audience. Maciunas's mother attended, and was appalled, describing it as a 'painful' experience, and felt her values were being undermined.[6] Playing the piano and attending concerts were indeed middle-class activities and instead of hearing the orchestrated sounds of a piano recital, the hall was filled with abrasive noises like the grating of a saw and the banging of a hammer. While one can appreciate her reaction, the performance had a funny side, drawing on the anarchic humour of Buster Keaton and Charlie Chaplin and most of the audience were in stitches.

Maciunas would go on to mastermind the Fluxus Festival, which featured a programme of performances by various artists. Probably influenced by his own itinerant childhood, internationalism was an integral part of his vision. The events ran in multiple cities including Amsterdam, Berlin, Poznań and Stockholm, and the make-up of the group was multinational. There was a continued focus on lived experience, and performances included chopping salads, cutting hair and listening to the sound of water dripping. The festival cemented the identity of the Fluxus group, and afterwards Maciunas released a manifesto, which stated their intentions, as can be seen from this extract:

> Purge the world of bourgeois sickness, 'intellectual', professional & commercialised culture, Purge the world of dead art, imitation, artificial art, abstract art, illusionistic art, mathematical art [...] Promote living art, anti-art, promote NON ART REALITY to be grasped by all peoples, not only critics, dilettantes and professionals.[7]

By the end of 1963, conflicts were appearing in the group, not helped by Maciunas sometimes playing dictator and expelling members. Maciunas decided to return to New York. While he was interested in selling art again, he was looking for alternative routes to do so. In 1961, the artist Claes Oldenburg had circumvented the gallery system and opened a shop selling his food sculptures directly to the public. Perhaps inspired by his example, on New Year's Day, 1964, Maciunas announced, 'I want to open a shop... A shop, not a gallery.'[8] He found a space at 359 Canal Street and opened the first Fluxus shop and concert hall. It soon became an international phenomenon, with several European outlets – the Dutch artist, Willem de Ridder (1939–2022), for example, ran the Fluxshop in Amsterdam. However, there were very few sales, and they had only a couple of dedicated collectors.

Another highly original route Maciunas took was selling art through a mail order scheme – items could be bought individually, or a collector could sign up and receive an item each month. As always, the promotional material was brilliantly conceived by Maciunas. The goods were advertised in the Fluxus newspaper. One ad listed the items on sale in a grid infographic. The seriousness and elegance of the format played against the silliness of the advertised 'artworks' which included a 'fire alarm' (at $3), 'stick-on medals' ($3) and 'timekit' ($8). Significantly, the artists' identities were obscured, with their names randomly placed through the grid, and not linked to a specific product. And their low price points made them affordable to almost everyone.

Acting as the interface between the artist and the buyer, Maciunas was playing the role of art dealer. However, he was also heavily involved in production. Typically, artists suggested a concept, which Maciunas then interpreted. On occasion, he would overstep. When Ken Friedman (b. 1949) presented the idea of *Flux Clippings* (1968), Maciunas boxed up some rather sinister-looking,

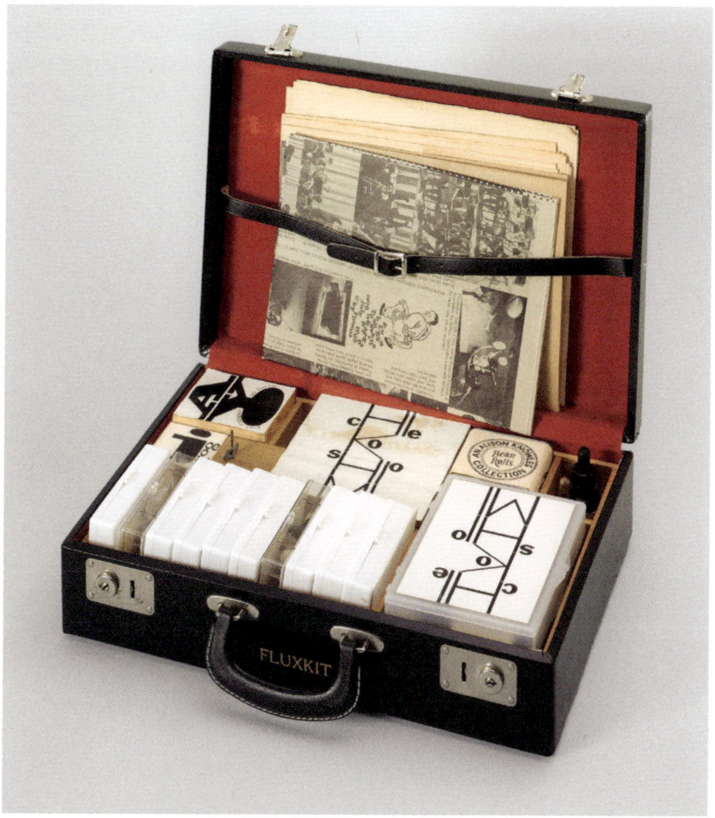

Fig. 35 Various artists, *Fluxkit*, 1965–66, vinyl-covered attaché case,
containing objects in various media, overall (closed): 34 × 44.5 ×
12.5 cm (13⅜ × 17½ × 5 in.), Museum of Modern Art, New York.

yellowed toenails, and added a macabre-looking label. However, Friedman's
original intent was to have a selection of newspaper cuttings that featured the
Fluxus movement. Maciunas's casual disregard ran contrary to traditional art
dealership practice, predicated on revering the artist, and sanctifying their
artworks. However, his primary concern was that the items were appreciated
on their own terms and were part of everyday life.

A particularly noteworthy line sold in the Fluxshops, and through
mail order was the limited-edition Flux Year boxes, and *Fluxkit* (1965–66,
fig. 35), which all contained a collection of works by different Fluxus artists.
The brainchild of Maciunas, they bore the imprint of his personality, his

compulsive organisation and his approach to design. The cubic boxes were meticulously subdivided into sections. In the case of *Fluxkit*, the container was a suitcase. Joseph Cornell's imaginative boxes, and Marcel Duchamp's *Box in a Valise* (1935–41) were important precedents; the latter contained miniature versions of his entire oeuvre. Maciunas's originality was to involve different artists, and curate a collection of their work.

The boxes and kits challenged fundamental practices in art dealership, questioning the need for a physical gallery space. They brought together artists' work in one small container. While art dealers typically sold artworks to be admired, and appreciated visually, Maciunas was offering an interactive and multisensory experience. The *Fluxkit* was an intensely intimate encounter: one could rummage through the box, pick the items up and play with them. *Bean Rolls* (1963) was the contribution of Alison Knowles (b.1933) to the *Fluxkit*. It comprises a small tin (adorned with a Maciunas label), which holds several beans, and 17 miniature rolls of paper which are inscribed with stories, songs and scientific facts about beans. The beans could be touched and enjoyed visually, but they also made a sound when the tin was shaken.

The *Fluxkit* and Flux Year boxes hardly sold, and yet now they are revered and part of key museum collections. In terms of art dealership, they offered an alternative to the physical gallery space. On a personal level, they answered Maciunas's quest for a collective experience. In the later years, Maciunas found an artistic community, and a partner, and began to wear women's clothes publicly. In the 1970s, he would be less involved in art-making; however, he continued with his collectivist dream, and went on to establish artists' cooperatives in warehouses in the then abandoned, and crime-ridden SoHo district of New York. Like all his projects, this enterprise was both highly innovative and fraught with tension.

Robert Fraser

(1937–1986)

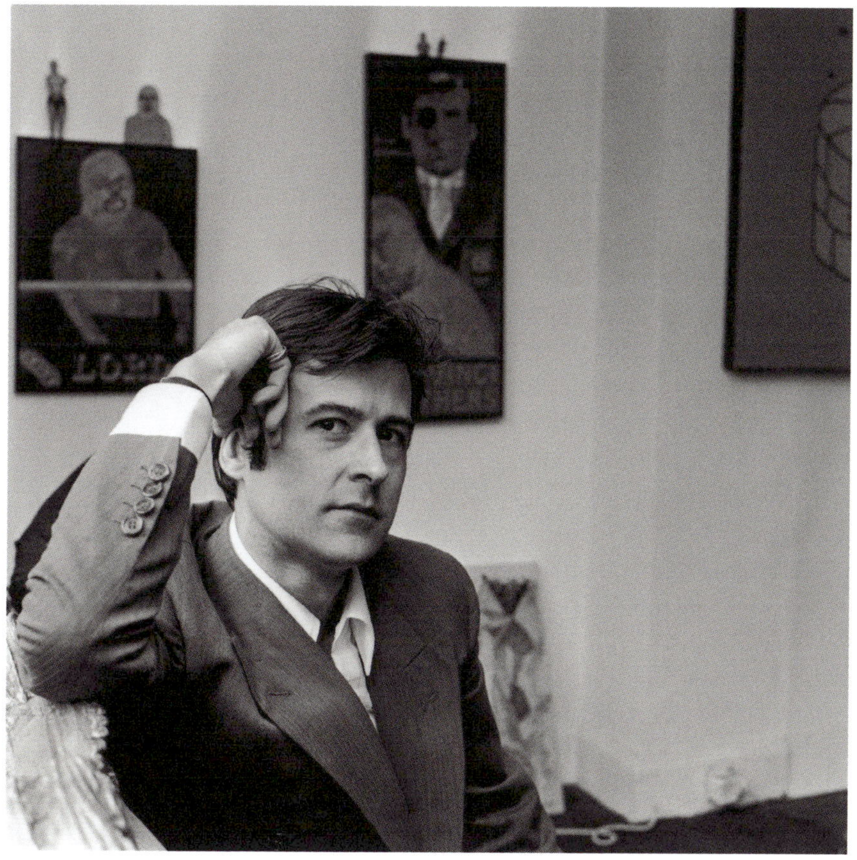

Fred Mott, *Robert Fraser*, c. 1965.

Robert Fraser was 25 years old when he opened his gallery on Duke Street in London. The glamorous dealer had the magnetic charm of the Pied Piper. According to Rolling Stones legend Keith Richards, 'He gathered the best and brightest around. They all flocked to him, the most interesting people.'[1] Rock stars, aristocrats and artists hung out at his gallery where Pop art was showcased throughout the 1960s. Fraser had a heightened sensitivity to life's promises. As a dealer, he had conviction and an instinctive sense of what made good art. His directness endeared him to rock musicians and Pop artists who were mostly from working-class backgrounds, and had no time for high-minded art talk. Beatles icon Paul McCartney remembers asking Fraser about a sculpture by Eduardo Paolozzi (1924–2005) and him coolly replying, 'What is it? I don't know. It's a mantelpiece, a bit of car, who knows?'[2] It wasn't the considered pitch of the typical art dealer. But this was 'Groovy Bob', and as McCartney tells it: 'I was very happy with that attitude, not too academic. There was no dour art talk. It was much more razzy, loose, lively discussion with him.'[3]

Born in 1937, Fraser had a privileged upbringing. His father, Lionel, was a banker and self-made millionaire. Both parents were Christian Scientists, and though Fraser rejected the religion, his conviction about art bordered on belief. He showed this confidence around art from an early age, once writing home from prep school to tell his parents he'd read a book on Picasso and found his art to have 'great rythm [*sic*]'.[4] As a young boy, he was equally enamoured by his parents' social life, and already believed that certain people were special, and clothes also had appeal. In a letter to his parents, he writes, 'You seemed to have a very busy week, what with the luncheon partys at the Ritz etc. Did Daddy wear White tie and tails at the City Ball, I hope you look lovely dancing.'[5]

His prep school headmaster reported, 'He enjoys the belief that he is "different" from other boys.'[6] In 1950, Fraser joined his brother Nicholas at Eton where he was one of the hip kids who smoked cigarettes and listened to jazz. Attending this elite public school later became part of his ambivalent identity. He would be the old Etonian, who dressed in Savile Row suits, yet sold what was considered 'vulgar' Pop art. After Eton, he trained as an officer, serving in the King's African Rifles in Uganda. The humdrum of army life bored him and, as always, he chased excitement. He got himself a sports car, dined with the Kabaka (king) of Buganda, and, according to the singer Marianne Faithfull, had a fling with the future politician Idi Amin.

Fraser's career in art took off when he was living in America between 1958 and 1962. Initially, he was in Philadelphia, and working on the Carnegie Institute's biennial, an experience which brought him into contact with an international art scene. He later moved to New York, which he described as 'the garden of enchantment'[7]. Interior designer Bill Willis emphasises the optimism in the city during that period:

> The time Robert was in NY was a very exciting period of history... The sixties were an era of social liberation, social barriers were falling, very creative. Those were glamorous times, but we didn't realise it. We were just so curious about life, feeling young, feeling our oats, the world was our oyster.[8]

Immersed in the art scene, he connected with significant art dealers including Betty Parsons and Sidney Janis, and became attuned to the cultural climate, detecting the move away from Minimalism. In 1960, he visited proto-Pop artist Jim Dine (b. 1935) at his studio. Dine describes what unfolded: 'Robert bought $1,400 worth of work, which was enormous then. And he was the first person who put down some money for me.'[9] Fraser continued buying artworks and soon had a collection worth $50,000. Towards the end of his time in New York, he became romantically involved with Michael Warren, who had a gallery in the city, and they started talking about opening a gallery in London. Fraser returned home to speak with his father about his gallery plans, and to tell him he was gay. He was worried how his father would react to the latter, but Lionel was accepting, saying, 'that as long as he was a *good* homosexual it was all right.'[10]

In 1962, he opened the Robert Fraser Gallery at 69 Mount Street in Mayfair, London. The stark interior was very different to London's plush, Victorian-looking galleries. Designed by architect Cedric Price, the walls were white, and had no skirtings or mouldings. Fraser launched with an exhibition of Jean Dubuffet whose work had never been seen before in Britain. Their black and white aesthetic complemented the pristine white gallery space. Fraser had an instinctive sense for what looked good. When Bridget Riley (b. 1931) had a show of small drawings with him in 1966, the day before it opened Fraser and Riley desperately tried to make the hang work, but the works always seemed lost. Disappointed, Riley went home only to be called a few hours later by Fraser to say he'd had an idea. Riley relates:

> And when I went to the gallery first thing in the morning I was
> amazed. He had painted the entire place black – walls, ceiling,
> all the woodwork, everything was completely black. And so
> these little light, pale studies, very fragile pieces of paper, shone,
> and were set in an amazing way. And the whole place looked
> absolutely beautiful.[11]

The English curator Bryan Robertson (1925–2002) credits Fraser as being central to London's cultural revolution. He explains: 'People's perception of things began to alter and Robert was certainly primary in all of this. I think that what he stood for and what he produced at the gallery, what he made people aware of, affected things a lot.'[12] In 1965, Fraser held an exhibition of Dine's paintings and, in the following year, showed his pioneering drawings. Dine was embracing the commonplace. His work *Two Palettes (Sears, Roebuck; Francis Picabia)* (1963) depicts artist's tools and heating system pipes. The startling clarity of his drawing style foreshadowed the matter-of-fact approach that defines American Pop art. Not everyone appreciated Dine's show; a retired general complained that some works were offensive – in particular a collage of a gift-wrapped penis. Charged with displaying indecent imagery, in court Fraser was unrepentant, and argued: 'I consider these pictures to be as pornographic as Cezanne.'[13] The notoriety of the trial brought kudos to the gallery, and more scandal was to follow.

As well as bringing American artists to the United Kingdom, Fraser presented a local London scene. Not interested in ideology, he embraced very different interpretations of Pop art. In 1967, he held an exhibition with Patrick Caulfield (1936–2005) who was not following the trend amongst Pop artists of using mass media images, but was interested in traditional subject matter. In *The Hermit* (1967), a hooded figure meditates in a cave which overlooks the setting sun. His blissful state is expressed by radiant primary colours. Fraser also showed Jann Haworth (b.1942), a pioneer of soft sculpture who was fashioning life-size, textile figures. And he persuaded The Beatles to drop their original designers for the *Sgt Pepper's Lonely Hearts Club Band* album and instead use Haworth and Peter Blake (b.1932) who came up with their iconic cover. Blake and Haworth agreed to a fee of £200 with no royalty, which they bitterly regretted later. Fraser was renowned for being awful at business, and particularly bad at paying. Riley says, 'Not only did we have difficulties getting what he owed us, he also arranged almost nothing for anybody, any sort of contracts, any sort of exhibitions.'[14] Oblivious to practicalities, as Fraser became caught up in a hedonistic flow, the boundaries between his gallery and life dissolved.

Situated above Scott's Oyster Bar, his flat at 23 Mount Street became an extension of the gallery. It was sparsely decorated with black leather chairs from Italy, an Yves Klein coffee table and Jean Dubuffet (1901–1985) works on the wall. Here, rock legends Mick Jagger, Brian Jones and John Lennon hung out with aristocrats like Lord Londonderry and the Bonham-Carters. Fraser was experimenting with drugs, and offered them out. Anita Pallenberg says, 'Robert introduced me to acid. He was the first person I know of who had LSD in London.'[15]

Art was part of their heady conversations. Andy Warhol (1928–1987) and his entourage showed up after the Cannes Film Festival refused to show *The Chelsea Girls* (1966), and McCartney brought over a projector, and they had a private viewing in the flat. Art sales unfolded informally. Fraser knew McCartney had his eye on René Magritte's painting *Le Jeu De Morre* (1966), which depicts a Surreal-sized apple. The Beatles icon tells how Fraser turned up at his home:

> I think I was filming Mary Hopkin with a film crew, just getting her
> to sing live in the garden with bees and flies buzzing around... and
> Robert didn't want to interrupt, so when we went back in the big
> door from the garden to the living room, there on the table he'd just
> propped up this little Magritte. It was of a green apple.[16]

In 1967, Fraser, Jagger and Richards were arrested for drug possession. Artist Richard Hamilton (1922–2011) made *Swingeing London* (1968–69), the infamous portrait of Jagger and Fraser handcuffed together in the back of a police van. Heroin was found in Fraser's coat, and at the trial the judge decided to make an example of the old Etonian, and he was made to serve six months at Wormwood Scrubs. When he got out, he was off heroin, and for a while continued with the gallery, but he was disenchanted, and felt, 'modern art and England had nothing to say to him any more.'[17] Caulfield's *The Hermit* (1967) resonates with the broad cultural interest in Eastern faiths, and spirituality circulating in London's Swinging Sixties. Attuned to this, Fraser would spend five years in India where he swapped his smart suits for free-flowing pyjamas, and explored tantra, and studied classical Kuchipudi dance.

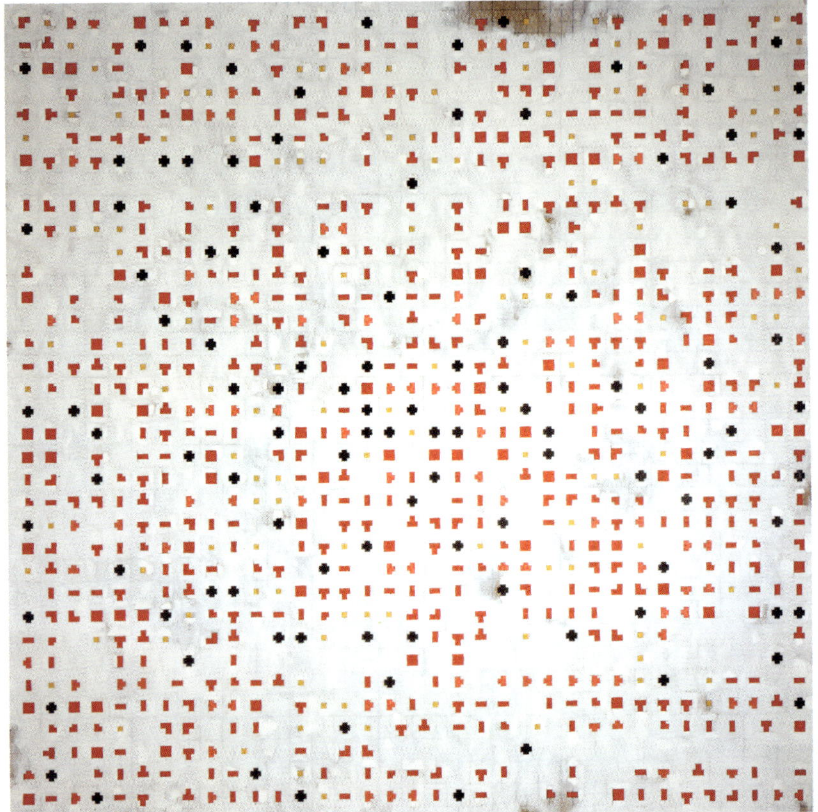

Fig. 36 Brian Clarke, *Marks on a White Background*, 1980,
oil on canvas, 183 × 183 cm (72⅛ × 72⅛ in.).

When he returned to London, he started dealing privately, but was restless. According to the fashion designer and music manager Malcolm McLaren, 'he was a bit like a rebel without a cause.'[18] In 1983, Fraser opened a new gallery at 21 Cork Street with a show of paintings by Brian Clarke (b. 1953). The gallery was filled with flowers sent from art dealers who wanted to welcome Fraser back. The art world had felt stagnant for years, and everyone was hoping Fraser would reignite things. Clarke's exhibition showcased his recent experiment with computer technology. The geometric motifs, and repetitive patterns in *Marks on a White Background* (1980, fig. 36) reference the light-metering computergrams from Olympus OM cameras. In these later years, Fraser also showed work by Jean-Michel

Basquiat (1960–1988) and had a solo show with Keith Haring (1958–1990) who painted murals across the shutters, and handed out doodles on the opening night; one of the first exhibitions for a graffiti artist – Fraser was ahead of the curve again. Clarke reflects on the dealer's brilliant, but short-lived return: 'Robert came along and suddenly it was a party, a party that lasted about two years, intense, really creative, like a Catherine wheel shooting sparks.'[19]

In 1986 Fraser died of an AIDS-related illness. The newspapers did not run obituaries, which was a terrible oversight. Before he died, Hamilton wrote to his old dealer, 'The opportunity to show in the best gallery London has seen in 50 years was a real privilege.'[20] Fraser had exhibited the most exciting art, and through his lifestyle had connected his gallery and artists with the vibrant Swinging Sixties and the music scene. Essentially, he made art lively.

Conclusion

For the inaugural exhibition at her second New York gallery in 1971, Ileana Sonnabend invited Gilbert and George to perform *The Singing Sculpture*.[1] Wearing well-tailored suits, their faces sparkling with metal powder, the duo stood on a table, and sang the music hall classic, 'Underneath the Arches'. The song gained popularity during World War II and remained connected to that era, symbolising a mythic moment when society pulled together. In a similar way, the art dealer fosters a sense of cohesion by taking artworks from the private realm of the artist's studio, and presenting them to the public. And by doing so, they enchant our lives.

As the artists sang, 'Underneath the arches, We dream our dreams away', they moved with mechanical precision to the rhythm. Gilbert held a glove, and George had a cane, which at one moment in the song he pressed down on, making the rubber toy attached to the tip squeak. The randomness of the objects, including the very ordinary table they sang from, brought a tender fallibility to the performance, which echoed the sentiment of the song. George explains, 'We felt very close to the ideas in the text, these two tramps trying to be sort of cheerful under very difficult circumstances... We did feel in some way lost and homeless.'[2] Notably, Sonnabend had provided a shelter, not just for the artists, but for the crowds that came to watch them. For eight hours, the artists repeated their act, later admitting their intention was to transfix their audience, and immerse them in the soulful performance.[3]

Gilbert and George's performance is the perfect swan song to this book on dealers. A failure to fully understand their talents and historical influence has contributed to dealers being erroneously sidelined as unsavoury guests in the art world. There are distasteful practices within the industry. However, Sonnabend, and the many other dealers covered here, provided a unique space where an audience could participate in the magical universe of art. Without them as organisers, some of these effervescent experiences may never have come about. These extraordinary dealers undeniably played a precious role in the history of art.

Notes

Extraordinary Art Dealers

Introduction

1 Marcel Duchamp quoted in Philip Hook, *Rogues' Gallery: A History of Art and Its Dealers* (London: Profile Books, 2017), 1.

2 Kant mainly explores the subject of aesthetics in his text, first published in 1790, *Critique of Judgment*, trans. Werner S. Pluhar (Indianapolis: Hackett Publishing Company, 1987).

3 F. Scott Fitzgerald, *The Great Gatsby* (Global Publishers, Kindle Edition, 2023), 75.

4 Betty Parsons interviewed for the television programme, *About the Arts*, 1977.

5 Leo Castelli interviewed on *About the Arts*, 1976.

6 Larry Rivers is quoted in James Meyer, 'The Art Gallery in an Era of Mobility', James Meyer (ed.), *Los Angeles to New York: Dwan Gallery, 1959–1971* (Chicago: University of Chicago Press, 2016), 34.

CHAPTER 1: EARLY DEALINGS

Introduction

1 Philip Hook, *Rogues' Gallery: A History of Art and its Dealers* (London: Profile Books, 2017), 9.

Arthur Pond

1 J. M. Robertson (ed.), *Characteristics of Men, Manners, Opinions and Times* (1711) 2 vols. (Indianapolis: Bobbs-Merrill, 1964), 279.

William Hogarth

1 William Hogarth quoted in Hester Thrale Piozzi, *Anecdotes of the Late Samuel Johnson* (1786), published with introduction by S. C. Roberts (Cambridge: Cambridge University Press, 1925), 89.

2 Pierre Bourdieu, *The Rules of Art* (Cambridge: Polity Press, 1996).

3 William Hogarth quoted in Jenny Uglow, *William Hogarth: A Life and a World* (London: Faber and Faber, 1998), 22.

4 William Hogarth quoted in Uglow, *William Hogarth*, 348.

William Buchanan

1 William Buchanan, *Memoirs of Painting, With A Chronological History of The Importation of Pictures by the Great Masters Into England Since The French Revolution* (London: R. Ackermann, Strand, 1824), 9.

2 William Buchanan quoted in Philip Hook, *Rogues' Gallery: A History of Art and Its Dealers* (London: Profile Books, 2017), 48.

3 Buchanan quoted in Hook, *Rogues' Gallery*, 48.

4 Buchanan quoted in Hook, *Rogues' Gallery*, 45.

5 Buchanan quoted, in Hook, *Rogues' Gallery*, 46.

6 Buchanan quoted in Hook, *Rogues' Gallery*, 48.

7 Buchanan quoted in Hook, *Rogues' Gallery*, 52.

8 Buchanan, *Memoirs*, 49.

9 Buchanan quoted in Hook, *Rogues' Gallery*, 44.

10 Hook, *Rogues' Gallery*, 53.

Ernest Gambart

1 Pamela Fletcher, 'Creating the French Gallery: Ernest Gambart and the Rise of the Commercial Art Gallery in Mid-Victorian London', *Nineteenth Century Art Worldwide*, 6, 1 (Spring 2007).

2 Pierre Bourdieu, 'The Economic World Reversed', *The Field of Cultural Production: Essays on Art and Literature*, Randal Johnson (trans. and ed.), (New York: Columbia University Press, 1993), 29–73.

3 John Everett Millais to his wife, Effie Millais, 17 May 1859, letter in Pierpont Morgan Library, New York.

4 Unknown writer, *London Illustrated News*, 17 November 1860. Quoted in Jeremy Maas, *Gambart: Prince of the Victorian Art World* (London: Barrie and Jenkins, 1975), 133.

5 William Holman Hunt quoted in Maas, *Gambart*, 90.

6 Arthur Munby quoted in Derek Hudson, *Munby: Man of Two Worlds: The Life and Diaries of Arthur J. Munby, 1828–1910* (London: John Murray, 1972), 59.

Paul Durand-Ruel

1 Paul-Louis Durand-Ruel and Flavie Durand-Ruel, *Paul Durand-Ruel: Memoirs of the First Impressionist Art Dealer (1831–1922)* (Paris: Flammarion, 2014), 110.

2 Auguste Renoir quoted in Pierre Assouline, *Discovering Impressionism: The Life of Paul Durand-Ruel* (London: Thames and Hudson, 2005), 109.

3 Assouline, *Discovering Impressionism*, 88.

4 Durand-Ruel and Durand-Ruel, *Memoirs*, 19.

5 Eugène Boudin quoted in Sylvie Patry (ed.), *Inventing Impressionism: Paul Durand-Ruel and the Modern Art Market* (London: National Gallery

Company, 2015), 102.

6 Boudin quoted in Patry, *Inventing Impressionism*, 104.

7 Émile Zola quoted in Durand-Ruel and Durand-Ruel, *Memoirs*, 158.

8 Paul Durand-Ruel quoted in Royal Cortissoz, *Personalities in Art* (New York: Bowen Press, 1925), 269–70.

9 Durand-Ruel quoted in Sylvie Patrie, Anne Robbins, Christopher Riopelle, Joseph J. Rishel and Jennifer A. Thompson, 'Paul Durand-Ruel: An Unrepentant Risk-taker', *Inventing Impressionism: Paul Durand-Ruel and The Modern Art Market* (London: National Gallery Company, 2015), 28.

10 Durand-Ruel quoted in Paul-Louis Durand-Ruel and Flavie Durand-Ruel, 'Paul Durand-Ruel (1831–1922): A Portrait', in Patry, *Inventing Impressionism*, 32.

11 Durand-Ruel quoted in Assouline, *Discovering Impressionism*, 95.

CHAPTER 2: THE BRANDED DEALER

Introduction

1 Don Thompson, *The $12 Million Stuffed Shark: The Curious Economics of Contemporary Art* (London: Aurum Press, 2008), 34.

2 Thompson, *The $12 Million Stuffed Shark*, 41.

3 Brian O'Doherty, 'Notes on the Gallery Space', *Inside the White Cube: The Ideology of the Gallery Space* (Berkeley, CA: University of California Press, 1999), 15.

Joseph Duveen

1 Andrew Mellon quoted in S. N. Behrman, *Duveen* (New York: Random House, 1952), 13.

2 Philip Hook, *Rogues' Gallery: A History of Art and its Dealers* (London: Profile Books, 2017), 76.

3 Duveen quoted in Behrman, *Duveen*, 15.

4 Duveen quoted in Behrman, *Duveen*, 15.

5 Behrman, *Duveen*, 50.

6 Duveen quoted in Behrman, *Duveen*, 61.

7 Jules Bache quoted in Behrman, *Duveen*, 60.

8 Duveen quoted in Behrman, *Duveen*, 75.

9 Duveen quoted in Behrman, *Duveen*, 54.

10 The official title of this work is *A Portrait of a Young Boy*. It has become popularly known as *The Blue Boy*.

11 Duveen was, in fact, right to contest the attribution. The version Andrée Hahn owned was not by Leonardo, but was a copy done by another painter. It is dated, before 1750.

12 Hook, *Rogues' Gallery*, 90.

13 Duveen quoted in Behrman, *Duveen*, 15.

Ambroise Vollard

1 Pablo Picasso quoted in Françoise Gilot and Carlton Lake, *Life with Picasso* (London: McGraw Hill, 1964), 49.

2 Gertrude Stein, *The Autobiography of Alice B. Toklas* (New York: Harcourt, Brace and Company, 1933), 36.

3 Stein, *Autobiography*, 36.

4 Philip Hook, *Rogues' Gallery: A History of Art and its Dealers* (London: Profile Books, 2017), 128.

5 Stein, *Autobiography*, 36.

6 Ambroise Vollard, *Recollections of a Picture Dealer* (first published in French, 1936; English edition, New York: Dover Publications, 1978), 230.

7 Vollard, *Recollections*, 52.

8 Vollard, quoted in Philip Hook, *Rogues' Gallery*, 127.

9 Vollard, *Recollections*, 317.

10 Paul Gauguin quoted in Rebecca A. Rabinow (ed.), *Cezanne to Picasso: Ambroise Vollard, Patron of the Avant-Garde* (New Haven, CT: Yale University Press, 2006), 76.

11 Vollard quoted in Brassaï, *The Artists of My Life* (English edition, London: Thames and Hudson, 1982), 212.

12 Ann Dumas outlines Apollinaire's negative reaction to the show in her essay, 'Ambroise Vollard, Patron of the Avant-garde' in Rabinow, *Cezanne to Picasso*, 20.

13 Brassaï, *Artists*, 210.

14 Henri Matisse, *Matisse on Art* (New York: E.P. Dutton, 1978), 75.

15 André Billy, *La Terrasse du Luxembourg* (Paris: Fayard, 1945), 150.

Samuel M. Kootz

1 Samuel Kootz, excerpt from his promotional banner for winter holiday show in 1952, held in Archives of American Art, Smithsonian Institute, Washington, DC.

2 Advertisement in *The New York Times*, 4 January, 1942.

3 Oral history interview with Samuel M. Kootz, 13 April 1964, transcript and recording held in Archives of American Art.

4 Françoise Gilot relates that Picasso mentioned to her that one bullet passed his head by only a few inches. Françoise Gilot, *Life with Picasso* (New York: McGraw-Hill Book Co., 1964), 61.

5 'Pictures on Exhibit', newspaper unknown, February 1947, cutting from Scrapbook 1 , Series 5: Scrapbooks, 1931–1966, Box 3, Smithsonian Institute, Washington, DC.

6 Unnamed reporter, *Art Digest,* 15 January 1947, cutting from Scrapbook 1, Series 5: Scrapbooks, 1931–1966, Box 3, Smithsonian Institute.

7 Samuel Kootz, 'Introduction', *The Intrasubjectives* (New York: Samuel. M Kootz Gallery), 1949.

8 This exhibition was also called *Talent 1950*.

9 When interviewer Dorothy Seckler asks Kootz to explain the sudden upsurge of interest in Abstract Expressionism, he replies, 'Lord knows, I couldn't tell you. I have no concept as to what.' Oral history interview with Samuel M. Kootz, 13 April 1964, transcript and recording held in Archives of American Art.

10 Oral history interview with Samuel M. Kootz, 13 April 1964, transcript and recording held in Archives of American Art.

Betty Parsons

1 Saul Steinberg quoted in Peter Ward, *From Manet to Manhattan: The Rise of The Modern Art Market* (London: Hutchinson, 1992), 28.

2 Betty Parsons quoted in Lee Hall, *Betty Parsons: Artist, Dealer, Collector* (New York: H.N. Abrams, 1991), 20.

3 Parsons quoted in Hall, *Betty Parsons*, 102.

4 Parsons quoted in Hall, *Betty Parsons,* 23.

5 Parsons describes her conversation to Hall, which Hall then recounts in Hall, *Betty Parsons,* 71.

6 Parsons quoted in Hall, *Betty Parsons*, 77.

7 Don Thompson, *The $12 Million Stuffed Shark: The Curious Economics of Contemporary Art* (London: Palgrave Macmillan, 2008), 27.

8 Thomas McEvilley 'Introduction', Brian O'Doherty, *Inside the White Cube: The Ideology of the Gallery Space* (San Francisco, CA: Lapis Press, 1986), 7. Internal quotes reflect O'Doherty's words.

9 Barnett Newman quoted in Hall, *Betty Parsons*, 73.

10 Betty Parsons constantly refers to the four main Abstract Expressionists as the 'Giants'. In one instance, she remarks, 'My artists were giants and the critics refused to know it,' Parsons quoted in Hall, *Betty Parsons*, 94.

11 Leo Castelli interview with Paul Cummings, New York, 14 May–8 June 1969, Archives of American Art, Smithsonian Institution, Washington, DC.

12 Parsons quoted in Hall, *Betty Parsons*, 90.

13 Parsons quoted in Hall, *Betty Parsons*, 90.

14 Parsons quoted in Hall, *Betty Parsons*, 53.

15 Parsons recalls a statement by Barnett Newman, quoted in Hall, *Betty Parsons*, 102.

16 Parsons quoted in Hall, *Betty Parsons*, 29.

17 Parsons quoted in Hall, *Betty Parsons*, 95.

Leo Castelli

1 Rosalind Krauss mentions this in her lecture 'Art in the Twenty-First Century' which she gave on the occasion of her retrospective at the University of Chicago, 28 January 2008.

2 Leo Castelli interview with Paul Cummings, 1969, transcript held in Archives of American Art, Smithsonian Institute, Washington, DC.

3 Castelli quoted in Meryle Secrest, 'Leo Castelli, Dealing in Myths', *ARTnews* (Summer 1982), 62-63.

4 Castelli interview with Cummings, 1969.

5 Ivan Karp interview with Annie Cohen-Solal, New York, 26 April 2007, quoted in her book, *Leo and His Circle: The Life of Leo Castelli* (New York: Knopf, 2010), Ch. 21.

6 Ann Hindry, *Claude Berri rencontre/meets Leo Castelli* (Paris: Renn, 1990), 90.

7 Jasper Johns quoted in Cohen-Solal, *Leo and His Circle*, Ch. 26.

8 Leo Castelli interview with Cummings, 1969.

9 Castelli quoted in Cohen-Solal, *Leo and His Circle*, Ch. 24.

10 Leo Castelli interview with Cummings, 1969.

11 Jean-Christophe Castelli interview with Annie Cohen-Solal, New York, 25 September 2008, quoted in Cohen-Solal, *Leo and His Circle*, Ch. 28.

12 Leo Castelli interview with Russell O'Connor, 1979, Leo Castelli archives, Archives of American Art, Smithsonian Institute, Washington, DC.

13 Calvin Tomkins, *Off The Wall: Robert Rauschenberg and the Art World of Our Time* (New York: Doubleday, 1980), 282.

14 Leo Castelli interview with Cummings, 1969.

CHAPTER 3: THE IDEALISTS

Introduction

1 Virginia Dwan interviewed for the video accompanying *Los Angeles to New York: Dwan Gallery, 1959–1971*, held at the National Gallery of Art, Washington, DC in 2016.

2 The response in *The Times* is quoted by Martin Harrison in his text 'Painting 1946', on *Francis Bacon MB Art Foundation:* https://www.mbartfoundation.com/francis-bacon-the-artist/foundation-focus/painting-1946/

3 Dwan interviewed for the video accompanying *Los Angeles to New York: Dwan Gallery, 1959–1971*

Daniel-Henry Kahnweiler

1 Daniel-Henry Kahnweiler, *My Gallery and Painters* (trans. H. Weaver), (London: Thames and Hudson, 1971), 32.

2 Kahnweiler, *My Gallery*, 22.

3 Pierre Assouline, *An Artful Life: A Biography of D.H. Kahnweiler, 1884–1979* (New York: Fromm International Pub. Corp, 1991), 4.

4 Kahnweiler, *My Gallery*, 39.

5 Kahnweiler discusses Braque's position in *My Gallery*, 39.

6 Georges Braque quoted in Pierre Cabanne, *Cubism* (Paris: Terrail, 2001), 36.

7 Braque quoted in Assouline, *An Artful Life*, 103.

8 Kahnweiler, *My Gallery*, 41.

9 Yve-Alain Bois and Katharine Streip, 'Kahnweiler's Lesson', *Representations*, 18 (1987), 34.

10 Kahnweiler, *My Gallery*, 100.

11 Assouline, *An Artful Life*, 168.

Alfred Stieglitz

1 Marie Rapp Boursault quoted in William Innes Homer, *Alfred Stieglitz and the American Avant-Garde* (Boston, MA: New York Graphic Society, 1977), 80.

2 Charles Caffin, *Photography as a Fine Art* (Mishawaka, IN: Watson-Guptill Publications, 1972), 199.

3 Stieglitz quoted in Homer, *Alfred Stieglitz*, 39.

4 Stieglitz in conversation with Paul Haviland, interview printed in the magazine, *291*, 1, (01/03/1915).

5 Stieglitz quoted by Guido Bruno in 'The Passing of *291*', *Pearson's Magazine*, 38 (March 1918), 402.

6 Stieglitz to Rodin, 17 January 1907, *Correspondance de Rodin, vol. II, 1900–1907* (Paris: Éditions du Musée Rodin, 1986), 29, n3.

7 Stieglitz to Rodin, 17 January 1907, 29, n3.

8 Stieglitz quoted in Sarah Greenough, 'Alfred Stieglitz, Rebellious Midwife to a Thousand Ideas', in Greenough, *Modern Art and America: Alfred Stieglitz and His New York Galleries* (Washington, DC: National Gallery of Art, 2000), 32.

9 Paul Strand, 'Photography and the New God', *Broom* 3 (November 1922), 256.

10 Strand, 'Photography and the New God', 256.

11 Sarah Greenough, 'Alfred Stieglitz, Facilitator, Financier and Father Presents Seven Americans', in Greenough, *Alfred Stieglitz and His New York Galleries*, 279.

12 The full exhibition title was *Alfred Stieglitz Presents Seven Americans: 159 Paintings, Photographs and things, Recent & Never Before Publicly Shown by Arthur G. Dove, Marsden Hartley, John Marin, Charles Demuth, Paul Strand, Georgia O'Keeffe and Alfred Stieglitz.*

13 Stieglitz quoted in Greenough, 'Alfred Stieglitz, Rebellious Midwife', 51.

André Breton

1 André Breton quoted in Adam Jolles, *The Curatorial Avant-Garde: Surrealism and Exhibition Practice in France, 1925–1941* (Pennsylvania: Penn State University Press, 2015).

2 Jacqueline Lamba quoted in Jean-Claude Blachère, *Les Totems d'André Breton: Surréalisme et primitivisme littéraire* (Paris: Éditions L'Harmattan, 1996), 138.

3 André Breton, 'Manifesto for Surrealism', first published in 1924, reprinted in *Manifestoes of Surrealism* (Michigan: University of Michigan Press, 1972), 9.

4 Breton, 'Manifesto for Surrealism', 26.

5 André Breton, letter to Pablo Picasso, 15 March 1937, call no. MP 3649, Archives Picasso, Musée National Picasso–Paris.

6 Raymond Queneau, 'Connaissez-vous Paris?' *L'Intransigeant*, 8 November 1937; translated and quoted by Paul Franklin, 'Décor in Dialogue: Marcel Duchamp's and Salvador Dalí's Projects for the Galerie Gradiva', *Avant-garde* Studies, 3 (Spring/Summer 2018), 9.

7 Breton, 'Manifesto for Surrealism', 20. Breton was quoting Pierre Reverdy in *Nord-Sud*, 1918.

8 Breton, 'Manifesto for Surrealism', 26.

9 Louise Tythacott, 'A "Convulsive Beauty":
Surrealism, Oceania and African Art', *Journal of
Museum Ethnography*, 11 (May 1999), 44.

10 René Magritte, Letter to Edward James, 3 July
1937, Edward James Foundation.

11 Magritte, Letter to Edward James, 3 July 1937.

12 Maurice Henry, 'Gradiva, magasin surréaliste:
sur le pont qui relie le rêve à la réalité,'
Marianne: grand hébdomadaire littéraire illustré,
11 August 1937.

Topazia Alliata

1 Emilio Villa quoted in Carlotta Sylos Calò,
'Topazia Alliata, Piero Manzoni, and the
Coincidence between Idea and Visual Language.
The Case of Riducibili, Rome 1960' in Véronique
Chagnon-Burke and Caterina Toschi (eds),
*Women Art Dealers: Creating Markets for Modern
Art, 1940–1990* (London: Bloomsbury Visual Arts,
2024), 224.

2 Italo Calvino 'Lightness', *Dancing on the Ceiling:
Art and Zero Gravity*, Online Catalogue.

3 Toni Maraini, *Topazia Alliata* (Rome: Luca
Editori d'Arte, 2022), 15. All translations from
Maraini are author's own.

4 Jiddu Krishnamurti, *Freedom from the
Known* (Bombay, Delhi, Calcutta, Madras: B.i.
Publications, 1959), 19.

5 Topazia Alliata quoted in 'Obituary of Princess
Topazia Alliata', *The Telegraph*, 17 February 2016.

6 Felicita Alliata, comment remembered by
Maraini in *Topazia Alliata*, 21.

7 Fabrizio D'Amico, quoted in Sylos Calò, 'Topazia
Alliata', 221.

8 Melehi in conversation with Reem Fadda.

9 Journalist's comment remembered by Maraini in
Topazia Alliata, 11.

10 Details recounted by Maraini in *Topazia Alliata*, 6.

11 Toni Maraini describes the press picking up
Alliata's interest in abstract art in *Topazia
Alliata*, 47.

12 Journalist's comment remembered by Maraini
in *Topazia Alliata*, 47.

13 Maraini, *Topazia Alliata*, 6.

14 Sylos Calò, 'Topazia Alliata', 225.

Virginia Dwan

1 Virginia Dwan quoted by Paige Rozanski in the
chronology of James Meyer (ed.), *Los Angeles
to New York: Dwan Gallery, 1959–1971* (Chicago:

University of Chicago Press, 2016), 286.

2 The family money originally came from her
grandfather who was one of the five founders of
Minnesota Mining and Manufacturing Company.

3 Recounted in the accompanying video to the
exhibition *Los Angeles to New York: Dwan Gallery,
1959–1971*, held at the National Gallery of Art,
Washington, DC in 2016.

4 Claes Oldenburg in video *Los Angeles to New
York: Dwan Gallery, 1959–1971*.

5 Rozanski in Meyer, *Los Angeles to New York*, 292.

6 Virginia Dwan writes an essay on the subject of
the silence engendered by Minimalist sculpture,
'Selling Silence', reprinted in Meyer, *Los Angeles
to New York*, 247–50.

7 Virginia Dwan, 'Star Axis' reprinted in Meyer, *Los
Angeles to New York*, 278.

8 Virginia Dwan, 'Ils sont tous venus', reprinted in
Meyer, *Los Angeles to New York*, 245.

9 Virgina Dwan, 'Selling Silence', reprinted in
Meyer, *Los Angeles to New York*, 247–50.

10 Virginia Dwan, 'Earthworks', reprinted in Meyer,
Los Angeles to New York, 265.

CHAPTER 4: CULTURAL STEWARDS

Introduction

1 Anne Helmreich, '"On or About 1910", London's
New Bond Street, and the Global Art Market',
Irina D. Costache and Clare Kunny (eds),
Historical Narratives of Global Modern Art (New
York: Routledge, 2023).

2 This book is also called *Life in the Woods*.

3 Lucy R. Lippard, *On the Beaten Track: Tourism,
Art and Place* (New York: The New Press, 2016).

4 E. F. Schumacher, *Small is Beautiful: Economics
as if People Mattered* (New York: Harper
Colophon Books, 1975), 187.

5 E. F. Schumacher, *Small is Beautiful*, 33.

Herwarth Walden

1 Herwarth Walden, Unpublished letter, 2 October
1912, quoted in Monica Strauss, 'Kandinsky and
"Der Sturm"', *Art Journal*, 43, 1 (1983), 32.

2 This is recounted in Philip Hook, *Rogues' Gallery:
A History of Art and Its Dealers* (London: Profile,
2017), 186–87.

3 Wilhelm II, 'True Art' (1901): Wilhelm II, 'True
Art' (1901): https://germanhistorydocs.ghi-dc.org/
pdf/eng/301_Wilhelm%20II_True_Art_50.pdf, 2.

4 Paul Fechter quoted in Donald E. Gordon, 'On the Origin of the Word "Expressionism"', *Journal of the Warburg and Courtauld Institutes*, 29 (1966).

5 This is recounted in Benedetta Ricci, 'The Shows that Made Contemporary Art History: The First Exhibition of Der Blaue Reiter', *Artland Magazine*, https://magazine.artland.com/the-shows-that-made-contemporary-art-history-the-first-exhibition-of-der-blaue-reiter/.

6 This painting is also known as *Blue Horses*.

7 Franz Marc quoted in Christopher P. Jones, 'The Modern Artist who Found Creative Awakening in Animals', *Medium,* 3 November 2023.

8 Wassily Kandinsky quoted in Riccardo Marchi, 'October 1912: Understanding Kandinsky's Art "Indirectly" at Der Sturm', *Getty Research Journal,* 1 (2009), 58–59.

9 Kate Winskell, 'The Art of Propaganda: Herwarth Walden and "Der Sturm", 1914–1919', *Art History,* 18, 3 (September 1995), 318.

10 Winskell, 'The Art of Propaganda', 329–30.

11 Letter from the head of the press office of the German Embassy in Copenhagen to Chancellor Count von Hertling dated 3 June 1918, discussed in Winskell, 'The Art of Propaganda', 332.

Edith Halpert

1 Press release, November 1926, R-ND/46, Downtown Gallery Records, Archives of American Art, Smithsonian Institute, Washington, DC.

2 A. Deirdre Robson argues this in her essay, 'The Girl with the Gallery: Edith Halpert in the Mid-Twentieth-Century New York Art Market' in *Women Art Dealers: Creating Markets for Modern Art, 1940–1990*, eds Véronique Chagnon-Burke and Caterina Toschi (London: Bloomsbury Visual Arts, 2023), 32.

3 This view was explored by A. Deirdre Robson in her paper 'The Girl with the Gallery: Agency, Orientation, and Women Dealers in the Mid-Twentieth Century New York Art Market', for the Arts Education Conference, Christie's Education, New York, June 2018.

4 Halpert interviewed by Harland Philips, transcript of interviews from 1962–63 held in the Archives of American Art.

5 Halpert quoted by John X. Christ, 'Stuart Davis as Public Artist: American Painting and the Reconstruction of the Public Sphere', *Oxford Art Journal*, 37, 1 (March 2014), 76.

6 Christ, 'Stuart Davis as Public Artist', 80.

7 Edward Alden Jewell, 'Plaster Cast of Zorah's "Spirit of the Dance" Banned in Radio City is Shown Downtown', *The New York Times,* 28 December 1932.

8 Robson, 'The Girl with the Gallery', 34–5.

9 Edith Halpert quoted by Jackson Arn in 'Edith Halpert: The Art World Needs You More Than Ever', *Forward*, 3 November 2019.

10 Halpert interviewed by Harlan Philips.

11 Halpert interviewed by Harlan Philips.

12 Halpert interviewed by Harlan Philips.

Manuel and Lola Álvarez Bravo

1 Rufino Tamayo, quoted in the artist's biography on The Art Story, https://www.theartstory.org/artist/tamayo.

2 MacKinley Helm quoted in Agustín Arteaga, *México 1900–1950* (New Haven, CT: Yale University Press, 2017), 30.

3 André Breton quoted in 'Memories of a Surreal Journey: Property from an Important San Francisco Bay Area', Press Release, Christie's, 2 February 2023.

4 André Breton, 'Souvenir du Mexique' was included as well as reproductions of works of art, *Minotaure*, 11/12 (Paris, 1939).

5 André Breton quoted by Christina Burrusin. *Frida Kahlo: Painting her Own Reality* (New York: Harry N. Abrams, 2008), 55.

6 This term was coined by André Breton. It appears in his novel *Nadja* (1928), and later in *Mad Love* (1937). It refers to a beauty that is contorted and communicates a disturbed state of being.

7 Rosa Castro quoted in Ana Garduño, 'Documentary traces of Galeria de Arte Contemporáneo', *Lola Álvarez Bravo and the Photography of an Era* (Barcelona, Spain: R. M. Verlag, 2012).

8 Lola Álvarez Bravo in *Lola Álvarez Bravo: The Frida Kahlo photographs* (Dallas, TX: Society of Friends of Mexican Culture; New York: Distributed Art Publishers, 1991).

Kekoo and Khorshed Gandhy

1 Sidharth Bhatia refers to Kekoo Gandhy as the accidental gallerist in his article 'The Accidental Gallerist and the Making of Indian Modern Art', *The Wire* (08 July 2020).

2 Behroze Gandhy discusses her father's desire to

tell the Indian story in the lecture 'Catalysts for Creative Space: Kekoo and Khorshed Gandhy' for Jiyo Parsi Friday Forum (24 September 2021).

3 Kekoo Gandhy, 'The Beginnings of the Art Movement', 'City of Dreams', special issue of *Seminar*, 539, August 2003.

4 Shireen Gandhy is quoted in Meher Marfatia, 'Kekoo Gandhy: Guru, mentor, patron', *Mumbai Mirror,* 11 November 2012.

5 Gandhy, 'The Beginnings of the Art Movement'.

6 Gandhy describes Langhammer's thinking in 'The Beginnings of the Art Movement'.

7 M. F. Husain quoted in Margit Franz, 'From Dinner Parties to Galleries: The Langhammer-Leyden-Schlesinger Circle in Bombay – 1940s through the 1950s', in Burcu Dogramaci, Mareike Hetschold, Laura Karp Lugo, Rachel Lee, Helene Roth (eds), *Arrival Cities: Migrating Artists and New Metropolitan Topographies in the 20th Century* (Leuven, Belgium: Leuven University Press, 2020), 77.

8 Gandhy, 'The Beginnings of the Art Movement'

9 Gandhy describes these different exhibition sites in 'The Beginnings of the Art Movement'.

10 Gandhy, 'The Beginnings of the Art Movement'.

11 He held an exhibition of Indian Art at the Upper Grosvenor Gallery, London, and there were several shows in Switzerland.

12 M. F. Husain quoted in lot essay for Christie's: https://www.christies.com/en/lot/lot-6277042/

13 Zehra Jumabhoy in conversation with Karin Zitzewitz and Sonal Khullar, 'The Progressive Artists' Group & the "Idea of India"', *Borderlines* (9 October 2019).

14 S. H. Raza quoted in Kabir Jhala, 'Leading Indian Modernist SH Raza gets first public museum retrospective at Centre Pompidou in Paris', *The Art Newspaper* (16 March 2023).

15 Shireen Gandhy describes her mother's involvement: 'She would travel to Baroda (Valadora) to find newer artists, and was in the office every day, involved with every show... She was good sense, and he was all idealism.' Quoted in Sanjukta Sharma, 'Gallery Chemould: The alchemists', *Mint* (2 September 2013).

16 Jerry Pinto in *Citizen Gallery: The Gandhys of Chemould and the Birth of Modern Art in Bombay* (New Delhi: Speaking Tiger, 2022), 120.

17 Khorshed Gandhy quoted in Pinto, *Citizen Gallery*, 183.

18 Khorshed Gandhy quoted in Pinto, *Citizen Gallery*, 184.

19 Kekoo Gandhy quoted in Meher Marfatia, 'Kekoo Gandhy: Guru, mentor, patron, critic and more', *Mumbai Mirror* (11 November 2012).

Malick Sidibé

1 Manthia Diawara, 'The 1960s in Bamako: Malick Sidibé and James Brown', in Mona Hadler and Kalliopi Minioudaki (eds), *Pop Art and Beyond: Gender, Race, and Class in the Global Sixties* (London: Bloomsbury, 2022), 48.

2 Malick Sidibé in *Dolce Vita Africana* (dir. Cosima Spender, Tiger Lily Productions, for BBC Storyville, 2006).

3 Malick Sidibé in interview with Jerome Sother in *Lens Culture*, 2008: https://www.lensculture.com/articles/malick-sidibe-interview-with-malick-sidibe

4 Interview with Malick Sidibé in *ASX*, 2009: https://americansuburbx.com/2011/02/interview-interview-with-malick-sidibe.html

5 Interview with Malick Sidibé in *ASX*, 2009: https://americansuburbx.com/2011/02/interview-interview-with-malick-sidibe.html

6 Michelle Lamuniere, introduction to 'Ready to Wear: A Conversation with Malick Sidibé', *Transition*, 88, 10, 4 (2001), 132.

7 Sidibé in *Lens Culture*, 2008.

8 Diawara, 'The 1960s in Bamako', 49–50.

9 Interview with Malick Sidibé in *ASX*, 2009: https://americansuburbx.com/2011/02/interview-interview-with-malick-sidibe.html

10 Sidibé in *Lens Culture*, 2008.

11 Roland Barthes, *Camera Lucida*, 27: https://archive.org/details/BarthesRolandCameraLucidaReflectionsonPhotography/page/n1/mode/2up?q=punctum

12 Malick Sidibé, interviewed by Lucas Michael, *Index Magazine*, 1999: http://www.indexmagazine.com/interviews/malick_Sidibé.shtml

13 Malick Sidibé in *Incontent* (dir. Douglas Sloan).

14 Sidibé in *Incontent*.

CHAPTER 5: COURTING CONTROVERSY

Introduction

1 Yaëlle Biro explores this in the essay 'Amedeo Modigliani: Paul Guillaume and African Art', Simonetta Fraquelli and Cécile Girardeau

(eds), *Modigliani: A Painter and His Art Dealer* (Paris: Musée d'Orsay, Flammarion, 2023).

2 Quoted in Philippe Peltier 'Fénéon's Collection of Art from Africa and Oceania', Starr Figura, Isabelle Cahn and Philippe Peltier (eds), *Félix Fénéon: The Anarchist and the Avant-Garde* (New York: Museum of Modern Art, 2020), 184.

Paul Guillaume

1 Paul Guillaume, *Primitive Negro Sculpture* (New York: Harcourt, Brace and Company, 1926), 64.

2 Adolph Basler, 'M. Paul Guillaume et sa collection de tableaux', *L'Amour de l'Art*, 7 (July 1929), 255.

3 Alain Locke, 'A Note on African Art', *Opportunity: A Journal of Negro Life*, 2, 17 (May 1924), 136.

4 Alain Locke, 'African Art in America', *Nation* (16 March 1926), 290.

5 Guillaume, *Primitive Negro Sculpture*, 3.

6 Guillaume, *Primitive Negro Sculpture*, 10.

7 Guillaume, *Primitive Negro Sculpture*, 9.

8 Guillaume, *Primitive Negro Sculpture*, 7.

9 Ijeoma Oluo, *So you want to talk about race* (New York: Hachette, 2018), 140.

10 Locke, 'African Art in America', *Nation*, 290.

11 Paul Guillaume, 'Actualités', *Les arts à Paris*, I (March 15, 1918), 3.

12 John Monroe, 'Surface Tensions: Empire, Parisian Modernism, and "Authenticity" in African Sculpture, 1917–1939', *The American Historical Review* 117, 2 (2012), 456.

13 Marcel Astruc, 'A une idole noire', *Vogue*, 8, 3 (1 March 1927), 39.

14 Chinua Achebe, *From The Education of a British-Protected Child* (London: Penguin, 2010), 136–7.

Dikran Kelekian

1 The business card for his uncle's shop Magasin Kéork Kélékian mentioned it sold *'curiosités orientales, antiquités diverses'*. The details of this are discussed by Luiza De Camargo, in 'Content and Character: Dikran Kelekian and Eastern Decorative Arts Objects in America', MA Dissertation (The Smithsonian Associates and the Concoran College of Art and Design, 2012), 4.

2 The Metropolitan Museum of Art, New York, did not have an Islamic art department until 1932.

3 Edward Said, 'Introduction', *Orientalism: Western Conceptions of the Orient* (London: Penguin 1995), I.

4 Unnamed writer, 'A Connoisseur's Advice', *Chicago Daily Tribune*, 3 September 1893, 3.

5 John J. Flinn recounts the typical bargain prices on offer, 'Bazaars may be found here in abundance, and there is ample opportunity for spending a dollar or two in curiosities', *World's Fair Grounds, Buildings and Attractions Illustrated* (Chicago: Stanford Guide Co., 1893), 67.

6 These evaluations appear in the pamphlet Dikran Kelekian, *Works of Art and Antiquities: Faiences, Carpets, Statuettes, Greek and Roman Old Coins, and Precious Stones* (1893).

7 Wellesley Reid Davis, *Notes of Le Musée de Bosphore* (New York City: Dikran G. Kelekian, 1898), 3.

8 Unnamed writer, 'The Kelekian Collection', *The Collector*, 6, 1 (1894), 13.

9 'Persian Textiles', *The Art Amateur* 44, 3 (1901), 68.

10 Kelekian quoted by Marilyn Jenkins-Madina in 'Collecting the "Orient" at the Met: Early Tastemakers in America', *Ars Orientalis*, 30 (2000), 74.

11 Friedrich Sarre quoted by David J. Roxburgh in 'After Munich: Reflections on Recent Exhibitions', in 'After One Hundred Years: The 1910 Exhibition "Meisterwerke muhammedanischer Kunst" Reconsidered', Andrea Lermer and Avinoam Shalem (eds), *Islamic History and Civilization*, 82, (2010), 362.

12 Roxburgh, 'After Munich', 365.

13 Kelekian quoted by Marianna Shreve Simpson in 'A Gallant Era: Henry Walters, Islamic Art, and the Kelekian Connection', *The Journal of the Walters Art Museum*, 59 (2001), 108.

14 Kelekian's obituary in *The New York Times* from 31 January 1951 mentions that he was awarded the Legion of Honor. Regarding Kelekian's commitment to modern art, the dealer had his portrait painted by many modern artists whose careers he supported. In 1944, the Durand-Ruel gallery in New York brought together a number of these portraits for the exhibition, *Kelekian as the Artist Sees Him* (17 October–4 November).

The Wildenstein Family

1 Daniel Wildenstein and Yves Stravidès, *Marchands d'art* (Paris: Plon, 1999), 170. (All quotes authors' own.)

2 Charles Dellheim discusses Nathan's background in Chapter 1 of Charles Dellheim, *Belonging*

and Betrayal: How Jews Made the Art World (Waltham, MA: Brandeis University Press, 2021), 36–75.

3 Wildenstein, Stravidès, *Marchands d'Art*, 15.

4 In 1907, he and Duveen jointly acquired Rudolph Kann's art collection.

5 Wildenstein, Stravidès, *Marchands d'Art*, 14.

6 This is recounted by Charles Dellheim in *Belonging and Betrayal: How Jews Made the Art World* (Waltham, MA: Brandeis University Press, 2021), 45.

7 Wildenstein, Stravidès, *Marchands d'Art*, 13.

8 Wildenstein, Stravidès, *Marchands d'Art*, 39–40.,

9 Georges' comment is remembered by Wildenstein in *Marchands d'Art*, 40.

10 Michel Foucault discusses the relationship between knowledge and power in Michel Foucault and Colin Gordon, *Power/Knowledge: Selected Interviews and Other Writings 1972–1977* (New York: Vintage Books, 2015).

11 Douglas Cooper quoted in Suzanna Andrews, 'Bitter Spoils', *Vanity Fair* (March 1998).

12 Daniel Wildenstein writes, 'One day, an art historian wrote a vitriolic article on my Dad's and Raymond Cogniat's *Gauguin*. He was called Douglas Cooper: it was him who interrogated Haberstock after the war. In his article, he had just things and unjust remarks. My father therefore said to Cooper: "Ah good, come work with us. Go for it. Do it again." That's what he did. He died in 1984. He had just finished cataloguing all the paintings,' in Wildenstein and Stravidès, *Marchands* d'Art, 193.

13 The events around this sale are recounted by Suzanna Andrews in 'Bitter Spoils', *Vanity Fair* (March 1998).

14 Daniel had two sons, Alec and Guy. Guy ran his father's art business, while Alec was more interested in the family's other great passion: racehorses.

15 Alec Wildenstein, quoted in Andrews, *Vanity Fair*.

16 Philip Hook, *Rogues' Gallery: A History of Art and Its Dealers* (London: Profile, 2017), 102.

17 Wildenstein, Stravidès, *Marchands d'Art*, 134.

18 Haberstock quoted in Dellheim, *Belonging and Betrayal*, 782. Dellheim discusses Haberstock's interrogation, and evaluates Georges Wildenstein's potential involvement with the Nazi art dealer: 782–93.

19 Daniel Wildenstein dismisses the idea that the family were involved with the Nazis. He says of Dequoy, 'When one has been as crooked as he was before my father hired him, I say that one can stay that way... During the Occupation, Dequoy did business with Haberstock. He did some beauties. He bought a superb apartment on Rue Saint-Florentin, and it was not with what we gave him in London that he was able to afford it,' Wildenstein, Stravidès, *Marchands d'Art*, 111.

20 The manuscripts were inscribed with the letters 'ka', which indicates how the Nazis had catalogued the family's collection ('ka' standing for Kann, Alphonse). The Wildensteins contested the validity of the inscriptions. This case is recounted in detailed by Alan Riding, 'Collector's Family Tries to Illuminate the Past of Manuscripts in France', *The New York Times* (3 September 1997).

21 *Marchands d'Art* (Paris: Plon, 1999) is an attempt by Daniel Wildenstein to clear up contentious stories like this. He insists, the 'nine medieval illuminated manuscripts... my grandfather and my father had bought from the Kann family and from dealers, between 1909 and 1930', 130–31.

22 This raid was the result of Sylvia Wildenstein's case against her stepchildren, Alec and Guy, which is discussed in detail by Rachel Corbett in 'The Inheritance Case That Could Unravel an Art Dynasty', *New York Times* (23 August 2023).

23 The discovery of the frames with swastikas is recounted in Corbett, *The New York Times*.

24 Andrews, *Vanity Fair*.

25 Wildenstein, Stravidès, *Marchands d'Art*, 172.

26 Daniel Wildenstein quoted in Corbett, *The New York Times*.

27 This is mentioned in Corbett, *The New York Times*.

28 Daniel Wildenstein quoted in Corbett, *The New York Times*.

29 This case is documented in Corbett, *The New York Times*.

30 How Sylvia Wildenstein's evidence was used in the second trial is discussed by Anca Ulea in 'To trust or not to trust? Wildenstein art family back in court for tax fraud', *euronews.culture*, 20 September 2023.

31 Quoted in *Apollo*, 10 March 2024.

32 *Apollo*, 10 March 2024.

Notes

Hildebrand Gurlitt

1 Hildebrand Gurlitt, Diary, undated, quoted in Meike Hoffmann 'The Long Shadows of the Past: A Critical Appraisal of Hildebrand Gurlitt's Life', in Andrea Baresel-Brand, Meike Hopp, Agnieszka Magdalena Lulińska (eds), *Gurlitt Status Report* (Munich, Germany: Hirmer, 2017), 16.

2 Fydor Dostoevsky, *The Idiot* (London; Vizetelly and Co; New York: Bretano's, 1887), 2. The original line reads, 'A coward is a man who is afraid and runs away; the man who is frightened but does not run away, is not *quite* a coward.' It is worth noting that Gurlitt has misinterpreted Dostoevsky who is not saying that remaining is uncowardly.

3 This is recounted by Johannes Kayser in 'Museumswürdig: Ein Wort zu der letzten Ansprache des Museumsdirektors Dr. Gurlitt in Zwickau', *Zwickauer Zeitung*, 21 October 1929.

4 His father (being classified as half Jewish) was dismissed from his position at the university, and his brother, who was married to a Jewish woman, lost his job in 1937.

5 The accepted opinion is that Gurlitt acquired 3,879 works of art, including 78 paintings, 3,471 prints, 278 watercolours and 52 drawings. He bought far more than the other three dealers: Ferdinand Möller (848 works), Karl Buchholz (883 works) and Bernhard A. Böhmer (1,187 works).

6 Probably because there were no repercussions, Gurlitt would admit to dealing in degenerate art.

7 Susan Ronald, *Hitler's Art Thief: Hildebrand Gurlitt, the Nazis, and the Looting of Europe's Treasures* (New York: St. Martin's Griffin, 2017), 206.

8 The Linz Commission sourced art for the Führermuseum, which was to be located in Linz, Austria, where Hitler was born.

9 These figures are based on the accounting records of the Linz Commission.

10 In 1943 Voss took over the Linz Commission after his predecessor Hans Posse died in 1942. Voss knew Gurlitt from his museum days, and he appointed him as chief buyer. He asked Gurlitt to look out for drawings by Jean-Baptiste Huet, François Boucher and Jean-Honoré Fragonard to complement their eighteenth-century paintings.

11 These financial details are discussed by Birgit Schwarz 'Hildebrand Gurlitt and the "Special Commission Linz"' in Baresel-Brand, Hopp, Lulińska (eds), *Gurlitt Status Report*, 55.

12 In 1946, the Law of Liberation from National Socialism and Militarism was passed. This stated that a profiteer was 'anyone who, at the expense of those persecuted for political, religious or racial reasons, directly or indirectly gained, or strove for excessive advantages for himself or others,' quoted in Hoffmann, 'The Long Shadows of the Past', 24. Gurlitt's income was well beyond the 36,000 RM annual limit set by the Law of Liberation. Gurlitt argued that his higher profits reflected his expertise in the field and knowledge of art history.

13 Renate Gurlitt quoted in Gramlich and Hopp, 'Occasionally Spirit is Turned into Money', 44–5.

14 Jeevan Vasagar and Elizabeth Paton, 'Art: Lost and Found', *Financial Times*, 8 November 2013.

15 Ronald Lauder, quoted in Alex Shoumatoff, 'The Devil and the Art Dealer', *Vanity Fair*, 19 March 2014.

16 Cornelius Gurlitt quoted in Philip Oltermann, 'Reclusive Art Collector Cornelius Gurlitt to Return Nazi-looted Works', *Guardian*, 27 March 2014.

Stephen Radich

1 Yayoi Kusama, *Infinity Net: The Autobiography of Yayoi Kusama*, translated by Ralph McCarthy (Chicago IL: University of Chicago Press, 2021), 33.

2 'Obituary Stephen Radich', *Artforum*, 27 December 2007.

3 Hilton Kramer's defence is described in Ken Johnson, 'Stephen Radich, Owner of Controversial Art Gallery, Is Dead at 85', *New York Times*, 26 December 2007.

4 Leon Golub quoted in Lippard, *Different War*, 13.

5 Faith Ringgold, video interview for Glenstone Museum, 21 October 2021: https://youtube.com/watch?v=RU5x-xc7xrQ.

6 Assistant District Attorney Gerald Slater quoted in Lippard, *Different War*, 27.

7 Lippard, *Different War*, 17.

CHAPTER 6: THE PERSONALITY DEALER

Introduction

1 Tom Wolfe, 'The "Me" Decade', *New York*, 23 August 1976: https://nymag.com/article/tom-wolfe-me-decade-third-great-awakening.html.

2 Christopher Lasch, *The Culture of Narcissism* (New York, London: W. W. Norton and Company, 1978), 4–5.

3 Joan U. Halperin, *Félix Fénéon and the Language of Art Criticism* (Ann Arbor, I: UMI Research Press, 1980), 8.

4 Alexander Iolas quoted in Regina Marler, 'Every Time I Look at It I Feel Ill', *The New York Review,* 25 October 2018.

5 Wolfe, 'The "Me" Decade'.

Félix Fénéon

1 Remy de Gourmont quoted in Joan U. Halperin, *Félix Fénéon and the Language of Art Criticism* (Ann Arbor, Michigan: UMI Research Press, 1980), 8.

2 Stéphane Mallarmé, 'Crisis in Poetry' in *Stéphane Mallarmé: Selected Poetry and Prose,* trans. Mary Ann Caws (New York: New Directions Publishing, 1982), 75.

3 Arthur Rimbaud, *Illuminations,* trans.by John Ashbery, new edition (Manchester, England: Carcanet Press, 2018).

4 Félix Fénéon, *Au-delà de l'impressionnisme,* ed. Françoise Cachin (Paris: Hermann, 1966), 43

5 Téodor de Wyzewa quoted in Marnin Young 'Fénéon's Art Criticism' in Starr Figura, Isabelle Cahn and Philippe Peltier (eds), *Félix Fénéon: The Anarchist and the Avant-Garde* (New York: Museum of Modern Art, 2020), 37.

6 Patricia Leighton, 'Feneon's Anarchist Avant-Gardism', in *Félix Fénéon: The Anarchist and the Avant-Garde,* 95.

7 Camille Pissarro, Georges Seurat and Paul Signac were all anarchists, as were many of the Nabis artists including Félix Vallotton.

8 In a diary entry dated 26 December 1894, Fénéon wrote 'anarchist acts of terrorism have done a lot more for propaganda than 20 years of pamphlets by Reclus or Kropotkin.' This is also cited in Starr Figura, Isabelle Cahn and Philippe Peltier 'Félix Fénéon: The Anarchist and the Avant-Garde' in *Félix Fénéon: The Anarchist and the Avant-Garde,* 23.

9 Félix Fénéon quoted in Julian Barnes, 'Behind the Gas Lamp', *London Review of Books*, 29, 19 (14 October 2007).

10 Philip Hook, *Rogues' Gallery: A History of Art and its Dealers* (London: Profile Books, 2017), 172.

11 This street is now called rue du Chevalier-de-Saint-George.

12 Many of the Fauve artists had worked with the Neo-Impressionists. Matisse had spent the summer of 1904 painting with Signac in Saint-Tropez, and his works around this time show the influence of Neo-Impressionism. It is highly likely that Signac introduced Matisse to Fénéon.

13 Gertrude Stein, *The Autobiography of Alice B. Toklas* (New York: The Modern Library, 1992), 79.

14 Stein described the camps as 'Picassoites and Matisseites' in *The Autobiography of Alice B. Toklas,* 124–25.

15 Fénéon quoted by Halperin in *Félix Fénéon and the Language of Art Criticism,* 69.

16 Hook, *Rogues' Gallery,* 174.

17 Félix Fénéon quoted in Julian Barnes, 'Behind the Gas Lamp', *London Review of Books,* 29, 19 (4 October 2007).

Julien Levy

1 Joella recalled, 'He never wanted to leave a party. He'd always say something might happen, something amazing might happen,' quoted in Steven Watson, 'Julien Levy: Exhibitionist and Harvard Modernist,' quoted in Ingrid Schaffner and Lisa Jacobs (eds), *Julien Levy: Portrait of an Art Gallery* (Cambridge, MA: MIT Press, 1998), 92.

2 Julien Levy, oral history interview, 30 May 1975.

3 Dorothea Lang, 'The Julien Levy That I Knew' in Ingrid Schaffner and Lisa Jacobs (eds), *Julien Levy: Portrait of an Art Gallery* (Cambridge, MA: MIT Press, 1998), 15.

4 Levy, oral history interview, 30 May 1975.

5 For more information on Mina Loy's apartment, and her relationship with Julien Levy, see Carolyn Burke, 'Loy-alism: Julien Levy's Kinship with Mina Loy' in *Julien Levy: Portrait of an Art Gallery,* 60–78.

6 Levy, oral history interview, 30 May 1975.

7 Levy quoted in Ingrid Schaffner 'Alchemy of the Gallery' in *Julien Levy: Portrait of an Art Gallery,* 24.

8 Sallie Faxon Saunders 'Middle Men of Art,' *Vogue,* 15 March 1938.

9 Levy quoted in Schaffner, 'Alchemy of the Gallery', 21.

10 Levy, oral history interview, 30 May 1975.

11 Levy, oral history interview, 30 May 1975.

12 Schaffner, 'Alchemy of the Gallery', 21.

13 Julien Levy, *Memoir of an Art Gallery* (Boston, MA: MFA Publications, 2003), 150.

14 This is the title of the last chapter of *Memoir of an Art Gallery*. There are differing stories around Gorky's last words. Others say he had written a note. Also, some report that this read 'Goodby all my loved'. For an account of this discrepancy, see 'The Mysterious Art of Arshile Gorky', *Guardian*, 6 February 2010.

Peggy Guggenheim

1 Peggy Guggenheim recounts this in her last interview with Jacqueline B. Weld, included in the film *Peggy Guggenheim, Art Addict* (dir. Lisa Immordino Vreeland, 2015).

2 Peggy Guggenheim published her autobiography *Out of this Century: Confessions of an Art Addict* in 1946.

3 When Peggy Guggenheim closed her New York gallery in 1947, Clement Greenberg said, 'In the three or four years of her career as a New York gallery director, she gave first showings to more serious new artists than anyone else in the country. I am convinced that Peggy Guggenheim's place in the history of American art will grow larger as time passes,' quoted in Grace Glueck, 'Paying Tribute to the Daring Peggy Guggenheim,' *The New York Times*, 1 March 1987.

4 Peggy Guggenheim in her last interview with Jacqueline B. Weld, in *Peggy Guggenheim, Art Addict*.

5 Peggy Guggenheim, *Out of this Century: Confessions of an Art Addict* (London, Welbeck, 2018), 6.

6 Guggenheim, *Out of this Century*, 5.

7 Guggenheim, 'I have no pleasant memories of any kind. It seems to me now that it was one long protracted agony. When I was very young I had no friends. I didn't go to school until I was fifteen. Instead, I studied under private tutors at home,' in *Out of this Century*, 6.

8 Guggenheim describes this in *Out of this Century*, 5.

9 Guggenheim describes this in *Out of this Century*, 13.

10 The operation on her nose was unsuccessful, and so painful that Guggenheim asked the surgeon to stop. Biographer Francine Prose devotes a chapter to Guggenheim's nose, *Peggy Guggenheim: The Shock of the Modern* (New Haven, CT: Yale University Press, 2015), 52–6.

11 John Richardson in interview in *Peggy Guggenheim, Art Addict*.

12 In 1919 Peggy Guggenheim received $450,000 inheritance (equivalent to around $5 million today) from her father who had made a fortune from mining metals. On her mother's death in 1937, she received a further $450,000.

13 Marina Abramović interviewed in *Peggy Guggenheim, Art Addict*.

14 Guggenheim in interview in *Peggy Guggenheim, Art Addict*.

15 Guggenheim quoted by Jennifer Blessing in 'Peggy's Surreal Playground' in Clare Bell, Jennifer Blessing, Julia Brown, Lisa Dennison, Andrea Feeser, Michael Govan, Thomas Krens, Nancy Spector, Diane Waldman, *Art of this Century: the Guggenheim and Museum and its Collection* (New York: Solomon R. Guggenheim Foundation, 1993), 195 and 198.

16 Guggenheim quoted in Amy Fine Collins, 'The 20th Century Enfant Terrible', *Airmail* (13 April 2024).

17 Guggenheim quoted in Thomas Krens, 'The Genesis of a Museum: The History of the Guggenheim', *Art of this Century: The Guggenheim Museum and its Collections*, 24.

18 Guggenheim in interview in *Peggy Guggenheim, Art Addict*.

19 Guggenheim in interview in *Peggy Guggenheim, Art Addict*.

20 In a later interview, Guggenheim, reflecting on her decision to stay in Paris, said, 'I wouldn't leave until I could get the pictures out,' in interview in *Peggy Guggenheim, Art Addict*.

21 Picasso quoted in Claudia Pierpont, 'The Collector', *The New Yorker* (5 May 2002).

22 Guggenheim quoted in Jennifer Blessing, 'Peggy's Surreal Playground' in *Art of this Century: The Guggenheim Museum and its Collections*, 181.

23 Guggenheim in interview in *Peggy Guggenheim, Art Addict*.

George Maciunas

1 Milan Knížák quoted by Emmett Williams and Ann Noel (eds) in *Mr. Fluxus: A Collective Portrait of George Maciunas 1931–1978* (London: Thames and Hudson, 1997), 322.

2 Footage of Leokadija Maciunas recounting

their wartime experience is included in the biographical film *George: The Story of George Maciunas and Fluxus* (dir. Jeffrey Perkins, 2019).

3 This is recounted in *George: The Story of George Maciunas and Fluxus*.

4 Yoko Ono in interview with MoMA curator Christopher Cherix, https://www.moma.org/audio/playlist/15/370.

5 Ono in interview with Cherix.

6 This is recounted by Leokadija Maciunas in *George: The Story of George Maciunas and Fluxus*.

7 Fluxus manifesto quoted by Clive Phillpot in 'Manifesto I: Fluxus: Magazines, Manifestos. Multum in Parvo' on https://georgemaciunas.com/about/cv/manifesto-i/

8 Fluxus artist AY-O recounts Maciunas saying this in conversation. AY-O is quoted in *Mr Fluxus*, 127.

Robert Fraser

1 Keith Richards quoted in Harriet Vyner, *Groovy Bob* (London: Faber and Faber, 1999), 103.

2 Paul McCartney quoted in *Groovy Bob*, 102.

3 McCartney quoted in *Groovy Bob*, 102.

4 Robert Fraser quoted in *Groovy Bob*, 9. Susan Loppert also reports that Fraser's mother said, 'He saw a Vuillard when he was six and he just *knew*,' quoted in *Groovy Bob*, 131.

5 Fraser's letter to parents, undated, quoted in *Groovy Bob*, 8.

6 Mr Elliot, Headmaster of Fraser's prep school, Fan Court School, quoted in *Groovy Bob*, 13.

7 Fraser quoted in *Groovy Bob*, 52.

8 Bill Willis quoted in *Groovy Bob*, 47.

9 Jim Dine quoted in *Groovy Bob*, 55.

10 The conversation between Robert and Lionel Fraser is related by Arne Ekstron in *Groovy Bob*, 62-63.

11 Bridget Riley quoted in *Groovy Bob*, 131.

12 Bryan Robertson quoted in *Groovy Bob*, 80.

13 Fraser quoted in Barry Miles, *Paul McCartney: Many Years From Now* (London: Vintage, 1997), 251.

14 Riley quoted in *Groovy Bob*, 114.

15 Anita Pallenberg quoted in *Groovy Bob*, 117.

16 McCartney quoted in 'Paul McCartney acquires a painting', *The Paul McCartney Project*, https://www.the-paulmccartney-project.com/1968/06/paul-mccartney-acquires-le-jeu-de-mourre-a-painting-by-magritte/.

17 Chris Jagger quoted in *Groovy Bob*, 237.

18 Malcolm McLaren quoted in *Groovy Bob*, 256.

19 Brian Clarke quoted in *Groovy Bob*, 271.

20 Richard Hamilton quoted in *Groovy Bob*, 292.

CONCLUSION

1 Gilbert and George first performed *The Singing Sculpture* in their studio in 1969. This rendition was simpler (for example, their faces were not painted). They went on to perform the piece on many other occasions.

2 George talking in the South Bank Show two-part television documentary, *The Fundamental Gilbert & George* (1997).

3 Gilbert talks about this in *The Fundamental Gilbert & George*.

Selected Bibliography

CHAPTER 1: EARLY DEALINGS

Arthur Pond

Anthony Ashley Cooper, 3rd Earl of Shaftesbury, 'Concerning Virtue or Merit', in John M. Robertson (ed.), *Characteristics of Men, Manners, Opinions and Times* (1711), 2 vols. (Indianapolis: Bobbs Merrill, 1964).

Philip Hook, *Rogues' Gallery: A History of Art and its Dealers* (London: Profile Books, 2017).

Louise Lippincott, *Selling Art in Georgian London: The Rise of Arthur Pond* (New Haven, CT: Yale University Press, 1983).

Harry Mount, 'The Monkey with the Magnifying Glass: Constructions of the Connoisseur in Eighteenth-Century Britain', *Oxford Art Journal*, 29, 2 (June 2006), 167–84.

William Hogarth

Pierre Bourdieu, *The Rules of Art* (Cambridge: Polity Press, 1996).

Alice Insley, *William Hogarth: Visions in Print* (London: Tate Publishing, 2021).

Joseph Monteyne, *From Still Life to the Screen: Print Culture, Display, and the Materiality of the Image in Eighteenth-Century London* (New Haven, CT: Yale University Press, 2013).

Hester Lynch Piozzi, *Anecdotes of the Late Samuel Johnson* (1786), published with introduction by S. C. Roberts (Cambridge, UK: Cambridge University Press, 1925).

Michael Rosenthal, *Hogarth* (London: Chaucer Press, 2005).

Jenny Uglow, *William Hogarth: A Life and a World* (London: Faber and Faber, 1998).

William Buchanan

Hugh Brigstocke (ed.), *William Buchanan and the Nineteenth Century Art Trade: 100 letters to his Agents in London and Italy* (London: Paul Mellon Centre for Studies in British Art, 1982).

William Buchanan, *Memoirs of Painting, With A Chronological History of The Importation of Pictures by the Great Masters Into England Since The French Revolution* (London: R. Ackermann, 1824).

Philip Hook, *Rogues' Gallery: A History of Art and Its Dealers* (London: Profile Books, 2017).

Charles Sebag-Montefiore, *A Dynasty of Dealers: John Smith and Successors, 1801–1924. A Study of the Art Market in Nineteenth Century London* (London: The Roxburghe Club, 2013).

Ernest Gambart

Pierre Bourdieu, *The Field of Cultural Production: Essays on Art and Literature*, Randal Johnson (trans. and ed.), (New York: Columbia University Press, 1993).

Pierre Bourdieu, *The Rules of Art* (Cambridge, UK: Polity Press, 1996).

Pamela Fletcher, 'Creating the French Gallery: Ernest Gambart and the Rise of the Commercial Art Gallery in Mid-Victorian London', *Nineteenth Century Art Worldwide*, 6, 1 (Spring 2007).

Philip Hook, *Rogues' Gallery: A History of Art and Its Dealers* (London: Profile Books, 2017).

Jeremy Maas, *Gambart: Prince of the Victorian Art World* (London: Barrie and Jenkins, 1975).

Paul Durand-Ruel

Pierre Assouline, *Discovering Impressionism: The Life of Paul Durand-Ruel* (London: Thames and Hudson, 2005).

Jan Dirk Baetens and Dries Lyna (eds), *Art Crossing Borders: The Internationalisation of the Art Market in the Age of Nation States, 1750–1914* (Leiden, The Netherlands: Brill, 2019).

Paul-Louis Durand-Ruel and Flavie Durand-Ruel, *Paul Durand-Ruel: Memoirs of the First Impressionist Art Dealer (1831–1922)*, (Paris: Flammarion, 2014).

Philip Hook, *Rogues' Gallery: A History of Art and Its Dealers* (London: Profile Books, 2017).

Philip Hook, *The Ultimate Trophy: How the Impressionist Painting Conquered the World* (London: Prestel Publishing, 2009).

Sylvie Patry (ed.), *Inventing Impressionism: Paul Durand-Ruel and the Modern Art Market* (London: National Gallery, 2015).

Martha Ward, 'Impressionist Installations and Private Exhibitions', *The Art Bulletin* 73, 4 (1991), 599–622.

CHAPTER 2: THE BRANDED DEALER

Introduction

Brian O'Doherty, *Inside the White Cube: The Ideology of the Gallery Space* (Berkeley, CA: University of California Press, 1999).

Don Thompson, *The $12 Million Stuffed Shark: The Curious Economics of Contemporary Art* (London: Aurum Press, 2008).

Extraordinary Art Dealers

Joseph Duveen

S. N. Behrman, *Duveen* (New York: Random House, 1952).

Rachel Cohen, *Bernard Berenson: A Life in the Picture Trade* (New Haven, CT: Yale University Press, 2013).

Edward Fowles, *Memories of Duveen Brothers* (London: Times Books, 1976).

Christopher Gray, 'Where Old Masters Flew off the Walls', *The New York Times* (5 December 2015).

Anne Helmreich, Edward Sterrett, Edward and Sandra van Ginhoven, 'Purpose Built: Duveen and the Commercial Art Gallery', *Nineteenth-Century Art Worldwide* 20, 2 (Summer 2021).

Philip Hook, *Rogues' Gallery: A History of Art and Its Dealers* (London: Profile Books, 2017).

Meryle Secrest, *Duveen: A Life in Art* (New York: Knopf, 2004).

Colin Simpson, *Artful Partners: Bernard Berenson and Joseph Duveen* (New York: Macmillan, 1986).

Ambroise Vollard

Elza Adamowicz, 'The Surrealist Artist's Book: Beyond the Page', *Princeton University Library Chronicle* 70, 2 (2009), 265–92.

Jan Dirk Baetens and Dries Lyna (eds), *Art Crossing Borders – The Internationalisation of the Art Market in the Age of Nation States, 1750–1914* (Leiden, The Netherlands: Brill, 2019).

Philip Hook, *Rogues' Gallery: A History of Art and Its Dealers* (London: Profile Books, 2017).

Robert Jensen, *Marketing Modernism in Fin-de-Siècle Europe* (Princeton, NJ: Princeton University Press, 1994).

Rebecca A. Rabinow (ed.), *Cezanne to Picasso: Ambroise Vollard, Patron of the Avant-Garde* (New Haven, CT: Yale University Press, 2006).

John Russell Taylor and Brian Brooke, *The Art Dealers* (New York: Hodder and Stoughton, 1969).

Ambroise Vollard, *Recollections of a Picture Dealer* (London: Constable, 1936; New York: Dover Publications, 1978).

Ambroise Vollard, *Paul Cezanne: His Life and Art* (New York: Crown, 1937).

Samuel M. Kootz

Marcia Bystryn, 'Art Galleries as Gatekeepers: The Case of the Abstract Expressionists', *Social Research*, 45, 2 (Summer 1978), 390–408.

Samuel Kootz, *The Intrasubjectives* (New York: Samuel M. Kootz Gallery, 1949).

Samuel Kootz, *New Frontiers in American Painting* (New York: Hastings House, 1943).

Oral history interview with Samuel M. Kootz, 13 April 1964, transcript and recording held in Archives of American Art, Smithsonian Institute, Washington, DC.

Kootz Gallery Records, 1923–66, Archives of American Art, Smithsonian Institute, Washington, DC.

Emily S. Warner, 'Marketing the Monumental: Wall Painting at Midcentury', *Archives of American Art Journal*, 56, 2 (2017), 26–49.

Betty Parsons

Marcia Bystryn, 'Art Galleries as Gatekeepers: The Case of the Abstract Expressionists', *Social Research*, 45, 2 (Summer 1978).

Paul Cummings interviews Leo Castelli, New York, 14 May–8 June 1969, Archives of American Art, Smithsonian Institute, Washington, DC.

Lee Hall, *Betty Parsons: Artist, Dealer, Collector* (New York: H. N. Abrams, 1991).

Titia Hulst, (ed.), *A History of the Western Art Market: A Sourcebook of Writings on Artists, Dealers, and Markets* (Oakland, CA: University of California Press, 2017).

Brian O'Doherty, *Inside the White Cube: The Ideology of the Gallery Space* (San Francisco, CA: Lapis Press, 1986).

Don Thompson, *The $12 Million Stuffed Shark: The Curious Economics of Contemporary Art* (London: Palgrave Macmillan, 2008).

Calvin Tomkins, 'A Keeper of the Treasure', *New Yorker* (9 June 1975), 44–69.

Peter Ward, *From Manet to Manhattan: The Rise of The Modern Art Market* (London: Hutchinson 1992).

Leo Castelli

Castelli and his Artists: Twenty-Five Years (Aspen, CO: Aspen Center for Visual Arts, 1982).

Annie Cohen-Solal, *Leo and His Circle: The Life of Leo Castelli* (New York: Knopf, 2010).

Laura de Coppet and Alan Jones (eds), *The Art Dealers: The Powers Behind the Scene Tell How the Art World Really Works* (New York: Clarkson N. Potter, 1984).

Malcolm Goldstein, *Landscape with Figures: A History of Art Dealing in the United States* (Oxford: Oxford University Press, 2000).

Titia Hulst, 'The Leo Castelli Gallery', *Archives of American Art Journal*, 46, 3/4 (September 2007), 14–27.

Steven Naifeh, *Culture Making: Money, Success and the New York Art World* (Princeton, NJ: Princeton University Press, 1976).

Peter Schjeldahl, 'How Leo Castelli's Gallery Changed the Art World', *New Yorker*, 7 June 2010.

Meryle Secrest, 'Leo Castelli: Dealing in Myths', *Art News*, 81 (Summer 1982), 66–72.

John Russell Taylor, *The Art Dealers* (London: Hodder and Stoughton, 1969).

Calvin Tomkins, *A Tribute to Leo Castelli* (London: Mayor Gallery, 1985).

Peter Watson, *From Manet to Manhattan: The Rise of the Modern Art Market* (New York: Random House, 1992).

CHAPTER 3: THE IDEALISTS

Daniel-Henry Kahnweiler

Pierre Assouline, *An Artful Life: A Biography of D. H. Kahnweiler, 1884–1979* (New York: Fromm International Pub. Corp, 1991).

Yve-Alain Bois and Katharine Streip, 'Kahnweiler's Lesson', *Representations*, 18 (1987), 33–68.

Malcolm Gee, *Dealers, Critics and Collectors of Modern Painting: Aspects of the Parisian Art Market, 1910–1930* (New York and London: Garland Publishing, 1981).

Daniel-Henry Kahnweiler, *My Galleries and Painters* (trans. H. Weaver), (London: Thames and Hudson, 1971).

Daniel-Henry Kahnweiler, *The Rise of Cubism* (New York: Wittenborn, 1949).

John Richardson, *A Life of Picasso II: The Cubist Rebel, 1907–1916* (New York: Knopf, 2007).

Alfred Stieglitz

Debra Bricker Balken and Jay Bochner, *Debating American Modernism: Stieglitz, Duchamp, and the New York Avant-Garde* (New York: American Federation of Arts, 2003).

Guido Bruno, 'The Passing of "291"', *Pearson's Magazine*, 38 (March 1918), 402–3.

Sarah Greenough, *Modern Art and America: Alfred Stieglitz and His New York Galleries* (Washington, DC: National Gallery of Art, 2000).

William Innes Homer, *Alfred Stieglitz and the American Avant-Garde* (London: Secker and Warburg, 1977).

Lisa Mintz Messinger (ed.), *Stieglitz and His Artists: Matisse to O'Keeffe* (New York: Metropolitan Museum of Art, 2011).

Christian A. Peterson, *Alfred Stieglitz's Camera Notes* (New York: W.W. Norton and Co., 1993).

Alfred Stieglitz and Bettina L. Knapp, 'Alfred Stieglitz's Letters to David Liebovitz 1923–1930', *Modern Language Studies*, 15, 3 (1985), 3–37.

Alfred Stieglitz, Sarah Greenough and Juan Hamilton, *Alfred Stieglitz: Photographs and Writing*, 2nd edn (Washington, DC: National Gallery of Art, 1999).

Richard Whelan, *Alfred Stieglitz: A Biography* (Boston, MA: Little Brown, 1995).

Mahonri Sharp Young, *Early American Moderns: Painters of the Stieglitz Group* (New York: Watson-Guptill Publications, 1974).

André Breton

André Breton, *Manifestoes of Surrealism* (Ann Arbor, MI: University of Michigan Press, 1972).

Gérard Durozoi, *History of the Surrealist Movement* (Chicago, IL: University of Chicago Press, 2002).

Paul B. Franklin, 'Décor in Dialogue: Marcel Duchamp's and Salvador Dalí's Projects for the Galerie Gradiva', https://beta.thedali.org/wp-content/uploads/2018/05/Franklin_Final.pdf

Adam Jolles, *The Curatorial Avant-Garde: Surrealism and Exhibition Practice in France, 1925–1941* (Pennsylvania: Penn State University Press, 2015).

Louise Tythacott, 'A Convulsive Beauty: Surrealism, Oceania and African Art', *Journal of Museum Ethnography*, 11 (1999), 43–54.

Ghislaine Wood (ed.), *Surreal Things* (London: V and A, 2007).

Topazia Alliata

Véronique Chagnon-Burke and Caterina Toschi (eds), *Women Art Dealers: Creating Markets for Modern Art, 1940–1990* (London: Bloomsbury Visual Arts, 2024).

Jiddu Krishnamurti, *Freedom from the Known* (New York: Harper and Row, 1969).

Toni Maraini, *Topazia Alliata* (Rome: De Luca Editori d'Arte, 2022).

Virginia Dwan

Los Angeles to New York: Dwan Gallery, 1959–1971, film accompanying exhibition at National Gallery of Art, Washington, DC, 2016, https://www.nga.gov/audio-video/video/los-angeles-to-new-york-dwan-gallery.html.

Robert J. Kett, 'Monumentality as Method: Archaeology and Land Art in the Cold War', *Representations* 130, 1 (2015), 119–51, https://doi.org/10.1525/rep.2015.130.1.119.

James Meyer (ed.), *Los Angeles to New York: Dwan Gallery, 1959–1971* (Chicago, IL: Chicago University Press, 2016).

James Stuckey, 'Game Changer: Virginia Dwan', *Gagosian Quarterly* (Winter 2022).

CHAPTER 4: CULTURAL STEWARDS

Introduction

Irina D. Costache and Clare Kunny (eds), *Historical Narratives of Global Modern Art* (New York: Routledge, 2023).

E. F. Schumacher, *Small is Beautiful: Economics as if People Mattered* (New York: Harper Colophon Books, 1975).

Herwarth Walden

Shulamith Behr, *Expressionism: Movements in Modern Art* (London: Tate Publishing, 2000).

Helen Boorman, 'Rethinking the Expressionist Era: Wilhelmine Cultural Debates and Prussian Elements in German Expressionism', *Oxford Art Journal, 9, 2* (1986), 3–15.

Donald E. Gordon, 'On the Origin of the Word "Expressionism"', *Journal of the Warburg and Courtauld Institutes*, 29 (1966), 368–85.

Riccardo Marchi, 'October 1912: Understanding Kandinsky's Art "Indirectly" at Der Sturm', *Getty Research Journal*, 1 (2009), 53–74.

Monica Strauss, 'Kandinsky and "Der Sturm"', *Art Journal*, 43, 1 (1983), 31–35.

Kate Winskell, 'The Art of Propaganda: Herwarth Walden and "Der Sturm", 1914–1919', *Art History* 18, 3 (September 1995), 315–37.

Edith Halpert

John X. Christ, 'Stuart Davis as Public Artist: American Painting and the Reconstruction of the Public Sphere', *Oxford Art Journal*, 37, 1 (March 2014), 65–82.

A. Deirdre Robson, 'The Girl with the Gallery: Edith Halpert in the Mid-Twentieth-Century New York Art Market', in Véronique Chagnon-Burke and Caterina Toschi (eds), *Women Art Dealers: Creating Markets for Modern Art, 1940–1990* (London: Bloomsbury Visual Arts, 2023), 31–46.

Diane Tepfer, *Edith Gregor Halpert and the Downtown Gallery/Downtown, 1926–1940: A Study in American Art Patronage* (PhD. diss., University of Michigan, Ann Arbor, MI, 1989).

Manuel and Lola Álvarez Bravo

Lola Álvarez Bravo, *Lola Álvarez Bravo: The Frida Kahlo Photographs* (London: Art Data, 1991).

James Oles, Adriana Zala and Rachel Arauz, *Lola Álvarez Bravo and the Photography of an Era* (Barcelona, Spain: R.M. Verlag, 2012).

Agustín Arteaga, *México 1900–1950: Diego Rivera, Frida Kahlo, Jose Clemente Orozco and the Avant-Garde* (New Haven, CT: Yale University Press, 2017).

Adrian Locke, *Mexico: A Revolution in Art 1910–1940* (London: Royal Academy of Arts, 2013).

Kekoo and Khorshed Gandhy

Kekee Manzil: A House of Art (documentary, dir. Dilesh Korya), 2022.

Nancy Adajania, 'Beyond the Commodity Fetish: Art and the Public Sphere in India', *Guggenheim Articles* (28 January 2013).

Sidharth Bhatia, 'The Accidental Gallerist and the Making of Indian Modern Art', *The Wire* (8 July 2020).

Shraddha Jahagirdar-Saxena, 'Meeting the Gandhys through "Kekee Manzil: The House of Art"', *Verve Magazine* (3 March 2020).

Zehra Jumabhoy in conversation with Karin Zitzewitz and Sonal Khullar, 'The Progressive Artists' Group and the "Idea of India"', *Borderlines* (9 October 2019).

Helena Khandelwal, 'How a framing company became Mumbai's iconic Gallery Chemould', *The Indian Express* (15 September 2023).

Jerry Pinto, *Citizen Gallery: The Gandhys of Chemould and the Birth of Modern Art in Bombay* (New Delhi: Speaking Tiger, 2022).

Sanjukta Sharma, 'Gallery Chemould: The Alchemists', *Mint* (2 September 2013).

Karin Zitzewitz, *The Perfect Frame: Presenting Modern Indian Art, Stories and Photographs from the Collection of Kekoo Gandhy* (Mumbai, India: Chemould, 2003).

Malick Sidibé

Mona Hadler and Kalliopi Minioudaki (eds), *Pop Art and Beyond: Gender, Race, and Class in the Global Sixties* (London: Bloomsbury Visual Arts, 2022).

Michelle Lamuniere, Malick Sidibé and Lia Brozga, 'Ready to Wear: A Conversation with Malick Sidibé', *Transition*, 88, 10, 4 (2001), 132–59.

Malick Sidibé and Manthia Diawara, *Malick Sidibé: Photographs* (Göttingen, Germany: Hasselblad/Steidl, 2003).

Malick Sidibé and Florian Ebner, *Malick Sidibé: Bagadadji* (St. Brieuc, France: Gwinzegal, 2008).

Malick Sidibé et al., *Malick Sidibé: The Portrait of Mali* (Milan, Italy: Skira, 2011).

Malick Sidibé: Mali Twist (Paris: Éditions Xavier. Barral, 2017).

Selected Bibliography

CHAPTER 5: COURTING CONTROVERSY

Introduction
Simonetta Fraquelli and Cécile Girardeau
(eds), *Modigliani: A Painter and His Art Dealer*
(Paris: Musée d'Orsay, Flammarion, 2023).

Paul Guillaume
*Catalogue de la collection Jean Walter et Paul
Guillaume* (Paris: Musée de l'Orangerie, 1984).
Modigliani: A Painter and His Art Dealer
(Paris: Musée d'Orsay, Flammarion, 2023).
Joshua I Cohen, 'Fauve Masks: Rethinking Modern
"Primitivist" Uses of African and Oceanic Art,
1905–8', *The Art Bulletin*, 99, 2 (2017), 136–65.
Raymond Corbey, *Tribal Art Traffic: A Chronicle of
Taste, Trade and Desire in Colonial and Post-Colonial
Times* (Amsterdam: Royal Tropical Institute, 2000).
Paul Guillaume, *Primitive Negro Sculpture* (New York:
Harcourt, Brace and Company, 1926).
John Warne Monroe, 'Surface Tensions: Empire,
Parisian Modernism, and "Authenticity" in African
Sculpture, 1917–1939', *The American Historical
Review* 117, 2 (2012), 445–75.
John Warne Monroe, *Metropolitan Fetish: African
Sculpture and the Imperial French Invention of Primitive
Art* (Ithaca, NY: Cornell University Press, 2019).
Ijeoma Oluo, *So You Want to Talk About Race* (New
York: Hachette, 2019).
William Rubin, *'Primitivism' in 20th Century Art:
Affinity of the Tribal and the Modern* (New York:
Museum of Modern Art, 1984).

Dikran Kelekian
René Brimo, *The Evolution of Taste in American
Collecting,* trans. K. Haltman, (University Park, PA:
Penn State University Press, 2017).
Luiza De Camargo, 'Content and Character: Dikran
Kelekian and Eastern Decorative Arts Objects in
America (M.A. diss., The Smithsonian Associates and
the Corcoran College of Art and Design, 2012).
Marilyn Jenkins-Madina, 'Collecting the "Orient"
at the Met: Early Tastemakers in America', *Ars
Orientalis*, 30 (2000), 69–89.
William R. Johnston, *William and Henry Walters: The
Reticent Collectors* (Baltimore, MD: Johns Hopkins
University Press, 1999).
Dikran Kelekian, *The Kelekian Collection of Persian and
Analogous Potteries, 1885–1910* (Paris: H. Clarke, 1910).
Andrea Lermer and Avinoam Shalem (eds), 'After One
Hundred Years: The 1910 Exhibition "Meisterwerke
muhammedanischer Kunst" Reconsidered', *Islamic
History and Civilization*, 82, (2010).
Mariana Shreve Simpson, 'A Gallant Era: Henry
Walters, Islamic Art, and the Kelekian Connection',
Ars Orientalis, 30 (2000), 91–112.

The Wildenstein Family
Suzanna Andrews, 'Bitter Spoils', *Vanity Fair*
(March 1998).
Rachel Corbett, 'The Inheritance Case That Could Unravel
an Art Dynasty', *The New York Times* (23 August 2023).
Charles Dellheim, *Belonging and Betrayal: How
Jews Made the Art World* (Waltham, MA: Brandeis
University Press, 2021).
Hector Feliciano, *The Lost Museum: The Nazi
Conspiracy to Steal the World's Greatest Works of Art*
(New York: Basic Books, 1997).
Jonathan Petropoulos, *Goering's Man in Paris: The
Story of a Nazi Art Plunderer and His World* (New
Haven and London: Yale University Press, 2021).
Magali Serre, *Les Wildenstein* (Paris: J. C. Lattès, 2013).
Daniel Wildenstein, *Claude Monet: Biographie et
catalogue raisonné*, 5 vols (Paris and Lausanne,
Switzerland: La Bibliothèque des Arts, 1974–91).
Daniel Wildenstein and Yves Stravidès, *Marchands
d'Art* (Paris: Plon, 1999).
Georges Wildenstein, *Ingres* (London: Phaidon, 1956).
Georges Wildenstein, *The Paintings of Fragonard:
Complete Edition* (London: Phaidon, 1960).
Georges Wildenstein, *Chardin* (Oxford: Cassirer, 1969).

Hildebrand Gurlitt
Andrea Baresel-Brand, Meike Hopp, Agnieszka
Magdalena Lulińska (eds), *Gurlitt Status Report*
(Munich, Germany: Hirmer, 2017).
Bianca Gaudenzi and Astrid Swenson, 'Looted Art
and Restitution in the Twentieth Century – Towards
a Global Perspective', *Journal of Contemporary
History*, 52, 3 (2017), 491–518.
Meike Hoffmann, 'Hildebrand Gurlitt and His
Dealings with German Museums during the "Third
Reich"', *New German Critique*, 130 (2017), 35–55.
Jonathan Petropoulos, 'Art Dealer Networks in the
Third Reich and in the Postwar Period', *Journal of
Contemporary History*, 52, 3 (2017), 546–65.
Susan Ronald, *Hitler's Art Thief: Hildebrand Gurlitt,
the Nazis, and the Looting of Europe's Treasures*
(New York: St. Martin's Griffin, 2017).

Extraordinary Art Dealers

Stephen Radich

'Obituary Stephen Radich', *Artforum* (27
  December 2007).
Albert Boime, 'Waving the Red Flag and
  Reconstituting Old Glory', *Smithsonian Studies in
  American Art*, 4, 2 (1990), 3–25.
Ken Johnson, 'Stephen Radich, Owner of
  Controversial Art Gallery, Is Dead at 85', *The New
  York Times* (26 December 2007).
Lucy Lippard, *A Different War: Vietnam in Art*
  (Bellingham, WA: Whatcom Museum of History and
  Art, 1990).
Nicole Rudick, 'Faith Ringgold Debunks the Myth of
  the American Dream', *Apollo* (5 April 2024).
Deborah Wye, *Committed to Print: Social and Political
  Themes in Recent American Printed Art,* (New York:
  Museum of Modern Art, 1988).

CHAPTER 6: THE PERSONALITY DEALER

Introduction

Christopher Lasch, *The Culture of Narcissism* (New
  York, London: W. W. Norton and Company, 1978).
Richard Sennett, *The Fall of the Public Man* (London,
  Boston: Faber and Faber, 1993).
Tom Wolfe, 'The "Me" Decade', *New York*, 23 August 1976.

Félix Fénéon

Julian Barnes, 'Behind the Gas Lamp', *London Review
  of Books*, 29, 19 (4 October 2007).
Félix Fénéon, *Au-delà de l'impressionnisme*, ed.
  Françoise Cachin (Paris: Hermann, 1966).
Starr Figura, Isabelle Cahn and Philippe Peltier (eds),
  Félix Fénéon: The Anarchist and the Avant-Garde
  (New York: Museum of Modern Art, 2020).
Joan U. Halperin, *Félix Fénéon and the Language of Art
  Criticism* (Ann Arbor, MI: UMI Research Press, 1980).
Faye Hirsch, 'The Well-Dressed Anarchist', *Art in
  America* (22 December 2020).
Philip Hook, *Rogues' Gallery: A History of Art and its
  Dealers* (London: Profile Books, 2017).
Samuel Reilly, 'The Secret Sharer: Felix Fénéon, the
  publicity-averse critic, collector and anarchist
  who moved in avant-garde circles and was an early
  champion of African art, is being celebrated in a
  series of exhibitions in Paris and New York', *Apollo
  Magazine*, 190, 677 (July–August 2019).
Roberta Smith, 'Félix Fénéon, the Collector-Anarchist
  Who Was Seurat's First Champion, *The New York
  Times* (27 August 2007).

Julien Levy

Julien Levy, *Memoir of an Art Gallery* (Boston, MA:
  MFA Publications, 2003).
Julien Levy, *Surrealism* (New York: De Capo Press, 1995).
Oral history interview with Julien Levy, by Paul
  Cummings, 30 May 1975, Archives of American Art,
  Smithsonian Institute, Washington, DC.
Ingrid Schaffner and Lisa Jacobs (eds), *Julien Levy:
  Portrait of an Art Gallery* (Cambridge, MA: MIT
  Press, 1998).

Peggy Guggenheim

Francine Prose, *Peggy Guggenheim: The Shock of the
  Modern* (New Haven, CT: Yale University Press, 2015).
*Art of this Century: Objects, Drawings, Photographs,
  Paintings, Sculpture, Collage 1910–42* (New York:
  Arno, 1968).
Peggy Guggenheim, *Out of this Century: Confessions of
  an Art Addict* (London: Welbeck, 2023).
Clare Bell, Jennifer Blessing, Julia Brown, Lisa
  Dennison, Andrea Feeser, Michael Govan, Thomas
  Krens, Nancy Spector, Diane Waldman, *Art of this
  Century: The Guggenheim Museum and its Collections*
  (New York: Solomon R. Guggenheim Foundation, 1993).

George Maciunas

Jacquelynn Baas (ed.), *Fluxus and the Essential Questions
  of Life* (Chicago, IL: University of Chicago Press, 2011).
Janet Jenkins, *In the Spirit of Fluxus* (Minneapolis,
  MN: Walker Art Publications, 1993).
Thomas Kellerin, *The Dream of Fluxus, George
  Maciunas: An Artist's Biography*, trans. Fiona Elliott
  (London: Thames and Hudson, 2007).
Emmett Williams and Ann Noel (eds), *Mr. Fluxus: A
  Collective Portrait of George Maciunas 1931–1978*
  (London: Thames and Hudson, 1997).

Robert Fraser

Brian Clarke, Arne Glimcher and Harriet Vyner, *A
  Strong Sweet Smell of Incense: A Portrait of Robert
  Fraser* (London: Pace Gallery, 2015).
Uta Grosenick and Raimar Stange (eds), *International
  Art Galleries: Post-War to Post-Millennium. A
  Chronology of the Dealers, Places and Personalities of
  Modern Art* (London: Thames and Hudson, 2005).
Barry Miles, *Paul McCartney: Many Years From Now*
  (London: Vintage, 1997).
Harriet Vyner, *Groovy Bob* (London: Faber and
  Faber, 1999).

Image Credits

Images listed by figure number.

1 Harris Brisbane Dick Fund, 1917/The Metropolitan Museum of Art, New York (p.21)

2 Harris Brisbane Dick Fund, 1932/The Metropolitan Museum of Art, New York (p.22)

3 Gift of Bella C. Landauer, 1926/The Metropolitan Museum of Art, New York (p.23)

4 Gift of Bella C. Landauer, 1926/The Metropolitan Museum of Art, New York (p.25)

5 SJArt/Alamy Stock Photo (p.27)

6 Album/Alamy Stock Photo (p.28)

7 Gift of Cornelius Vanderbilt, 1887/The Metropolitan Museum of Art, New York (p.34)

8 Wikipedia CC0 (p.35)

9 Photo by Birmingham Museums Trust, licensed under CC0 (p.36)

10 Wikipedia CC0 (p.41)

11 Wikipedia CC0 (p.44)

12 Purchase, special contributions and funds given or bequeathed by friends of the Museum, 1961/The Metropolitan Museum of Art, New York (p.52)

13 The Picture Art Collection/Alamy Stock Photo (p.55)

14 Wikipedia CC0 (p.55)

15 Petit Palais, Museum of Fine Arts of the City of Paris (p.62)

16 Gift of Mr. and Mrs. Peter A. Ruebel. 1516.1968, Digital image, The Museum of Modern Art, New York/Scala, Florence. © ARS, NY and DACS, London 2024 (p.68)

17 Alfred Stieglitz Collection/Art Institute of Chicago (p.93)

18 adoc-photos/Corbis via Getty Images (p.101)

19 Collection of Barjeel Art Foundation, Sharjah. © ADAGP, Paris and DACS, London 2024 (p.107)

20 Michael Heizer, Double Negative, 1969, Mormon Mesa, Overton, Nevada © Michael Heizer. Courtesy of the artist and Gagosian. Photo: John Weber (p.116)

21 Collection Dia Art Foundation, New York. Gift of Virginia Dwan. © Estate of Walter De Maria. Courtesy Walter De Maria Archive (p.116)

22 Photo © NPL - DeA Picture Library/Bridgeman Images (p.125)

23 Photograph © 2024 Museum of Fine Arts, Boston/Bequest of William E. Teel/Bridgeman Images (p.159)

24 Art Gallery of Ontario/Gift of Sam and Ayala Zacks, 1970/Bridgeman Images (p.159)

25 The Michael C. Rockefeller Memorial Collection, Bequest of Nelson A. Rockefeller, 1979/The Metropolitan Museum of Art, New York (p.161)

26 Gift of Edward S. Harkness, 1917/The Metropolitan Museum of Art, New York (p.164)

27 The William Hood Dunwoody Fund/ Minneapolis Institute of Art (p.165)

28 Gift of Beatrice Kelekian, in memory of her husband, Charles D. Kelekian, 1983/The Metropolitan Museum of Art, New York (p.168)

29 Bequest of Joseph V. McMullan, 1973/The Metropolitan Museum of Art, New York (p.169)

30 The Jules Bache Collection, 1949/The Metropolitan Museum of Art, New York (p.173)

31 © Kunsthaus Lempertz (p.182)

32 The Abby Aldrich Rockefeller Endowment for Prints/Digital image, The Museum of Modern Art, New York/Scala, Florence. © 2024 Faith Ringgold/ARS, NY and DACS, London 2024 (p.187)

33 Peter Horree/Alamy Stock Photo (p.199)

34 Science History Images/Alamy Stock Photo (p.203)

35 The Gilbert and Lila Silverman Fluxus Collection Gift. Digital image, The Museum of Modern Art, New York/Scala, Florence (p.217)

36 © Brian Clarke (p.224)

Chapter opener credits, listed by page number.

6 Wikipedia CC0

14 Yale Center for British Art, Gift of Jules David Prown, Yale MA (HON.) 1971

19 incamerastock/Alamy Stock Photo

31 Gift from Miss Mary Hulse, 1913/© The Atkinson/Bridgeman Images

38 Wikipedia CC0

50 Everett Collection Historical/Alamy Stock Photo

57 Photo Scala, Florence. © Succession Picasso/ DACS, London 2024

64 Maurice Berezov. Samuel Kootz in his studio, 195-?. Kootz Gallery records, 1923-1966. Archives of American Art, Smithsonian Institution. © Madelyn Berezov

70 Alexander Liberman photography archive/

Getty Research Institute, Los Angeles
(2000.R.19). © J. Paul Getty Trust

76 © Chris Felver. All rights reserved 2024/
Bridgeman Images

86 Wolfgang Kühn/United Archives GmbH/Alamy
Stock Photo

92 Granger/Historical Picture Archive/Alamy
Stock Photo

99 Roger Viollet via Getty Images

105 Photo Fosco Maraini/FAF Toscana - Fondazione
Alinari per la Fotografia/akg-images

111 Virginia Dwan, 1969. Dwan Gallery records,
1959-circa 1982. Archives of American Art,
Smithsonian Institution

122 Bridgeman Images. © Fondation Oskar
Kokoschka/DACS 2024

128 Charles Sheeler. Edith Gregor Halpert, 1935.
Downtown Gallery records, 1824-1974. Archives
of American Art, Smithsonian Institution

134l Jean Dieuzaide/akg-images. © DACS 2024

134r Archivo Tomas Montero

140 Courtesy Chemould Prescott Road Archives

146 Horst Friedrichs/Alamy Stock Photo

156 Photo © Photo Josse/Bridgeman Images

163 John D. Schiff Photograph Collection at the
Leo Baeck Institute New York/Bridgeman
Images

171 Associated Press/Alamy Stock Photo

177 Album/Alamy Stock Photo

194 GL Archive/Alamy Stock Photo

200 Photo © Art Institute of Chicago/Gift of
Patricia and Frank Kolodny in memory of
Julien Levy/Bridgeman Images. © Estate of
Jay Leyda

207 Bettman/Getty Images

219 Hulton-Deutsch/Hulton-Deutsch Collection/
Corbis via Getty Images

Index

References to images are in *italics*.

Author Acknowledgements

Thank you to Joe Hage, whose interest in the subject of the history of art dealers led to the commissioning of this book. I am deeply grateful to Rebecca Morrill for the inspiring direction she has brought to this project, and to Vincenza Napoli who skilfully guided the process from beginning to end. A heartfelt thanks to Simona Pignataro for her preliminary research on the history of the art market and to Alice Blow, Lois Haines and Meghan Montgomery for their research. And thanks to Alice Blow and Meghan Montgomery for also generously stepping in to act as readers. I am extremely grateful to Sara Harrison for her deft editing, and for bringing together the various elements. I would also like to thank Kirsty Watling who joined this project in the latter stages and patiently brought the book across the finish line. Huge thanks to the designer, Sylvia Ugga, for her beautiful layout, to Jen Veall for her efficient picture research, and to illustrator Celyn Brazier for his characterful front cover. And thank you to my husband, Matt Ingram, for his support throughout.

Author Biography

Catherine Ingram (Ph.D., Oxford) is a writer and art historian, who has lectured for the Tate, Christie's, Imperial College London and Magdalen College, Oxford. She conceived of and edited the illustrated art history series, *This is*, published by Laurence King Publishing, also writing four of the titles. The series won the Brand/Series Identity Award at the British Book Design and Production Awards in 2015 and several titles were nominated for the V&A Illustration Awards. *This is Dalí, This is Pollock* and *This is Warhol* also featured in the *Guardian*'s best graphic books of 2014.